The Aesthetics of Failure

The Aesthetics of Failure

Dynamic Structure in the Plays of Eugene O'Neill

by
ZANDER BRIETZKE

McFarland & Company, Inc., Publishers
Jefferson, North Carolina, and London

Front cover: Al Pacino in the role of Erie Smith, in *Hughie*, 1996, at the Long Wharf Theatre, directed by Pacino. Photograph by T. Charles Erickson.

Frontispiece: Jason Robards (1922–2000) as Cornelius Melody in *A Touch of the Poet*, 1977, at the Helen Hayes Theatre, directed by José Quintero. Photograph by John Bryson. Museum of the City of New York. Theater Collection.

Library of Congress Cataloguing-in-Publication Data

Brietzke, Zander, 1960–
    The aesthetics of failure : dynamic structure in the plays of
Eugene O'Neill / by Zander Brietzke.
       p.   cm.
    Includes bibliographical references and index.
    ISBN 0-7864-0946-0 (softcover : 50# alkaline paper) ∞
    1. O'Neill, Eugene, 1888–1953—Technique.   2. O'Neill, Eugene,
1888–1953—Aesthetics.   3. Failure (Psychology) in literature.
4. Drama—Technique.   5. Tragedy.   I. Title.
PS3529.N5Z5745   2001
812'.52—dc21   2001016262

British Library cataloguing data are available

Manufactured in the United States of America

*McFarland & Company, Inc., Publishers
  Box 611, Jefferson, North Carolina 28640
    www.mcfarlandpub.com*

For my family

Contents

Acknowledgments

This project started in 1995 with my realization that after two advanced degree programs and seven years of graduate school I had yet to study American drama. I decided to fill that void by creating and teaching a course on O'Neill. I am very grateful to the College of Wooster for adopting "O'Neill and His Contemporaries" and providing generous research funds for me to explore a new area of interest. Dale Seeds, chair of the Theatre Department, was particularly supportive of a curriculum drive to advance the study of American theatre and drama. Students, of course, taught me a lot. Kristina Stoll, Emily McClain, Cameron Nicholson, and Anthony Kokocinski not only mostly listened to my often windy tangents, but they actually inspired and challenged me to put them in writing. Blame them! I can only offer them my enduring respect and gratitude.

I presented papers which informed the writing of this book at the American Literature Association (ALA) Conference in San Diego (1996), the American Theatre in Higher Education Conference in Chicago (1997) and the ALA Conference in Baltimore in 1999. The single most important event I attended, without question, was the International O'Neill Conference in Bermuda in January 1999. I delivered the premise of my book there and received encouragement from newfound colleagues and friends. I will not forget the pleasures of sipping sherry at Spithead (O'Neill's house there) in the company of the Eugene O'Neill Society and feeling that like the hairy ape, perhaps, at last, I belonged! No one could have known the impact of that gathering upon me and there are several people whom I need to thank. I am forever indebted to Thierry Dubost and his unflagging optimism and cheerful spirit. Sheila Hickey Garvey gave me confidence that a director might find my project worthwhile. Stephen Black, whom I first met in San Diego, continued to express interest in my project, corresponded electronically, wrote recommendations for me, and read and commented upon an early draft of the manuscript. Michael Manheim proved invaluable as a mentor and friendly yet tough guide through several drafts. Were it not for his wisdom and expertise, I would have made many more mistakes of fact and opinion than I eventually did.

The directors with whom I've worked and trained have made a tremendous impression upon the way I see O'Neill and modern drama. Certainly, my father was the first to show me how a director prepares for work and plans a rehearsal. Edmond Williams at the University of Alabama gave me first insight into the director as an artist in the theatre. Stuart Vaughan taught me techniques and professional standards and invited me to write the student exercises for his directing textbook. At Stanford, Carl Weber taught me how to see. From the very first class, his question remained the same: What did you see? That foremost question led quite directly to my focus on vision and emphasis upon things visual in this manuscript. I must also thank a director whom I did not know at all but who ended up making a huge impact on me and my work. I never worked with José Quintero (1924–1999); I never even saw one of his productions. I did attend a series of lectures, talks really, that he gave for the Playwrights' Theatre Forum at the Provincetown Playhouse in August 1998. He was the most open and emotionally present and vulnerable man I had ever seen. I was just a face in the audience but I felt that he talked directly to me. I'm sure others around me felt the same thing. He had that gift. And he gave me the courage to see O'Neill in the simplest terms possible— through the emotions. He encouraged us "to make ourselves vulnerable to the material." That is the gauntlet that O'Neill's best work throws down, sure, but it's a pretty good life lesson too.

My former advisor, Alice Rayner, read the third draft and offered a much needed shot in the arm for the project. Her comments forced me to reconsider some of the easy assumptions that I had made. I owe many thanks to my graduate school colleague and fellow Brooklynite Humphrey Gyde, who generously pored through an early draft and was able to sift out in conversation with me what I was really trying to do. His keen perceptions allowed me to be much more forthright with my intentions for the book.

The research staffs at both the New York Library for the Performing Arts and the Museum of the City of New York were very helpful. Visually, I had a lot of help securing images from several people: Jeremy McGraw at the New York Library for the Performing Arts; Anne Easterling at the

Museum of the City of New York; Tom Lisanti at the New York Public Library; Richard Kimmel of the Wooster Group; Beth Hauptle and Roberto Aguirre-Sacasa at the Shakespeare Theatre; photographer Joan Marcus. Theodore Mann at the Circle in the Square Theatre School and Tim Judge, Al Pacino's New York agent, helped me track down the photographer for *Hughie*. Harley J. Hammerman, M.D., whose web site (eOneill.com) presents a treasure trove of useful stuff, verified the spelling of some names.

Finally, my family, including my parents and in-laws, has been extremely supportive, emotionally and financially, throughout the tenure of this project. I would not have written the book without my wife Carol's encouragement. This period has been especially difficult for my children, Sasha and Jack, who would have preferred to spend the hours playing Big Uno. Nevertheless, they got to use the backs of each draft for artwork. Seeing the odd pages scattered about the house, O'Neill on one side, Crayola on the other, produced postmodern, if not humbling, realizations of my connection to the world. I'm not certain which side of the page is more valuable. Actually, I do know.

Having thanked many of the people who made this effort possible, I take full responsibility for the contents herein (who else would?). One of my former teachers, the late Professor Charles Lyons (d. 1999), a prolific scholar, advised me once never to publish anything. He said that I would regret seeing my thoughts in print long after I'd changed my mind. I believe he was kidding, but I already anticipate the merit of his advice.

Abbreviations

Cargill   Cargill, Oscar, N. Bryllion Fagin, William J. Fisher, ed. *O'Neill and His Plays: Four Decades of Criticism.* New York: New York University Press, 1961.

CP1   O'Neill, Eugene. *Complete Plays.* Ed. Travis Bogard. Vol. 1. New York: The Library of America, 1988.

CP2   O'Neill, Eugene. *Complete Plays.* Ed. Travis Bogard. Vol. 2. New York: The Library of America, 1988.

CP3   O'Neill, Eugene. *Complete Plays.* Ed. Travis Bogard. Vol. 3. New York: The Library of America, 1988.

SL   O'Neill, Eugene. *Selected Letters of Eugene O'Neill.* Ed. Travis Bogard and Jackson R. Bryer. New Haven: Yale University Press, 1988.

"The only success is in failure. Any man who has a big enough dream must be a failure and must accept this as one of the conditions of being alive. If he ever thinks for a moment that he is a success, then he is finished."

—*Eugene O'Neill*

Preface

During my first year of full-time teaching several years ago, I assigned Eugène Scribe's *A Scrap of Paper* to my dramatic literature class. After having read Marlowe and Jonson, Wycherley and Farquhar, Molière, Kleist, Gogol and Buchner, they encountered the nineteenth century well-made-play to appreciate the difference between popular entertainment and great art. That was the pedagogical intent. In practice, my plan succeeded too well. To a person, the class loved Scribe; in fact, they loved his play more than anything else they had read. I discovered through discussion that what they enjoyed most about the play, apart from the sheer joy of a good story, was their sense of mastery of the material. Pressed for time to keep up with the rigors of the syllabus (the work of a naive professor), they habitually felt unprepared to discuss the dramatic text of the day. Scribe's intrigues and plot machinations excited them and immediately rewarded their diligent efforts to comprehend the play. Crisp divisions between right/wrong, good/evil, rich/poor, high/low heightened the drama and made reading easy and fun. I felt almost guilty admonishing them that this was not "good literature." Convincing them that the experience had less value than they thought seemed a bit fraudulent. Perhaps I could not entirely convince myself.

This book attempts to respond, albeit belatedly, to my first class who responded enthusiastically to the dramatic clarity of melodrama. Rather than negating their experience, I wish with hindsight that I had supplemented it with an alternative way of looking at literature that did not reward mastery. Confusion, doubt, and frustration are perfectly viable responses, too. Failure to perceive every aspect of a particular subject might indicate that there is a lot to see. Trying to make sense of that subject, piecing things together, inferring a whole from so many parts, might yield

1

more insights than an unobstructed view of the entire thing. Getting the right answers about that thing might be less interesting than asking the right questions. Things sometimes become less interesting as they become more clear. Neat beginnings and tidy endings, villains and vixens, heroes and heroines, moral certitudes, decisive victories and defeats, may be dramatically compelling and may represent wish fulfillment on the part of the audience (another form of mastery), but ambiguity is the condition under which many people live (another form of confusion). To present the world to students as anything less complex and multidimensional would be a disservice and a lie. The trick remains to make the study of such a world view as entertaining an experience as reading *A Scrap of Paper*.

I heard Peter Gomes, the Harvard minister, deliver a commencement address a few years ago in which he suggested that we (those who teach and administrate) had wronged our students by emphasizing their great potential for success. He reasoned that we should have prepared our students for failure, since they would surely encounter many opportunities for failure in the future. Any success that they would enjoy in life would be measured by their reaction and ability to deal with adversity. Herein, I thought, might lie an approach to teaching and studying literature!

Championing failure supports my understanding of the works of Eugene O'Neill, the "world's worst great playwright," in the words of Clive Barnes. In a letter to the *New York Tribune* (February 13, 1921) early in his career, O'Neill had this to say in praise of failure: "To me, the tragic alone has that significant beauty which is truth. It is the meaning of life — and the hope. The noblest is eternally the most tragic. The people who succeed and do not push on to a greater failure are the spiritual middle classers. Their stopping at success is the proof of their compromising insignificance. How petty their dreams must have been!" (Cargill 104). O'Neill challenges his admirers, who call him the Father of American Drama (a moniker which produces the collective groan of the nation), to account for embarrassing qualities in many, if not most, of his plays. No apologies will be forthcoming here. Even though American dramatic literature still divides in terms of pre–O'Neill (before 1916) and after, and even though he remains the only American playwright to win the Nobel Prize for Literature, I ask the reader to lay aside received opinion and accept O'Neill as a failure. I intend to make a virtue out of his kind of failure.

O'Neill's failures as a playwright are particularly inspiring. First of all, his theory of tragedy, or tragic vision, as expressed above, requires failure. That "Man's reach exceeds his grasp" is the tragic condition of humanity, made more so by the fact that there is no heaven above. Failure alone grants humanity nobility. With respect to particular works, no artist fails more than O'Neill. More than half of his published works are not good. Significantly, however, his last works number among the finest American dramas. O'Neill appears to be that rare artist who overcomes his limitations through a lifetime of struggle. The evidence of that struggle is found in the plays themselves, and the methodology of this study traces that struggle within the works.

Instead of defining what the plays are about, my critical perspective examines conflict at the structural level. Structure shapes the drama: it is the container for the thing contained. By examining the container, one begins to feel the shape of what's inside (the contents) as well. Genre, language or dialogue, characters, space and time are basic structural elements of the drama, but the dramatist's manipulation of them is not as straightforward as it might appear. I plan to point out conflicts within each element: O'Neill aspires to write tragedy, but melodrama often results; his narrative impulse in the form of stage descriptions and lengthy monologues and even interior monologues or thought asides threatens the theatrical mandate to "show" rather than "tell"; acting and role playing add depth and project character, but true identity remains hidden and in flux; scenic space is sometimes realistic, sometimes not, but the relationship between what's seen onstage and what's not forces a re-evaluation of style; action develops in time linearly, but repetition imposes a pattern of circularity upon the temporal scheme and effectively makes time the subject of the drama. Specific strategies for solving these problems recur in play after play, and these patterns make up what can be identified as an O'Neill drama.

I plan to show how O'Neill's plays stage these conflicts, but offer, in the end, no easy resolutions. Profound failure again proves vital to an appreciation of the plays. It is not just that the overall impression of O'Neill's work is that it tries for greatness (tragedy) and falls short of the mark (melodrama). At each structural level his plays attempt something, but fail. Pursuit of that failure, however, creates the contest that makes the work interesting in the first place. I identify O'Neill's tragic vision, for example, as nothing more than the desire to see destiny clearly; that necessary failure creates tension in the work. O'Neill attempts to write a novelistic drama that erases the need for performance, but the failure of that project results in stunning theatre. He tries to penetrate the mask of character only to discover that a multitude of different masks lie underneath. He perfects a realistic style in his final plays, but his realism transcends the boundaries of that style. His work explores the past, but the structure in each play reveals much more about the stagnant present and the devastating future.

A visual approach that emphasizes the shape of the drama and the patterns in the plays accords with my training as a stage director. I'm interested primarily in how a play looks as I read it. What does the scenery look like? How does the groundplan affect character relationships? What's the relationship between actor and audience? Where are the doors? What is the pattern of entrances and exits that determines the rhythm of each scene? Who are characters addressing? What do they look like? How does the play begin and how does it end? What's happening on stage at every moment? These simple questions are the nitty-gritty of directing, and the shape of the drama begins to emerge from satisfactory answers. Interpretation evolves from an understanding of the visible patterns in the play(s). I'm most interested in showing how to see the plays, but not so much what to see. My readings of the plays are certainly not definitive. As I review these pages, the commitment of the printed word belies the provisional status of my shifting and particular point of view in time. I don't presume to think that I provide any final answers here, but I do hope that my exploration of the shape of O'Neill's works will spark an appreciation of structure that will open the plays to new readings and imaginative possibilities for realizing them.

Introduction:
The Director's Perspective

"It is the task of the artist as explorer to look into the abyss
and to prevent the facile acceptance of simplified visions."
— *Gary Shapiro, "In the Shadows of Philosophy:*
Nietzsche and the Question of Vision"

In praise of Eugene O'Neill's Nobel Prize Award in 1936, critic Brooks Atkinson proclaimed him as "a tragic dramatist with a great knack for old-fashioned melodrama." This evaluation hints at a productive way to analyze O'Neill's drama by suggesting a mix of melodramatic and tragic elements within individual plays. Fluid classifications help to promote dynamic interpretations. The relationship between melodrama and tragedy, the struggle to transcend the former category and to achieve the latter, enacts a drama rife with tension. Throughout his career, O'Neill (1888–1953) tried to find techniques to rival melodramatic theatricality but also to reflect the complexity of life in tragic form. Thirty years of playwriting (1913–1943) produced staggering variations in length, form, genre, style, technical innovation and quality. Early one acts gave way to some of the longest plays in the American canon, and in the end, tragic dramas among the finest in any language or country. Imported European expressionism transformed into some of the most powerful realistic portrayals of American life. In travel romances, histories, a domestic comedy, and tragedies modeled upon Greek drama, subjects varied from figures at sea, about whom O'Neill wrote from personal experience, to historical figures such as Ponce de Leon, Marco Polo, and the Biblical Lazarus. While *Strange Interlude* (1927) projected into the future, his final plays explored

5

events from the past. A planned but never completed cycle of eleven plays, stretching from prior to the birth of the nation to the time of composition in the 1930s, remains today his most ambitious historical project. O'Neill joked to *The New York Times* that after seeing this event, audiences would "never want to see another play." Still, he wrote his two best plays, *The Iceman Cometh* (1940) and *Long Day's Journey Into Night* (1941), during a respite from the unfinished cycle ordeal.

The multifaceted surfaces of his plays, in addition to their supposed depth of subject matter, reveal elements which provide both visual payoff and a framework for resonant emotional experience. To determine how the plays function, not what they mean, is the primary purpose of this study. In essence, then, I adopt the critical perspective of the stage director, who sees the play as a visible mechanism and stages the struggle of form to reveal itself. Erasing hierarchical notions of surface and depth in which the superficial layer masks hidden meaning exalts a primitive simplicity without sophistication, a formalism which heeds Nietzsche's retrospective surmise of culture and civilization in *The Gay Science*: "Oh, those Greeks! They knew how to live. What is required for that is to stop courageously at the surface, the fold, the skin, to adore appearance, to believe in forms, tones, words, in the whole Olympus of appearance. Those Greeks were superficial—*out of profundity*" (*Portable Nietzsche* 683). My proposed readings of specific plays result from an engagement with their dramatic means of production. Analysis of dialogue, character, scene, action and genre reveals the drama in the act of creation. Texts stage a battle between novelistic innovations and dramatic compromises; between masks that both reveal and conceal character; between an oscillation of the seen and unseen on stage; between repetition of the past staged in the present; between tragic hopes and melodramatic realizations.

How to see clearly the struggle within the work requires a methodology that, first of all, advances structure over subject matter. O'Neill's literary pruning colludes with autobiography to obscure full-scale view of his remarkable accomplishments. As his career grew in stature, O'Neill concerned himself much more with his reputation and legacy. He did not begin with such vigilance as a fledgling playwright. His start shows a cavalier attitude epitomized by his friend Terry Carlin's legendary response to the query from the Provincetown Players: "Mr. O'Neill's got a whole trunk full of plays" (Glaspell 195). O'Neill evidently later wanted to hide much in that trunk from the light of day. He destroyed many manuscripts of unfinished plays and tried to suppress publication of plays he didn't like or didn't feel represented his best work. Even *"Anna Christie,"*[1] his second Pulitzer Prize winner, became in his own mind a play he detested, and he later refused to publish it in an edition of his selected works.[2] O'Neill published fewer and fewer plays as he matured, but he wrote longer and longer works and with greater discipline than in his early career. Preparing *Strange Interlude* in 1927, he confided to Kenneth Macgowan that his work had become much deeper and that he had to make sure that there was more in it than in earlier efforts (SL 209). During the thirties, O'Neill sheltered himself with his elaborate cycle plays on American history. That project ballooned from as few as three plays to as many as eleven, yet O'Neill completed only one, *A Touch of the Poet* (1939). *More Stately Mansions*, the following play in the cycle, survived in draft form only because O'Neill inadvertently placed it among his completed works instead of destroying it along with drafts of other unfinished works. The loss of these manuscripts fosters an illusion of *Long Day's Journey Into Night*, his most autobiographical play, as the summation of his career. O'Neill did not intend for that play to be published until twenty-five years after his death and he stipulated that it should never be produced. When Carlotta Monterey, his literary executor and widow, violated this wish and allowed Yale University Press to publish the manuscript and the Royal Dramatic Theatre of Sweden to produce the play only three years after O'Neill's death, the illusion transformed into a powerful myth and legend.

Similarly, a series of dramatic self-portraits throughout O'Neill's works also leads inevitably to *Long Day's Journey Into Night* and the autobiographical figure of Edmund Tyrone. Stage directions in early plays such as *Bread and Butter* (1914), *Servitude* (1914), *Beyond the Horizon* (1918), and *The Straw* (1919) physically describe male protagonists very much like the author. The description of novelist David Royleston in *Servitude* represents features found in all of O'Neill's fictional artists: "a tall, slender, dark-haired man of thirty-five with large handsome features, a strong, ironical mouth half-hidden by a black mustache, and keenly-intelligent dark eyes" (CP1 237). Judging from photographs of O'Neill as a young man, he created these characters by looking at himself in a mirror. Obviously, Edmund Tyrone is Eugene O'Neill. When I teach O'Neill in class, I begin with *Long Day's Journey Into Night* in order to impart expeditiously (and dramatically) important biographical information about the playwright. This entertaining and economical strategy sets up convenient readings, too, for all the preceding plays. *All God's Chillun Got Wings* (1923), a play about a black man named Jim who marries a white woman named Ella, becomes a play about O'Neill's parents' (James and Ella) unfortunate marriage of opposite sensibilities. *Desire Under the Elms* (1924), a play which O'Neill said that he had dreamed one night, becomes

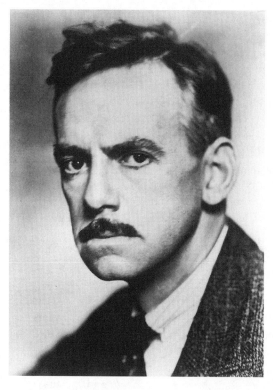

Eugene O'Neill in 1926, age 38. Descriptions of the author invariably mentioned the intensity of his eyes. Photograph by Nickolas Muray. Museum of the City of New York. Theater Collection.

a play mourning the recent death of his mother.[3] *Strange Interlude* dramatizes the guilt surrounding O'Neill's crumbling marriage and the slick motto "Be happy" provides license for O'Neill to abandon his second wife, Agnes Boulton, and their children and to escape to Europe with Carlotta Monterey. *Ah, Wilderness!* (1933) is a fantasy for the family the author wished that he had had, and *Long Day's Journey Into Night* shows the authentic picture of family life. Quite simply, this practice blurs the distinction between life and art. Seeing the plays through the author's life blinds the critical eye to the technical merits of the writing and legitimates personal experience as artistic truth.

O'Neill, who did lead a fascinating life, emerges in his self-portraits as a tortured artist. His dedication of *Long Day's Journey Into Night* to his third wife, Carlotta, offers evidence that this play finally expiated his demons: "Dearest: I give you the original script of this play of old sorrow, written in tears and blood. A sadly inappropriate gift, it would seem, for a day celebrating happiness [their 12th wedding anniversary]. But you will understand. I mean it as a tribute to your love and tenderness which gave me the faith in love that enabled me to face my dead at last and write this play—write it with deep pity and understanding and forgiveness for all the four haunted Tyrones" (CP3 714). What further proof of this great play as emotional and artistic breakthrough could one desire beyond a statement from the author? The Gelb biography paints an incredibly romantic portrait of the suffering artist who finally frees himself by confronting his past: "He worked every morning, many afternoons, and sometimes evenings as well. Often he wept as he wrote. He slept badly, and occasionally in the night he rose from the converted Chinese opium couch that served as his bed to go to his wife's room and talk of the play and of his anguish" (6). The effect of all this is to see O'Neill's entire career leading naturally up to this particular effort. The inescapable conclusion, then, is to spin a rich narrative that culminates in the Great American Play.

More importantly, the focus upon the subject matter (autobiography) deflects attention away from the necessary artistic skill to write the play. Granted, O'Neill is an autobiographical writer, perhaps more than any other. But the force of seeing the plays through the prism of his life focuses interpretation in one direction at the expense of other possibilities. You can't see the paint and the picture at the same time. O'Neill's paint includes dramatic form, use of language, the creation of roles for actors, and manipulations of scenic space and time. Collectively, these elements make up the dramatic illusion. Studied independently, they highlight the distinguishing characteristics and artistic techniques of O'Neill's dramaturgy. The portrait that emerges is of an accomplished playwright, who also happens to have been a compelling and complicated man.

Emphasis upon dramatic technique maintains a focus upon the surface of the text as opposed to the depth of the representation within the text. The struggle of characters within the plays reflects the analogous struggles of the writer to compose the drama. In *Beyond the Horizon*, for example, Robert Mayo longs to escape from his farm and to see what's on the other side of the hills. That desire set against the stultifying atmosphere and frustration of daily toil creates tension in the play. Edmund Tyrone, in *Long Day's Journey Into Night*, speaks of fleeting moments of seeing the meaning of life before an unseen hand drops a veil. While critics have identified transcendent desire in these characters and others, this same struggle is evident in the writing of the plays, too. At the outset of his playwriting career, immediately after the early success of *Beyond the Horizon*, which won him his first Pulitzer Prize at the age of 32, O'Neill wrote a letter to critic George Jean Nathan thanking him for his kind words of support. O'Neill explicitly refused to think of himself as more than a "beginner, with prospects." He went on to elaborate his artistic credo: "And in this faith I live: That if I have the 'guts' to ignore the megaphone men and what goes with them, to follow the dream and live for that alone, then my real significant bit of truth, and the ability to express it, will be conquered in time—not tomorrow nor the next day nor any near, easily-attained period, but after the struggle has been long enough and hard enough to merit victory" (SL 130).[4] The concept of struggle confirming human value, borrowed from Nietzsche, applies to O'Neill's estimate of himself as playwright as well as to his characters. His unique tragic vision sees the two as one, as his own words make clear: "The only success is in failure. Any man who has a big enough dream must be a failure and must accept this as one of the conditions of being alive. If he ever thinks for a moment that he is a success, then he is finished" (Gelb 337).

Recognized as the only American playwright to win the Nobel, O'Neill persevered to write his best plays *after* receiving the award. How many writers produce their finest work at the very end of long careers? Which ones have written their best efforts after winning the equivalent of a lifetime achievement award? Still, *Long Day's Journey Into Night* should not be interpreted as the grail at the end of years of struggle. O'Neill continued to write, continued to plan future dramas, long after this play. Virginia Floyd has discovered in O'Neill's private notebooks that he had plans for much more work including *The Last Conquest, Blind Alley Guy, The Visit of Malatesta*, and a series of eight one-acts under the title, *By Way of Obit*.[5] Based upon fragments of text, Floyd makes an extraordinary claim: "*Long Day's Journey Into Night* has rightfully been hailed America's finest tragedy; *The Visit of Malatesta* would have been its richest comedy—conceived as it was in the same last period of great creative maturity" (*Eugene O'Neill at Work* 301). While knowledge of plans and manuscripts of succeeding plays disrupts the notion of the autobiographical family plays as final statement, no evidence suggests that these plays would be superior to the earlier ones. It does imply, however, that O'Neill remained faithful to his dramatic quest throughout his career. Ultimately, failing health curtailed his career. He completed no plays during the last ten years of his life. A debilitating tremor prevented him from even holding a pencil and he was unable to write using any other means. Nevertheless, he aspired to continue. A typical literary curve of development, based upon a biological model, suggests a pattern of early promise, maturity, repetition and decline. Jaques puts it more bluntly in *As You Like It*:

> And so from hour to hour, we ripe, and ripe,
> And then from hour to hour, we rot, and rot,
> And thereby hangs a tale [2.7.26–28].

The story of O'Neill describes a Faustian playwright whose boundless aspiration and tragic vision sustain a remarkable career in which poetic titles and sometimes prosaic contents clash to do that which cannot be done. The plays themselves offer the most compelling argument for a tragic theory of drama. On the one hand, titles evoke vivid imagery: *Bound East for Cardiff*, *The Moon of the Caribbees*, *Beyond the Horizon*, *Desire Under the Elms*, *Strange Interlude*, *Mourning Becomes Electra*, *A Touch of the Poet*, *More Stately Mansions*, *The Iceman Cometh*, *Long Day's Journey Into Night*, *A Moon for the Misbegotten*. On the other hand, critics routinely carp on the failure of O'Neill's language to rise to the dramatic occasion and resonate poetically.[6] An aesthetics of failure emerges as the governing principle of struggle between visionary desire and artistic limitation. In the minds of many O'Neill's greatness does not rest in his having achieved the goal of writing a great play, but in his aspirations to reach that goal. Jean Chothia observes: "It is the promise latent in the plays that is valued rather than the plays themselves, the aspiration and enterprise of the writer rather than the writings" (93). O'Neill longed to be a poet; he was not a good one. In *Long Day's Journey Into Night*, after Edmund's disclosure about the mystery of life, Tyrone tells him that he has the makings of a poet, to which his son responds: "The *makings* of a poet. No, I'm afraid I'm like the guy who is always panhandling for a smoke. He hasn't even got the makings. He's got only the habit. I couldn't touch what I tried to tell you just now. I just stammered. That's the best I'll ever do. I mean, if I live. Well, it will be faithful realism, at least. Stammering is the native eloquence of us fog people" (CP3 812–813).

Harold Clurman concluded his review of the American premiere of *Long Day's Journey Into Night* with this summation: "O'Neill's work is more than realism. And if it is stammering—it is still the most eloquent and significant stammer of the American theatre. We have not yet developed a cultivated speech that is either superior to it or as good" (Cargill 216).[7] The following pages attempt to show what "more than realism" means and what it looks like. A stammer captures the best image of O'Neill's drama: a struggle to get the words out, constantly repeating itself, always striving for something more and settling for something less than desired.

The site of this struggle resides in the relationship between the literary act of writing the play and the theatrical spectacle of staging it for public performance. Tension exists between the act of writing/reading and the act of seeing/listening. That a drama is written to be performed speaks to its radical of presentation defined by Northrop Frye: "Words may be acted in front of a spectator; they may be spoken in front of a listener; they may be sung or chanted; or they may be written for a reader. … For all the loving care that is rightfully expended on the printed texts of Shakespeare's plays, they are still radically acting scripts, and belong to the genre of drama" (247). A performance may take place in the theatre of the mind as well as on stage, but the reference is always to a theatrical space rather than the mundane world. O'Neill writes for a proscenium space with an acute awareness of all visual elements, including spatial relationships of the actors on stage. It is irrelevant to distinguish between an imaginary and a physical theatre; drama depends upon, in Timo Tiusanen's words, the "presence of the idea of the stage" (4). In order to read a play, one must consider the fluid images of actors moving in time within a theatrical space. Theatrical demands to make elements of performance visually appealing diminish the sole authority of the playwright.

A director mediates the relationship between drama and theatre. The writer is to the play what the director is to the production, an "artist of occasions" to borrow vocabulary from Robert Edmond Jones, in the literal sense of the phrase. A director stages a material/visual event in space and time, a physical production which models literary interpretation. In terms of production choices, the director ponders historical and cultural forces at work during the time of composition and those which inform the represented period of the play, as well as the prevailing conditions of the day. This triadic matrix includes particular staging practices that forged the drama into being. At the same time, subsequent performances reveal different working conditions, values, staging conventions, and points of view. Shifting and changing values bring classical texts into and out of favorable performance conditions. Technological advances bring about new practices that shed new light and new possibilities for staging old plays. Computerized lighting systems and hydraulic turntables, to name only two obvious and omnipresent examples from the current professional theatre, provide efficient means to solve scenic problems. Production strategies mapped by directors impact meaning and interpretation and lead to, in the end, a version of the play. Different directors, different actors, different designers, produce different results. The relative permeability of the dramatic text to various interpretations determines viability in the theatre repertory. New interpretations keep old plays alive.

Son of one of the most famous actors of the nineteenth century, O'Neill rebelled against his father's old-fashioned school of performance and exhibited a vehement prejudice against actors and the theatre throughout his life. He valued the published drama much more than live performance of his plays on Broadway. Ironically, theatrical production salvaged O'Neill's sagging reputation. Posthumous productions of *Long Day's Journey Into Night* in Sweden, New York and all over the world secured O'Neill's international and domestic elite standing among dramatists. In the United States, the Off-Broadway revival of *The Iceman Cometh* in 1956 by the Circle in the Square Theatre, located only a couple of blocks from the old Provincetown Playhouse, flashed new light on O'Neill and established

The Shakespeare Theatre's production of *Mourning Becomes Electra*, directed by Michael Kahn, at the Lansburgh Theatre in Washington, D.C., 1997. Ming Cho Lee's starkly modern box-within-a-box design and a highly efficient revolve, upon which the three walls turned, allowed for seamless and theatrically arresting transitions from interior to exterior spaces. Neutral colors and formal arrangements suggested the textual imagery of a "whited sepulcher." Pictured above are (left to right) Michelle O'Neill as Hazel Niles, Kelly McGillis as Lavinia Mannon, and Robert Sella as Orin Mannon. Photograph by Carol Rosegg. Courtesy of the Shakespeare Theatre.

José Quintero as the foremost interpreter of O'Neill's plays. Thereafter Quintero gained rights to *Long Day's Journey Into Night* from Mrs. O'Neill and directed the American premiere of that play on Broadway. *A Moon for the Misbegotten* followed these successes and finally appeared on Broadway in May 1957. Harold Clurman directed *A Touch of the Poet* in October 1958. Several years after O'Neill's death, three of his major plays ran simultaneously in New York and a fourth lagged not far behind.[8] These last plays, along with *Hughie* and the lone comedy, *Ah, Wilderness!* form the core of the O'Neill repertory that sustains his legacy today.

While the ability of a play to hold multiple interpretations tests its enduring quality, the task of the director is simply to pursue one choice among many possibilities. Therefore, it is incumbent upon the director to understand and comprehend fully the ramifications of particular decisions. Directorial vision at its best, then, always partial and provisional, is analogous to Nietzsche's perspectivism. In *On the Genealogy of Morals*, Nietzsche warns fellow philosophers that there is no pure objectivity in which the viewer of a particular thing sees all sides of that object simultaneously. The will of the observer must recognize the challenge of limitations: "There is *only* a perspective seeing, *only* a perspective 'knowing'; and the *more* affects we allow to speak about one thing, the *more* eyes, different eyes, we can use to observe one thing, the more complete will our 'concept' of this thing, our 'objectivity,' be" (119). In *Twilight of the Idols*, Nietzsche addresses the first task for which educators are required. It is applicable to the challenge of the stage director as well: "Learning to *see*—accustoming the eye to calmness, to patience, to letting things come up to it; postponing judgment, learning to go around and grasp each individual case from all sides" (*Portable Nietzsche* 511). Is this not analogous to the director who, after imagining a production in the mind, opens the rehearsal period up to actors and designers who know the play far less well? The director allows the cast to learn the play during rehearsal, a process of starting, stopping, revising, and trying new things. It is not performance, but it represents a possibility out of which final production emerges. The director watches rehearsal in order to monitor the progress of a future event. During rehearsal the director moves around the hall in order to see rehearsal from every angle. Later, in the theatre, the director anticipates what the audience will see from particular vantage points, reconciling conflicts of perspective in order to build a complex yet coherent interpretation. In his article about Nietzsche and vision, Gary Shapiro writes: "It is the task of the artist as explorer to look into the abyss and to prevent the facile acceptance of simplified visions" (137). "Abyss," a favorite Nietzschean word, signifies the inability to know all things. One cannot readily peek into the abyss and see the bottom. Perspectival seeing warns the viewer not to accept what is readily apprehensible. It encourages exploration and attempts to see as others see and to compare vision from different positions. It issues caution to go slow, to see from every angle, to mull over the significance of things.

Just as each member of the audience sees a different production, each production offers only a perspective of the drama. There is no such thing as a definitive production. Such a designation would forever end the need to produce a particular play again. Each moment in the dramatic text implies immanent structure which every production must build in material terms. The process of selection determines the originality and creativity of a particular production but it by no means exhausts the possibilities of a text. Material choices establish originality and individuate the production from the drama. The task of the director is not to be right, but to be interesting, to add to an understanding of the text. To stick with a visual analogy, the text is a three dimensional object around which the director must move in order to see it and appreciate it from as many sides as possible. It is not a matter of getting more out of the text, but seeing more of it.

Each of the following chapters examines visual conflict in O'Neill's plays from a different formal perspective. Chapter 1, *Writing a Novel Drama*, traces the narrative impulse in the plays that results from O'Neill's profound antitheatrical prejudice. O'Neill routinely disparaged the theatre as the Show Shop. It is distinctly odd that America's greatest dramatist considered actual production of his plays as an inevitable disappointment. Actors rarely portrayed roles as he conceived them. It would

The Wooster Group's 1996 production of *The Emperor Jones*, directed by Elizabeth LeCompte, in Brussels. The nature of identity remains an open question for a production in which Jones is played by a white woman (Kate Valk) wearing blackface. Along with Smithers (Willem Dafoe), the two person acting ensemble embraced Western and Eastern performance styles. A high tech minstrel soft shoe number highlighted the performance. Given the layers of influence informing production choices, the play's essential unmasking action remained ambiguous. Photograph by Mary Gearhart. Courtesy of the Wooster Group.

be a mistake, however, to chalk his attitude up to either personal idiosyncrasy or to the tawdry theatrical practices of the day. I believe that the
visual spectacle of the theatre threatened to usurp the writer's pre-emi-
nence, and stimulated him to find new means of dramatic expression to
assert authorial control. O'Neill's attempt to master the drama results in
a number of innovative techniques which borrow from the novel form. A
recent lampoon in *The New Yorker*, "Unspoken O'Neill," highlights the
author's penchant for literary stage directions and descriptions at the
expense of dialogue.[9] An emphasis upon monologue further affords him
the luxury of narrative speech. Ultimately, he extends the monologue to
the inner monologue, or thought aside, in which characters speak their
"inner" thoughts in addition and in conjunction with their "external"
speech. Novelizing the drama, through copious stage directions, elaborate character descriptions, theatrical tricks such as the thought asides in
Strange Interlude, and lengthy monologues, resists the theatre's explicit
visual imperative in favor of storytelling. O'Neill's plays, then, stage a
revolt against the very medium which conveys them.

The drama between showing and telling, dramatic and narrative, plays
extremely well in *Hughie* (1942), a one-act comprised almost exclusively
of monologues, spoken by gambler Erie Smith, or described in the silent
monologues of the hotel night clerk. Dialogue, the main signifier of drama,
is virtually absent. Instead, the two-bit hustler tells stories out of the past
and describes the recently deceased Hughie. A novelistic urge to describe
fully past events and relationships belies the emptiness of life on stage.
Tension in this short play stems from the need to establish intimate contact by Smith and refusal to engage on the part of the hotel clerk. The
action ends, however, with the two men sharing a conversation and mutually passing the remainder of the early morning hours in company, away
from the silent terrors of the night outside or the loneliness of Room 492
upstairs. As Smith once did with Hughie, he again sees himself as he
wants to be seen in the eyes of the new night clerk. The action details the
restorative human powers of dialogue. Emphasis upon narrative in the play
ultimately reveals the triumph and importance of theatre. O'Neill's novelistic retreat from dialogue refreshes the drama.

Other than monologue, masks serve as a prominent device in O'Neill's
dramaturgy. Chapter 2, *Masks and Mirrors*, examines masks as means to
reveal character and to probe the question of identity: loneliness and sensitivity; dividedness and multiplicity. O'Neill advocated their use in his
only published contribution to dramatic theory, *Memoranda on Masks*
(1932-1933).[10] *The Great God Brown* (1925), in which characters wear
masks, take them off, even trade them, serves as the apotheosis of mask

technique. The barrier between the actor's face and the viewer provides tension between revelation and concealment. The mask graphically solves the problem of how to present the struggle between the inside and the outside; it reveals the public face but hides the private one. Perceived difference between the two creates the illusion of character. While O'Neill employed masks for the last time in *Days Without End* (1933), metaphorical masks provide the essence of character in all of his works. The gradual stripping away of uniformed finery in *The Emperor Jones* (1920) corresponds to the unmasking of character. The same action recurs in the naturalistic *A Touch of the Poet*, in which Melody's soiled and torn military uniform signifies that his aristocratic demeanor has also been removed. The presence of the mask demonstrates O'Neill's prevalent theme of the need for illusion or the pipe dream. Major Melody constantly poses in front of the mirror in order to see if his mask is in place. Mirrors, sometimes nothing more than another character's eyes, rebuke or sustain the illusions which make life bearable.

Energy devoted to creating a mask is means for protection, and the action of every play moves toward unmasking. What's at stake, what lies underneath the mask, is human vulnerability. Although no masks are used literally, nowhere is the concept of the mask more apparent than in *A Moon for the Misbegotten*. The three principal characters are all actors whose individual masks peel away as the action unfolds to reveal a tender love story. Action builds toward revelation and concludes after the masks totally disappear and tension no longer exists between exterior presentation and interior identity. Exposed vulnerability reveals depth of character, depth of sorrow, joy, and human feeling. Love as sacrifice, verbalized in early plays, including the end of *Beyond the Horizon*, receives visual expression with the image of Josie Hogan holding Tyrone's body through the moonlight until dawn. She expresses the magnitude of her sacrifice with a simple valuation of the gesture: "...because it costs so much" (CP3 927). Shedding her mask as a wanton woman and exposing herself as a virgin signals the end of the play. Tension between the two roles sustains the drama and leads to final revelation, after which nothing remains to see.

Chapter 3, *Beyond the Proscenium*, traces the oscillation between here and there, presence and absence, between inside the frame (proscenium) of representation and outside the frame. This movement creates compelling visual interest and alters the perception of O'Neill's realism. That style becomes the context, or rather, the confinement, of the action against which the play rebels. The act of rebellion forces the drama to turn out beyond the proscenium and gives it visual stature that it would not otherwise possess. The opposition between land and sea, for example, continually finds the characters searching for what they do not have. If they are from the sea, they want to be on land. If on land, they long for the sea. The Blessed Isles, another Nietzschean phrase, return again and again as safe havens, escapes, places of freedom, far away from the confined land and morality of New England. Unseen characters, talked about but never directly represented, fill in the action of the plays at crucial moments. Doors separating one space from another, seen and unseen, govern action in which the outside poses a threat to the inside. At the same time, characters aspire to leave the environment which constrains them. Visual diffusion occurs in the drama in which what's outside displaces what's inside.

The realistic detail of Harry Hope's saloon, a combination of three watering holes O'Neill frequented in New York, contrasts with the nebulous void of the Great City outside and creates tension in *The Iceman Cometh*. What begins in a kind of Plato's Cave, according to John Henry Raleigh, transforms into the only reality available to the inhabitants of the saloon at the end (*Plays* 165–167). Larry Slade's declaration voiced early in the play that the bums who live in the bar have no further to slide is a lie. The option to go outside represents an even more dangerous and degrading step for the men than remaining paralyzed at the table. By never going outside, characters indulge in pipe dreams that insist upon a glorious life "out there." Hickey's sermon of salvation turns the bums out of the bar to face their pipe dreams on the streets. Hickey's truth eliminates the dualism between inside and outside. By opening the door and throwing down the gauntlet, Hickey makes the men face the emptiness of their lives in the terror of the streets. An outsider, Hickey, displaces the bums. But that action only enforces the fact that the outside world is "dead" to them. As they exit on parade and return soon thereafter it is clear that there is nothing outside for them. The world gets smaller as the play progresses. The large cast of this play is notable for the lack of female characters (none, other than the three tarts). Absent women, referred to but never seen, nonetheless play an extremely important role in the events. Male characters invent Evelyn Hickman, Bessie Hope, and Rosa Parritt, but invoking them calls attention to an absence which indicates the failure of intimate relationships. If *Hughie* is about the need for intimacy and engagement, *The Iceman Cometh* examines the cost of intimacy and flight from its demands. The iceman, death, finds a group of damaged men huddled around a bottle as if it were a campfire in the wilderness. The booze provides the only warmth against the blast of cold air coming from the frightening outside.

Chapter 4, *Plays Without End*, deals with repetition and the question of how plays end. Suicides, murders, incestuous desires and clandestine affairs that fuel early plays give way to tidy Aristotelian depictions of everyday life in the final ones. Epic adventures mutate into episodic representations. Yet, as less and less happens, tragic resonance increases, due in part to O'Neill's masterful use of repetition. A famous anecdote survives about *The Iceman Cometh*, in which a phrase about pipe dreams is repeated 18 times. Lawrence Langner pointed this out to O'Neill, who responded by saying that he meant it to occur 18 times (Langner 405). Repeating a particular image magnifies it and also creates a pattern. Critics harp upon the excessive length of O'Neill's plays and what they deem as needless repetition within them, but repetition is fundamental to the essential action in all of them. Tension always exists between the narrative drive of the plot to end in closure (e.g., suicide), and the competing desire for the play to repeat itself and form part of what O'Neill might call, with echoes of Nietzsche, the recurring life force. O'Neill's plays can be seen as musical compositions in which developing themes recur and transmute over time. The effect of time upon character is the theme for a novel that O'Neill tried to explore in early experimental plays. He adopted a traditional form in his final plays but the action became entirely retrospective and time, in a novel way, became the definitive and tragic subject at last.

Backward movement to the past in the plays rubs against forward drive in the present. Mary Tyrone recognizes the equation between the two temporal modes when she says, "The past is the present. It's the future, too" (CP3 765). Repetition is the force of the past claiming its victims in the present, victims who try in vain to break free. Action in *Long Day's Journey Into Night* picks up at the precise moment in which the Tyrones have begun to hope again that Mary has licked her crippling drug habit. Subsequently, they learn that an old pattern has resumed and they anticipate the familiar ritual of addiction. The supposed happy ending of a much earlier play, *"Anna Christie,"* failed to balance momentary happiness in the present with future tragic necessity. *Long Day's Journey Into Night* brilliantly reverses the temporal flow in a final image. No better curtain line exists than the quotidian brilliance of Mary's final words: "I fell in love with James Tyrone and was so happy for a time" (CP3 828). The drunken Tyrone men, trying to forget what has happened to them, gaze upon Mary, whose pigtails recall lost adolescence. She carries her wedding dress but she speaks of the convent. Instead of projecting a future of uncertain happiness as in *"Anna Christie,"* the final image in *Long Day's Journey Into Night* eulogizes the passing of time and the poignancy of regret despite the presence and persistence of love.

The final chapter, *Tragic Vision*, looks at the question of genre and the ongoing debate between melodrama and tragedy. Historically, critical opinion of O'Neill weighs on one side or the other and ranges from the artist as longwinded melodramatist to sublime tragedian. Although he received the Nobel Prize for "dramatic works of vital energy, sincerity, and intensity of feeling, stamped with an original conception of tragedy" (Hallström), Francis Fergusson, never an admirer of O'Neill, wrote unflatteringly of his plays in 1930: "I take it that the essence of melodrama is to accept emotions uncritically; which, in the writing amounts to assuming or suggesting emotions that are never realized either in language or action. Melodrama in this sense is a constant quality of Mr. O'Neill's work" (Cargill 272–273).[11] Eric Bentley, perhaps the most ardent O'Neill critic, allowed in *The Life of the Drama* that O'Neill succeeds with melodrama where he fails with tragedy (214). While Fergusson and Bentley invoke melodrama to cast aspersions upon O'Neill's work, Robert Benchley compliments O'Neill for "thrilling the bejeezus" out of his audience in *Mourning Becomes Electra*. His review of that play in *The New Yorker* cites aspects of melodrama as a source of great appeal in O'Neill's plays.

My interest does not lie in the search for adequate definitions of terms. O'Neill, of course, thought that he was writing tragedy which he regarded as ennobling. He particularly admired Greek tragedy and *Mourning Becomes Electra* attempted to scale tragic heights, in the vein of the Greeks, even to the point of borrowing their myths, but without resort to gods and with only a modern psychology of fate. Sticking to the concrete, I draw a visual analogy to the genres of tragedy and melodrama. Melodrama embodies visual clarity in terms of the size of gesture, clash of opposites, contrast of colors, and purity of values that are readily readable. To say that melodrama goes "over the top" is to appreciate the excessive theatricality that defines the genre and makes it enjoyable. If struggle is the operative word in O'Neill's sense of the tragic, the visual aspect of the struggle is that characters cannot see where they are going and cannot foretell consequences of what they do. Fog is the principal motif in O'Neill which visually defines tragic experience. Characters cannot see, and the inability to see functions as the essence of O'Neill's tragic vision. The desire to see and failure to do so creates a context for tragic events to occur. If melodrama represents a kind of wish-fulfillment in which everything is clear and visible, tragedy represents recognition that dreams don't come true. Looking at genre in this way eliminates discussion of melodrama and tragedy as discrete categories. Tension between them, always present, sustains visual interest in the plays.

From the perspective of genre, O'Neill's tragic vision derives from

Nietzsche's view of the world as unfathomable. In the Nietzschean landscape, the black abyss threatens to swallow human endeavor. Just as Socrates and intelligibility foil Nietzschean tragedy, melodrama, with its high contrast and visual clarity opposes O'Neill's tragic fog of anxiety and ambiguity. In *Mourning Becomes Electra*, for example, O'Neill, himself, hoped that his audience would see past the surface melodrama to the real drama underneath (SL 379). The surface and depth paradigm asks that the diligent interpreter excavate the work in order to discover riches buried within the play. O'Neill places melodrama and tragedy in two separate places. My project aligns the terms and recognizes that these tendencies, while polar opposites, are not mutually exclusive in O'Neill's dramatic universe. Examination of a grand play such as *Mourning Becomes Electra* reveals the codependent relationship of melodramatic and tragic elements. The plot, a thrilling melodrama of lust, revenge, murder and incestuous desire, provides an excuse for a spectacle of watching. Beginning with the entrance of the town chorus at the start of the play, the audience observes characters watching each other perform a melodrama. Only Lavinia refuses ultimately to play. She refuses to publish her brother's lurid history of the Mannons, a generational melodrama. Her final act, self-entombment, pulls down the curtain on melodrama; opaqueness, inability to see, raises the possibility of tragedy.

My method appears to stack a series of binary oppositions against each other: narrative and dramatic; revelation and concealment; here and there; past and present; melodrama and tragedy. Indeed, these tensions sustain the drama, but I don't suggest that there is an Hegelian synthesis to the dialectic that I'm putting forward as a basic structuring principle in O'Neill's drama. I believe that the failure of the plays (that phrase again) to resolve these conflicts accounts for their enduring presentations. This claim may seem counter-intuitive given familiarity with O'Neill's works. One of the habits that he adopted in Professor Baker's English 47 playwriting class was the discipline of writing a detailed scenario of a play before he wrote it. It is impossible not to see the direction in which a particular O'Neill play travels. Even O'Neill's better plays, such as *A Touch of the Poet*, *The Iceman Cometh*, and *A Moon for the Misbegotten* chug through their respective plots along a formulaic track. O'Neill railroads the illusion/reality theme (a classic Western literature theme and the subject of many undergraduate essays) to the extent that his meaning seems inescapable, if not depressing: humanity cannot bear to face the truth. The highly architected plays seem to lead to a definitive and inevitable conclusion, but I don't think that they are as straightforward as they seem. The oppositions end in stalemates which don't provide answers but ask questions of the audience who witnesses the event. My critical project drives a wedge in this site of failure to open up space for interpretation to fill.

Problems, not plays, provide the organizational structure for all the chapters. Focus upon pervasive tendencies that appear throughout the entire canon replaces any need to deal with the plays in chronological order. The range of examples is limited to O'Neill's *Complete Plays*, edited by Travis Bogard, the three volume edition of 50 plays published by the Library of America in 1988 to mark the centennial of O'Neill's birth. Even among this group of plays, however, emphasis remains upon those plays which form part of an enduring repertory. Thus, *Lazarus Laughed* (1926), a play O'Neill always admired for containing some of his best writing (that's what he thought), gets short shrift because it has never been produced professionally. Technical and artistic demands of that text make any future production highly problematic. The "lost" plays, early unproduced work, find little representation in these pages, nor does the very lengthy draft of *More Stately Mansions* (1939).[12] The creative license that an unfinished manuscript offers to a production team often invites production, and successful stagings of this play credit the skillful editing and vision of a director. That said, there is no way to anticipate what changes O'Neill, himself, would have made to his manuscript, and thus, the text resists the kind of analysis that I'm employing in this study. In general, examples show preference to the late masterpieces. The reader will discover far more references to *Long Day's Journey Into Night* than to, say, *The First Man* (1921). The former play is one of the greatest plays in all of modern drama and a play that the reader will likely have an opportunity to see, or has seen, at some point. *The First Man*, on the other hand, appeals only to the most earnest O'Neill scholar and enthusiast. The weaknesses of that play, however, and others such as *Diff'rent* (1920), *Dynamo* (1928), and *Days Without End* (1933) often address particular problems more effectively than the strengths of better plays and bear inclusion for that reason. O'Neill frequently integrates obvious techniques in inferior plays into more subtle representations in superior efforts. The first part of each chapter lays the groundwork for a particular theoretical claim and concludes with extended analysis of a single play or plays in order to ground the argument within a sustained context. While the problems remain discrete in each chapter, the force of my project implies interchangeable examples. I use *A Moon for the Misbegotten*, for instance, to talk at length about character and unmasking as a principal action. This is doubtless a convenient pairing, but if there is any profound truth to my overall approach, then another play, say, *Hughie*, must also fit within the schema that I develop. The tensions that I see within the plays regarding genre, dialogue, character, scene, and action operate on all of the plays all of the time.

By way of example, *Bound East for Cardiff* (1914) shows how perspectives outlined in each chapter combine to form a composite picture of the drama. This early play, the first of O'Neill's to receive production, authentically represents all the later plays to come, according to Eugene M. Waith: "The movement of its action is the characteristic movement of an O'Neill play—a movement toward discovery or revelation or both—a kind of unmasking" (33). O'Neill recognized the importance of this play in a letter correcting dates for his plays in 1934 to Richard Dana Skinner, who was then writing a book on O'Neill's drama: "In it can be seen—or felt—the germ of the spirit, life-attitude, etc. of all my significant future work—and it was written practically within my first half-year as a playwright, before I went to Baker, under whose influence the following year I did nothing 1/10 as original. Remember in these U. S. in 1914 *Bound East for Cardiff* was a daring innovation both in form & content" (SL 438).

Beginning with the title, the play evokes tragic aspirations, despite the low class characters represented in the action and the mundane events portrayed. The play takes place in the crewmen's quarters of the S.S. *Glencairn*, a tramp steamer en route from New York to Cardiff. Action picks up *in medias res*, somewhere between the two ports on the Atlantic Ocean. Previous to the start, one seaman, Yank, fell from a ladder and mortally injured himself. The action of the play consists of his friend, Driscoll, comforting him during his dying moments. On a foggy night, fog remains as the dominant motif in the play (see Chapter 5). The titular word "bound" evokes a sense of fate in the play, a destination over which the sailors in the ship have no control. Days away from port, the ship strands them alone at sea, along with the fog, which prevents them from seeing.

At the outset of this short play, members of the crew, including a Swede and an Irishman, talk among themselves and smoke in the seamen's forecastle. A Norwegian plays a battered accordion from the top deck. Talk of the rotten weather and foul working conditions halts at the sound of a groan from the rear bunk. Only then do they realize that Yank lies with them, badly injured and slowly dying. The crew respectfully muffles their speech and leaves to relieve the watch. One group goes out, another comes in. Only Driscoll remains to tend to Yank. In the second section, the captain and first mate enter to take stock of the situation. Social divisions between officers and sailors manifest themselves in uniforms, titles, and the fact that the officers "come down" to see about Yank. One of the sailors, Davis, describes the relationship between haves and have nots in this way:

"Plenty o' work and no food—and the owners ridin' around in carriages!" (CP1 190). Significantly, owners are not present in the action. Ship's officers, including the captain, function as their surrogates. Cocky, confident that the captain can do nothing for Yank, expresses the contempt of the working men for their superiors: "That silly ol' josser! Wot the 'ell would 'e know abaht anythink?" (189). When the captain and mate do appear, expected antagonisms vanish in the humanity of the moment. The captain is genuinely interested in Yank's health. He expresses true sorrow that he cannot help Yank, but instructs Driscoll to stay with him and not to let him move. He captures the futility and fateful moment of the play with his lament: "I can't do anything else for him. It's too serious for me. If this had only happened a week later we'd be in Cardiff in time to—" (194). Use of the subjunctive indicates a grammar of fate. There is no doctor and no facility to help Yank. There is no hope, even though all the men pretend and hope that he won't die. The hopeless hope, or the need for illusion, surfaces in this play as a major theme.

Yank knows and feels that he's going to die. Monologue supplants dialogue in the form of confessions of the dying man to his best friend in the final part of the play (see Chapter 1). The monologue fulfills a narrative function and supplies a history of the mens' lives in terms of where they've been and what they want. Driscoll, the friend, becomes a silent auditor, whose bunkside presence gives Yank license to speak at length. Yank speaks of the repetition of life and tries to justify death as relief from it: "This sailor life ain't much to cry about leavin'—just one ship after another, hard work, small pay, and bum grub; and when we git into port, just a drunk endin' up in a fight, and all your money gone, and then ship away again. Never meetin' no nice people; never gittin' outa sailor town, hardly, in any port; travelin' all over the world and never seein' none of it; without no one to care whether you're alive or dead. [*with a bitter smile*] There ain't much in all that that'd make yuh sorry to lose it, Drisc" (195).

The reality of the sailor's lot is juxtaposed by Yank's dream of being buried on land and owning a farm. Driscoll joins in enthusiastically to say that he's had the same dream and that they'll live it together as soon as Yank gets better. Expression of the dream breathes life into the drama. The land/sea opposition transports the action of the play beyond the proscenium as the characters paint a picture of life away from the tiny quarters of the forecastle (see Chapter 3). Yank reveals his dream to Driscoll only when he knows that he's going to die. He says that he was always afraid that his friend would laugh at him if he spoke of his heartfelt dreams. Only with death upon him, can he unburden himself. The dire situation, however, forces Driscoll to agree with Yank and drop his tough pose. The unmasking of the characters reaches poignancy in their last scene together (see Chapter 2). They describe a brutal world in which they have played a part. Yank gives voice to his fear that he will be damned because he once stabbed a man. Driscoll eases his conscience by absolving him of the crime by asserting that it was self-defense. At last, Yank, who has no relations, asks Driscoll to buy a box of candy for Fanny the barmaid, who once "tried to lend me half a crown" (198). The tenderness and intimacy of the two sailors, beneath hard and coarse exteriors, engenders an empathetic response.

The image of the dying sailor flirts with melodrama. Near the end, Yank sees fog within the cabin. It is the fog of death, "a pretty lady dressed in black" come to take Yank away (198). The atmosphere of the *Glencairn* undercuts Yank's dying in the arms of his best friend. Repetition of the ship's routine, the change in the watch, the sound of the ship's bells, offsets the finality of death (see Chapter 4). While Yank lies dying, other sailors snore in their bunks, resting before their next watch. Snoring and sleeping effectively drain melodrama from the death scene. In fact, the routine of the ship heightens the impact of the dying sailor. According to Alan S. Downer, Yank's "dying against a background of his quarreling, disinterested mates, is an image of the loneliness and frustration of man" (469). Ironically, a sailor returns to the cabin at play's end to report that the fog has lifted. Clarity returns only after Yank has died. The drama expands from the cramped quarters of the seamen's forecastle, the represented scene of the dying sailor, to show the ship as part of a much larger scene, one tiny ship floating on an immense ocean. The sea as fate, a wild and untamed presence which surrounds and dwarfs the represented scene, potentially diminishes the importance of human action. The relative insignificance of Yank's death gives it dignity and tragic stature. Loss of his friend greatly impacts Driscoll. The fact that life goes on proffers a tough reminder of an undying reality.

The following chapters emphasize the technical means of expression in order to see the plays in a new way. Rather than exploring conflict between characters within the representation, this way of seeing explores tensions or conflict between the very elements that make up the drama. Foregrounding dramatic technique separates the representation from reality. By looking at O'Neill's plays, not as reflections of personal experience, but as works of art, they begin to appear as strange and wondrous as opposed to old and familiar. It is indisputable that the late plays surpass all of O'Neill's previous efforts. Abandoning classifications such as expressionistic and realistic, however, creates an opportunity to discover principles which bind all of O'Neill's dramas together. This approach reverses the traditional order of how to view a play: seeing the picture first and then trying to explain how it got that way. I look at the techniques first, and build an interpretation on the basis of pervasive tendencies. This strategy tries to liberate O'Neill from the shackles of autobiography and highlight the extraordinary achievements of a remarkable American playwright.

Chapter 1

Writing a Novel Drama

"Oh for a language to write drama in! For a speech that is dramatic and isn't just conversation! I'm so strait-jacketed by writing in terms of talk! I'm so fed up with the dodge-question of dialect! But where to find that language? Any suggestions on this question will be gratefully received."
—*letter to Joseph Wood Krutch, July 27, 1929*

Welded (1923) portrays a married couple, playwright and actress, who fight continually in order to form a more perfect union. The writer, Michael Cape, seeks an ideal state in which the two are one. O'Neill's staging techniques visualize this struggle perfectly. He dictates that the only light onstage should be two spotlights following each character, representing individual "auras of egoism" (CP2 235).[1] The action also introduces the first use of the thought aside, which becomes a dominant technique later in the decade with *Strange Interlude* (1927). More limited use here finds husband and wife, at one point, sitting side by side in chairs and speaking directly at the audience as if they were giving voice to inner thoughts. The stage picture at the end of the play overcomes division in an expression of unity as Michael ascends the stairs of his apartment to join Eleanor: "For a moment as their hands touch they form together one cross" (276). Judging from O'Neill's letters to his wives, he may have believed in the ideal of marriage to which the playwright in *Welded* aspires.[2] Indeed, critics have argued that O'Neill wrote this play as an attempt to work out problems with his marriage to his second wife, Agnes Boulton, to whom he had been married five years.[3]

As much as the play may reveal about O'Neill's personal struggles, *Welded* dramatizes the playwright's desire to suit the action to the word

27

and to subordinate the actor to the playwright. In one heated exchange between the couple, Cape ends the argument with the following attack: "Good God, how dare you criticize creative work, you actress!" (249). Celebrated and revered as a collaborative art, theatrical performance poses a threat to the playwright who seeks to have first and last word. For O'Neill, the ideal marriage of actor and playwright requires the actor to serve as an extension of the writer's will and to perform the role as written and conceived by the playwright. O'Neill considered the written drama as he wrote it superior to theatrical production. Throughout his career, he fastidiously prepared his manuscripts for publication. Adding descriptive narrative to the plays addresses a reading public, but it also attempts to compensate for shoddy theatrical productions. The plays reveal O'Neill's antitheatrical prejudice and novelistic impulse to stage his plays on the written page.[4]

Consequently, O'Neill writes a novel drama in at least three senses. In a letter to director George C. Tyler in 1920, O'Neill regarded *Chris Christophersen*, which closed in an out of town tryout, as "a special play, a technical experiment by which I tried to compress the theme for a novel into play form without losing the flavor of the novel" (SL 122).[5] O'Neill does not identify his theme for a novel. Evidence from the plays written during this period (1918–1927) implies that he means character development as it unfolds over a long period of time. Literally, O'Neill's plays throughout the experimental decade of the 1920s begin to resemble novels in terms of length of representation and amount of time covered by the representation. An inverse relationship develops between these two aspects in the last plays. These plays, some of the longest among all American plays, adhere to Aristotelian unities of time, place and action. I will delay a discussion of the temporal aspects of novelization until the fourth chapter.

Novel drama in a second sense, as new and innovative, brings an array of O'Neill's contributions to mind. O'Neill specified radical ideas for staging his plays, such as removable exterior (*Desire Under the Elms*) and shrinking interior walls (*All God's Chillun Got Wings*); he developed expressionistic pantomime in *The Emperor Jones* (1920) and *The Hairy Ape* (1921) and compounded the dramatic use of long monologues by developing a conceit of inner monologues or thought asides (*Strange Interlude*) whereby characters expressed thoughts aloud to the audience; he intended stage lighting to add tangible significance to the meaning of the play and not serve as mere illumination (*Welded*); the sound of the hydroelectric plant in *Dynamo* reaches for the structural quality of a musical composition. In *The Great God Brown* (1925), O'Neill made extensive use of masks in order to show the duality and multiplicity and dividedness of character; he later expanded the use of masks (subject of the next chapter on character) to include hundreds of permutations of them in *Lazarus Laughed* (1926). *Marco Millions* (1924), in which a thirteenth century Marco applauds the play he has just appeared in and then leaves the building for the waiting comfort of a long limousine, satirizes the babbitry of the American businessman. These largely self-conscious techniques are symptomatic of O'Neill's desire to trump theatrical productions with his master text.

The novel drama, in its most profound sense, stages a battle between showing and telling. The former is the tendency of the drama; the latter is the function of narrative. Narrative needs, according to Scholes and Kellogg, "a teller and a tale" (4). The presence of a story-teller, a filter to the events, a medium, allows great flexibility in terms of the way the story is told. It may be told chronologically in a straightforward manner, or in reverse order, or alternate between the two. The story-teller may pause at any moment to expound upon anything that seems appropriate. The teller stands outside the tale, spatially and temporally, and thus has the power to mediate the event. Drama, on the other hand, is "a story without a story-teller; in it characters act out directly what Aristotle called an 'imitation' of such actions as we find in life" (4). Historically, appealing aspects of the theatre include immediacy and the presence of the actor standing on a stage in front of an audience. A novel is, above all else, complete as written. It only needs a reader. Drama, conversely, must be produced. Directors, designers, and especially actors intervene between the playwright and audience to interpret the work and make it visible. In this chapter, I am concerned with the novelistic desire to tell all versus the resistant theatrical mandate to show events.

Any high school student can recognize drama by its most obvious formal attribute: dialogue. In *The Theory of the Modern Drama*, Peter Szondi writes that "The absolute dominance of dialogue—that is, of interpersonal communication, reflects the fact that the Drama consists only of the reproduction of interpersonal relations, is only cognizant of what shines forth within this sphere" (8). Unlike the novel, in which a narrator may establish a point of view and tell the reader valuable expository and descriptive information, provide commentary on events, or even present internal thoughts of characters directly, the drama places the burden upon dialogue, communication between two or more characters, to show everything. Dramatic texts are essentially comprised only of dialogue. Everything else is extraneous. Stage directions, which often try to accomplish the above novelistic purposes, remain unseen in the theatre, except through the interpretations of actors, directors, and designers. Combinations of language and gesture, in which one implies if not dictates the other, create meaning in the theatre. Szondi suggests that the drama does not enjoy the comparative looseness of form of the novel. At the same time, the demands of dramatic form create opportunities for other theatrical collaborators to produce the drama and to expand the possibilities for performance.

O'Neill resists the idea of collaboration expanding the text. For him, reading his play is preferable to seeing it. Complaining of theatrical conditions to Kenneth Macgowan in 1926, O'Neill lamented: "What's the use of my trying to get ahead with new stuff until some theatre can give that stuff the care and opportunity it must have in order to register its new significance outside of the written page in a theatre?" (SL 213–214). Concerning several productions of his plays in Stockholm, Budapest, Berlin, and Vienna, O'Neill rationalized his decision not to see any of them, even though he was living in France at the time, to Eleanor Fitzgerald in 1929: "My interest in the productions steadily decreases as my interest in plays as written increases. They always—with the exceptions you know—fall so far below or beside my intent that I'm a bit weary and disillusioned with scenery and actors and the whole uninspired works of the Show Shop" (SL 338). O'Neill follows a tradition of critics, notably Charles Lamb in Shakespeare criticism, who view the performance as inferior to the literary work.[6] The material performance and its interpretation interfered with the platonic structure that O'Neill built in his own imagination. In a 1924 interview, O'Neill put his case forward bluntly: "I don't go to the theatre because I can always do a better production in my mind than the one on stage. I have a better time and I am not bothered by the audience" (Cargill 112).[7] Actors, when all else is said and done, receive the brunt of O'Neill's disdain for the theatrical event. Despite liking many individual actors, O'Neill felt that actors rarely performed roles in his plays as he conceived them. In all of O'Neill's plays, he noted only three actors who played the roles as he imagined them: Louis Wolheim as Yank in *The Hairy Ape*; Charles Gilpin as Brutus Jones in *The Emperor Jones*; and Walter Huston as Cabot in *Desire Under the Elms*. Even Gilpin's performance, however, rubbed O'Neill the wrong way in time and caused him to replace him with a young Paul Robeson. To friend Michael Gold, O'Neill berated the deterioration of Gilpin's performance in 1923: "Yes, Gilpin is all 'ham' and a yard wide! Honestly, I've stood for more from him than from all the white actors I've ever known—simply because he was colored! He played Emperor with author, play & everyone concerned. There is humor in the situation but I confess mine has worn out" (SL 177). For his part, Gilpin had this to say about the play's success and his performance in it: "I created the role of the Emperor. That role belongs to me. That Irishman, he just wrote the play" (Gelb 450).[8]

O'Neill's disdain for actors extended from early to late in his career. He did not outgrow antipathy against the theatre over time. Protesting director George C. Tyler's request for his presence to attend an out of town tryout of *Chris Christophersen* in Philadelphia in 1920, O'Neill countered that he could make any necessary adjustments in the script without seeing a performance: "Up here I see the real faults inherent in the play itself—my faults. But the only thing I ever get out of seeing a presentation is the actors' faults which never fail to set me in a rage. I'd rather keep a pleasant memory of the *Chris* cast than to have to hate at least fifty percent of them for the rest of my life" (SL 121). At the very end of his career, contemplating the last Broadway production during his lifetime, *The Iceman Cometh*, O'Neill's prejudice against actors had increased, if anything. A letter to his friend and critic George Jean Nathan reveals an author confident of the play's worth, but skeptical about putting it in the hands of actors and in front of an audience to see. He confided to Nathan in 1940: "I'm not giving a thought to production. In fact, I hate to think of it being produced—of having to watch a lot of actors muscle in their personalities to make strange for me these characters of the play that interest me so much—now, as *I* have made them live!" (SL 501). He finished writing the play in 1940 but refused to allow production until after the war. *Iceman* aside, O'Neill's best works remained unperformed during his lifetime: *A Touch of the Poet, A Moon for the Misbegotten, Hughie*, and, of course, *Long Day's Journey Into Night*. *A Moon for the Misbegotten*, his last play, opened out of town in Columbus, Ohio, and closed on the road. When he published it in 1952, O'Neill wrote the following note to introduce the text: "It has never been presented on the New York stage nor are there outstanding rights or plans for its production. Since I cannot presently give it the attention required for appropriate presentation, I have decided to make it available in book form" (CP2 854). Despite poor productions or no productions at all of his last plays, O'Neill recognized their value. As a group they vindicate literally and literarily a lifetime waged against the commercial theatre.

O'Neill desired to probe character below the "banality of surfaces," as his literary mentor Strindberg did (Sheaffer *Son and Artist* 124), to explore beyond what characters say to express what they think and feel as well.[9] The novel form best accomplishes this task because the narrator may freely articulate through language whatever enters the mind of the represented character. The novel, which contains but is not constrained by dialogue, is an ideal form for the exploration of psychological depth: it reveals secrets and keeps secrets from visibility. In plays, reliance upon dialogue between characters shifts emphasis to action, external events, instead of internal battles within the human psyche. Accordingly, melodrama serves as the ideal form for drama in the late nineteenth and early twentieth centuries. During that same period, not surprisingly, the modern novel ascends as the most serious form to deal with complex human developments. The novel provided for O'Neill a set of tools which he wished to appropriate for dramatic means, as Normand Berlin explains: "O'Neill wanted drama to do what the novel did; the novel had a flexibility that O'Neill wished to claim for the drama. Simply stated, O'Neill wanted drama to do *more*, the more that he found in the novel form, so he pushed his dramatic art closer to the art of the novelist in his boldest experiments, experiments which stress a character's *inner* reality through such devices as masks and thought monologues and split personalities" ("O'Neill the Novelist" 50).

O'Neill's novelistic techniques include elaborate stage directions, highly specific character descriptions, and reliance upon monologues which stress a narrative, as opposed to dramatic, function. The description of the trees in *Desire Under the Elms* offers a particularly good example of narrative device obscuring dramatic function:

> Two enormous elms are on each side of the house. They bend their trailing branches down over the roof. They appear to protect and at the same time subdue. There is a sinister maternity in their aspect, a crushing, jealous absorption. They have developed from their intimate contact with the life of man in the house an appalling humanness. They brood oppressively over the house. They are like exhausted women resting their sagging breasts and hands and hair on its roof, and when it rains their tears trickle down monotonously and rot on the shingles [CP2 318].

The two trees function as a false proscenium through which the audience sees the rest of the play. They disappear as soon as the play starts and do not integrate with the action. The house, with its cutaway sections, and scenic oscillations between interior and exterior settings, commands all focus in the play. There is no rain. Appearing like exhausted women poses a huge challenge for the trees in the context of a realistic play. Jean Chothia argues that the literary stage directions hold no dramatic value (40). Furthermore, suggestion that the trees have a "jealous maternity" and an "appalling humanness" provides recipe for theatrical disaster once the literary transforms into material and theatrical form. Not surprisingly, O'Neill raged in a letter to Kenneth Macgowan against the theatre's inability to produce the poetic trees that he had described.[10] While a reading of the play might benefit from O'Neill's descriptions, a theatrical production must translate the literary into the theatrical. It is possible to imagine a production that dispenses with the elms altogether in response to materiality's inability to embody a verbal image.

Opening directions for *Long Day's Journey Into Night* present a second example of literary stage directions that seek to novelize the drama. Two bookcases in the Tyrone household, which is certainly none other than O'Neill's boyhood home at *Monte Cristo* cottage on Pequot Avenue in New London, Connecticut, receive elaborate attention concerning their contents. The first contains novels by Balzac, Zola, Stendhal, philosophical and sociological works by Schopenhauer, Nietzsche, Marx, Engels, Kropotkin, Max Sterner; plays by Ibsen, Shaw, Strindberg; poetry by Swinburne, Rossetti, Wilde, Ernest Dowson, and Kipling. A second glassed-in bookcase has sets of "Dumas, Victor Hugo, Charles Lever, three sets of Shakespeare, The World's Best Literature in fifty large volumes, Hume's History of England, Thiers' History of the Consulate and Empire, Smollett's History of England, Gibbon's Roman Empire and miscellaneous volumes of old plays, poetry, and several histories of Ireland" (CP3 717). Of the latter, O'Neill adds: "The astonishing thing about these sets is that all the volumes have the look of having been read and reread" (717).

Who can see the condition of these books, let alone read the titles? O'Neill's directions, and probably most productions, place the bookcases in the back of the room in order to keep sightlines clear. A typical audience member, even one on the front row, would not be able to judge the condition of the books as to whether or not they had been read frequently. And it is highly doubtful that anyone would be able to detect a tiny copy of *Thus Spake Zarathustra*. Stage directions give information that is available to the reader much earlier than to an audience sitting in the theatre. The two bookcases establish territory between father and son and the generational battle that will play out for the duration of the action. Books draw the line between father and son, old and new, progressive and reactionary. The titles themselves help define character even before anyone speaks in the play, but this experience is only privy to a reader. The first group of titles represents primary literary influences upon O'Neill. Literary quotation plays an enormous role in the action and characters refer to many of the books on the shelf in the course of the play. Only through the mouths of the actors do the books become part of the relevant action. Shakespeare is not a force until Jamie first invokes *Othello*.[11] Nietzsche is not important until Edmund quotes from *Zarathustra*.[12] Swinburne does not really appear until the end when Jamie quotes *A Leave-taking* as he watches his mother in a drug induced fog.[13] The books only exist insofar as the actors bring them into play. The descriptions prior to the play attempt to pre-empt a function that belongs to the actors in the unfolding action.

Character descriptions similarly seek to make performance unnecessary and almost impossible. The description of Josie Hogan from *A Moon for the Misbegotten* offers the most extreme example of specific physiognomy that defies performance: "She is so oversize for a woman that she is almost a freak—five feet eleven in her stockings and weighs around one hundred and eighty. Her sloping shoulders are broad, her chest deep with large, firm breasts, her waist wide but slender by contrast with her hips and thighs. She has long smooth arms, immensely strong, although no muscles show. The same is true of her legs. She is more powerful than any but an exceptionally strong man, able to do the manual labor of two ordinary men. But there is no mannish quality about her. She is all woman" (CP3 857). As if that were not enough to establish her character, O'Neill continues: "The map of Ireland is stamped on her face, with its long upper lip and small nose, thick black eyebrows, black hair as coarse as a horse's mane, freckled, sunburned fair skin, high cheekbones and heavy jaw. It is not a pretty face, but her large dark-blue eyes give it a note of beauty, and her smile, revealing even white teeth, gives it charm" (857).

Specific physical requirements, absolutely important to O'Neill's conception of the character, make production difficult. Much of the play relies upon a discussion of Josie's physical features: her breasts, her height, her hair, etc. While Hamlet may be conceived in any size or gender, it is hard to see Josie other than the way that O'Neill describes the character. For O'Neill, describing the physical character from the outside roots the character in a reality. Appearances dictate character. Each detail of character description, however, raises a further question to the extent that even a slave to O'Neill's perceived intent would not know how to follow his directions. Contradictions in the passage above demand interpretation. Josie, for example, is "almost a freak," but she is "all woman." She is more powerful than a man, but "there is no mannish quality about her." Her face is not pretty, but her eyes "give it a note of beauty." In fact, the description of Josie establishes a principle of contradiction that opens up her character. Disjunction between Josie's outer appearance and her inner reality lies at the heart of the play's unmasking action. For the producer, O'Neill's literary character descriptions invite interpretation to define the particular contradictions of a character and a production. The point is that there may not be an actress who fits O'Neill's description of Josie, but the textual energy expended to capture her asks the director, and later an audience, to consider the question of beauty, not just in terms of Josie's beautiful soul, but her physical appearance.[14]

The ubiquitous monologue is further evidence of O'Neill's novelistic urge to fill up the drama and replace the spaces between dialogue with words. Just as stage directions and character descriptions satisfy a reading public, the monologue, with its emphasis upon words, allows the playwright to speak directly through the actor to the audience. As early as *Before Breakfast* (1916), a short one-act modeled after Strindberg's *The Stronger*, O'Neill experimented with the monologue to see how much an audience could endure.[15] In the case of the thought aside, an extension of the monologue, the actor becomes a mouthpiece for the character as written by the dramatist. In *Dynamo*, for example, Reuben Light addresses the dynamo as if it were a deity. The final four scenes of the play, including the entire third act, are almost entirely monologic. O'Neill resorts to monologue in this case to fulfill a narrative function and wind up his drama about the "the death of the old God and the failure of Science and Materialism to give any satisfying new One for the surviving primitive religious instinct to find a meaning for life in, and to comfort its fears of death with" (SL 311). The inability of the boy to communicate with his god creates an absurd situation. The last scene in Act 2 is entirely a monologue in which Reuben beholds his electrical god. In the printed text, indentation indicates that this speech reflects Reuben's internal thoughts: "It's like a great dark idol ... like the old stone statues of gods people prayed to ... only it's living and they were dead ... that part on top is like a head ... with eyes that see you without seeing you ... and below it is like a body ... not a man's ... round like a woman's ... as if it had breasts ... but not like a girl ... not like Ada ... no, like a woman ... like her mother ... or mine ... a great, dark mother! ... that's what the dynamo is! ... that's what life is! ..." (871).

By making the internal thoughts and feelings of a character manifest in the text, there is nothing left for the actor to do in performance. These thought asides function purely as narrative devices. The explicitness of the above speech, the articulation of thought into language, the reification of thought into language, is quite silly. To conclude that the dynamo equals mother, equals God, equals the meaning of life is to indulge extreme banality. The idea behind the play (witness O'Neill's above statement in his letter), remains an interesting and valid idea for a drama. This particular play fails, however, in part because narrative speech, telling, gives no room for ambiguity in the text. There is no room left to show anything.

The most novelistic of all plays remains *Strange Interlude* (1927), in which O'Neill, as one anonymous published source allows, "is claiming for the stage the liberties that are the novel's natural inheritance" (Cargill 367). This comment refers both to the content of the play and, more significantly, the form in which it is realized. The action occurs over a time span of twenty-five years and chronicles Nina Leeds' search for happiness in the arms of a series of men: her young lover (whose wartime death precedes and precipitates the action in the play); her father; her businessman husband; her scientist lover; her young son (named after her first lover); her surrogate father, Charlie Marsden, a novelist. In the sixth of nine acts, Nina, pregnant with her lover's baby, surrounded by husband Evans, Dr. Darrell, and good old Charlie, surveys the living room scene triumphantly and speaks to herself in a thought aside: "My three men! ... I feel their desires converge in me! ... to form one complete beautiful male desire which I absorb ... and am whole ... they dissolve in me, their life is my life ... I am pregnant with the three! ... husband! ... lover! ... father! ... and the fourth man! ... little man! ... little Gordon! ... he is mine too! ... that makes it perfect! ..." (CP2 756). The passion which Nina extends outward to all of the men in this scene first flames, then diminishes and finally burns out over the next three acts in which over twenty-one years pass and Gordon, Jr., rises to early manhood and picks a bride, himself. Despite being only about forty-five years old at the end, stage directions in act 8 describe Nina as an old woman: "Nina's hair has turned completely white. She is desperately trying to conceal the obvious inroads of time by an over-emphasis on make-up that defeats its end by drawing attention to what it would conceal" (778). The change between the end of act 6 and here is remarkable, to say the least!

This shift reveals the episodic structure of the whole play and the rapid acceleration of time's movement as the action draws to a close. Time between the episodes assumes more importance than the action within the episodes themselves. Each act recapitulates unseen action that brings the past back into the present moment. These unseen moments, which are really where the bulk of the action takes place, are the true subject of the drama—the effects of time upon the characters. Regarding Darrell, her old lover, in scene 8, Nina reminisces to herself about days of passion in contrast to present conditions: "...the only living life is the past and future ... the present is an interlude ... strange interlude in which we call on past and future to bear witness we are living..." (784). The end of the play returns Nina to the arms of a father, this time Charlie Marsden instead of Professor Leeds. Comforting her at the end, he urges her to rest and to forget the past: "So let's you and me forget the whole distressing episode, regard it as an interlude, of trial and preparation, say, in which our souls have been scraped clean of impure flesh and made worthy to bleach in peace" (817). Youthful innocence and first love with Gordon grows into an afternoon, adulterous affair with Darrell, followed by the cool evening shade that Marsden welcomes. The literary quality to the preceding lines matches well to a drama which is actually a novelistic interlude, in which the unseen spaces of time are the true subject of the play and novelistic technique triumphs over the dramatic.

Marsden, a novelist afraid to embrace life, writes his timid books from a distance. He functions nearly as a narrator to the events in the play, always prescient regarding Nina and her sexual attractions. Regarding events in the play, Marsden remarks half-way through the action, "... what a plot for a novel!" (747). In the very first scene, Nina prepares to leave her father's house to work as a nurse, a job in which she plans to give herself sexually to wounded soldiers in recompense for the fact that she didn't give herself to Gordon before he went off to die in the war. To calm Marsden's excitement and confusion of the moment, Nina teases: "But some day I'll read it all in one of your books, Charlie, and it'll be so simple and easy to understand that I won't be able to recognize it, Charlie, let alone understand it!" (650). In the next act, Darrell muses about Marsden's writing: "...his novels just well-written surface ... no depth, no digging underneath ... why?" (662). In act 8, while Nina is too self-absorbed to listen to him, Marsden vows to her that he will finally write a novel of real flesh and blood. "I'll write the book of us!" he concludes (795). Charlie holds out to win the prize of Nina at the end. Twice in the final pages he remarks that he who has "passed beyond desire" is the one to win Nina. The coolness of the writer, detached from the action, removed from the present tense, triumphs over the athlete, the businessman, and the scientist, all three action figures. Sexual interludes, the sustaining interest in this drama, are ultimately subdued by a figure who earns his living writing about sex. Description wins the day in the end.

Marsden, by far, is the most interesting character in the play.[16] Accordingly, the other major characters are true to types that O'Neill establishes in other plays. Sam Evans, by the end, is a successful advertising executive, but he's still the same dupe from the beginning of the play. His bourgeois values are no different than the ones espoused by the businessman in *Fog*, an early one-acter. O'Neill consistently sides with the underclass in his plays and his attacks against greed, materialism and American business are a theme that frequents most of his plays and dominates the cycle plays in the 1930s. Dr. Darrell, too, while he opposes the businessman and speaks with the voice of enlightenment, remains a stock figure. O'Neill portrays the scientist with an objective view of the world who gradually gets entangled in an emotional relationship with Nina and loses himself during the course of the play. Nina is also a rather conventional figure despite her powerful sexuality. The action defines her completely in terms of her relationships with other men (e.g., the "My three men" speech) and she exerts no independence throughout the play as she travels from one man to another. Descriptions of her work as a nurse describe this act quite literally and graphically. The outlandish plot development in the third act concerning hereditary insanity running in Sam's family stifles Nina's chance to pursue her own happiness through the birth of her child. Significantly, this shared scene between two women, the only one of its kind, is about how to make Sam happy. When Nina does determine to have a baby she falls in love with the father, Darrell. Later, she becomes a doting mother to a son and still later, a jealous woman of her son's fiancée. The fact that Madeline appears at the end as a younger version of Nina further reduces the lead character to a type.

As a writer, Marsden joins company with the artists in O'Neill's plays such as John Brown in *Bread and Butter*, David Royleston in *Servitude*, Michael Cape in *Welded*, Dion Anthony in *The Great God Brown*, and John Loving in *Days Without End*. Unlike those characters, however, Marsden is not the central character in *Strange Interlude*. He stands outside the action, comments upon what is happening, and always anticipates correctly what will happen next. O'Neill's description of him says that he's "always willing to listen" (634), and he acts as a confidant to all the characters, especially Nina. Unlike O'Neill's other artist figures, Marsden is not a direct self-portrait of the author. He's not a typical O'Neill heterosexual hero who must choose between his art and love. Instead, "there is an indefinable feminine quality about him, but it is nothing apparent in either appearance or act" (633). This mysterious quality adds interest to his character. Like Mitch in *A Streetcar Named Desire*, Marsden dotes upon a sick mother. Other characters, particularly Darrell, regard him as a ninny. His love for Nina, however, is as great as any other character in the play and his perseverance triumphs over time. At the same time, "Dear Old Charlie" is avuncular with all the homosexual connotations associated with that term of endearment. As the character in the background who waits his turn in the spotlight until the very end of the play, Marsden emerges as an "open" character, easily the most engaging in the whole play, and perhaps even the hero at the end.

Marsden fears living life; he only wants to write about it. From the beginning, he's very afraid of sex and intimacy despite his desire for Nina. After Nina's first entrance, she makes a note of Charlie in her very first thought aside: "What has Charlie done? ... nothing ... and never will ... Charlie sits beside the fierce river, immaculately timid, cool and clothed, watching the burning, frozen naked swimmers drown at last... ." (643). The opposition between Nina's lover, Gordon, the athletic war hero who died in flames, and Charlie, is established from the beginning. Given Nina's statement, however, it is clear who will survive the contest. Charlie wins the battle between action and passivity. Later, he defeats Nina's new lover, Darrell, in order to have her at the end. In the middle of the play, Marsden interrupts the two lovers and immediately senses their attraction to one another as he begins a lengthy thought aside: "Darrell! ... and Nina! ... there's something in this room! ... something disgusting! ... like a brutal, hairy hand, raw and red, at my throat! ... stench of human life! ... heavy and rank!" (723). The sexual imagery repulses Marsden, but it is his own mind and imagination which produces these images. As he says a few lines later, he has a "prurient purity." This scene is indicative of the entire play. There is a lot of talk about sex but there is very little sex in the play. There is very little action in the play, only endless talk about action. Marsden's attraction to Nina characterizes action in the play. He's drawn to her and she inspires him to "talk dirty," but, in the end, he's afraid to do it. The play, itself, so controversial in its day, embodies a kind of "prurient purity." Charlie, the genteel man with the lovely manners, gets the girl in the end, though once in his arms, Nina falls asleep. Good Old Charlie vanquishes all his rivals. Evans grows increasingly fat and dies of a heart attack at the end of act 8. In the ninth and final act, Darrell's skin has turned "a Mongolian yellow. ... His expression is sad and bitter" (808). Only Marsden is "younger, calm and contented" (805). His inability or refusal to function sexually signifies the triumph of cool detachment. The novelist wins over the businessman/scientist. The urge to act burns out in favor of a strong narrative that describes events but does not participate in them. All the talk through all the years represented in *Strange Interlude* makes it a thoroughly novel drama.

Formally, the most outstanding technique to render the drama into a novel is the extensive use of the thought aside, whereby a character, in addition to regular dialogue, also speaks directly to the audience in order to give expression to inner thoughts without allowing other characters to hear. As noted at the beginning of this essay, O'Neill first used the thought aside in *Welded*, but only in one specific moment. *Dynamo* (1929), too, makes selective use of this convention, although when Reuben Light addresses the dynamo as a god the distinction between a thought aside and a monologue begins to blur. The manuscript of *More Stately Mansions* (1939) also calls for this convention in act 3, scene 3 of that play. Only in

Strange Interlude is the thought aside used extensively and pervasively throughout the play. The thought asides solve the visual problem of how to present private thoughts publicly. They serve as a rejoinder to Darrell's critique of Marsden's lack of depth as a writer. The very nature of the aside construction, an addition to the spoken text, adds psychological or novelistic depth to characterization.

Novelistic asides, in an attempt to fill out the drama and supply necessary information, create several problems for the drama. First of all, they are conceived in language identical in form to the regular dialogue. O'Neill renders the thought asides in a somewhat stream of consciousness method, but nonetheless they look on the page much like the dialogue. In the printed text, indentations on the page are the only indications to separate public and private utterance. What should thought look like? When it comes out of the mouth of an actor on the stage it achieves a physical and voiced presence, which it lacks, say, in a novel by Joyce, in which written language is the necessary medium for the complete text. A shared grammatical syntax in the theatre among all modes of speech, thought asides and regular dialogue, strains credulity. Secondly, constraints of language force a linear development of the thought asides. A character speaks, falls back into a thought aside, then perhaps speaks again. Sometimes the reverse happens and thought precedes speech. The relationship between thought and speech alternates, but remains linear in all cases. Realistically, thought intersperses with spoken language in a complex relationship. In performance, director Philip Moeller defined the two modes of articulation, public and private, in order to avoid confusing the audience. He tried several techniques to achieve this, including designating a special zone of the stage for the thought aside to take place, creating distinct lighting effects to indicate a change, and requiring actors to adopt a different monologue "voice" for each aside. Ultimately, he had the actors freeze onstage and the speaking actor simply directed speech toward the house (Moeller). Thought and speech, each defined as distinctly as possible, produced melodramatic contradictions of sharp contrast with no blurred divisions. The freeze stopped once the monologue ended. Such a technique, however graceful it may have been, stopped the forward drive of the drama.

The awkwardness of the freeze onstage addresses the larger problem of the thought aside and the living actor. Thought asides effectively replace the need for the actor. Robert Benchley's evaluation of the original production in *The New Yorker* offered this analysis of O'Neill's thought asides: "They create the impression that Mr. O'Neill has done the groundwork which every dramatist must do, so much to his own satisfaction that he hasn't been able to rub any of it out, or that, unwilling to trust anything to his actors, he is trying to do their work for them too" (Gelb 661). One of the primary tasks of the actor is to make the subtext of a particular line readable. A character may say one thing, but mean another thing entirely; the actor's task is to articulate the planes of thought and speech. Again, since the nature of drama is dialogic, an actor's job is to fill in the blank spaces, the subtext, and manifest that interpretation in performance. The simultaneous presentation of line and subtext creates tension in the modern theatre. The linear and literary expression of O'Neill's stream of consciousness technique denies the creation and development of an actor's subtext. The playwright reduces the role of the actor in *Strange Interlude* to a cipher.

Strange Interlude ran on Broadway for 414 performances and earned O'Neill his third Pulitzer Prize. Written without need for actors, it also found tremendous success among the reading public. *Strange Interlude* is the first drama to rank on the best seller list. All told, O'Neill earned $275,000 with the play, far more than he earned on any other drama before or after. Certainly, O'Neill's story of sexuality tapped into pop psychology and the teachings of Freud and Jung. Joel Pfister's book, *Staging Depth: Eugene O'Neill and the Politics of Psychological Discourse*, details social and historical forces which account for how such a play could appeal to a mass audience in the late twenties. An icon of popular culture of the 1920s, there have been only two revivals of this play, a method acting approach by the Actors Studio in 1963, which blurred division between asides and dialogue, and a British production, starring Glenda Jackson and directed by Keith Hack, which came to America in 1985. This production emphasized comedic elements in the play and received considerable critical praise. Frank Rich wrote in *The New York Times* that the play "often seems the most enjoyable, not to mention deranged, comedy of sexual anxiety that Noel Coward or Philip Barry never wrote." Norma Shearer and Clark Gable starred in the film version of the play. Much shorter than the play, the film handled the thought asides through voice-overs. The results of that cinematic technique fare artistically no better than the onstage freezes. The actor becomes a mere content provider without the necessary tension in place between speech and action. Melodramatic earnestness threatens to produce laughter at every turn, including many of the serious moments.

The Elizabethan aside convention creates an exchange between actor and audience in which the actor addresses the audience directly. In this dynamic, speech does something to the audience. Thought asides in *Strange Interlude* sailed over the heads of the audience in keeping with conventions of realism, as if there were no acknowledgment of the presence of an audience. That such a play ultimately fails as an artistic creation offers evidence that O'Neill overreaches his medium in an attempt to replace dialogue. Throughout his career, O'Neill referred to the Broadway Theatre as the Show Shop. His terminology reflects a bias against the visual demands of the theatre as opposed to the literary drama. Reflecting upon the failure of *Dynamo*, O'Neill described the battle in his plays to Barrett Clark in 1929 as a struggle between the author and the director, as if it were a struggle between the drama and the theatre. From France, to which he had fled with Carlotta in 1928, he wrote: "I certainly admit that my worst plays have all been built around a germ idea that was in its essence theatre first and life secondarily. In justice to myself, I don't mean this in any meretricious 'theatrical' sense; it simply means that my medium has at times taken the upper hand and become an end in itself and the slumbering director in me (son of the Count of Monte Cristo) has swamped the author" (SL 344). O'Neill had already begun work on his next venture, the monumental *Mourning Becomes Electra*, when he lamented his tribulations with language in a letter to Joseph Wood Krutch in 1929: "Oh for a language to write drama in! For a speech that is dramatic and isn't just conversation! I'm so strait-jacketed by writing in terms of talk! I'm so fed up with the dodge-question of dialect! But where to find that language? Any suggestions on this question will be gratefully received" (SL 351). O'Neill devised thought asides to put more into his drama, to make the talk more than talk. Unfortunately, in effect they became little more than just talk. The novelistic aspects of his dramas smothered the dramatic achievements.

O'Neill's best plays don't possess any of the obvious stage tricks from his experimental period. They restore balance between showing and telling which results in compelling dramatic tension. Monologues in these plays reveal simultaneously a narrative and dramatic function. Theatrical language shows and tells. Editing Hamlet's advice to the players, Normand Berlin comments: "...depth in drama can only be achieved when the spoken word is suited to the visible action... ." ("O'Neill the Novelist" 56–57). For example, description by one character of an approaching character delivers information about that unseen character and prepares for an entrance. It is even more important, though, to see the effect of the impending arrival of the new character upon the visible character on stage describing the scene. In other words, the outside stimulus in the form of the approach of another character does something to the onstage character and produces a visual change in the onstage character. Monologues convey information and tell a story, but they also fulfill a dramatic function and do something to the other character or characters onstage. In *The Emperor Jones*, the power discrepancy between Smithers and Jones, with attendant threats of violence, elevates Jones to the dominant speaking position. The following scenes in which he encounters images from his past, all non-speaking images, undermine his authority and his speech tries to fend off fear and create an illusion to dispel loneliness. Inarticulate stokers in *The Hairy Ape* flank Yank, a thinking subject formulating a new consciousness, along with two other voices in the form of Long, who preaches a future of union labor and socialist class consciousness, and Paddy, whose speeches of the old days sailing in the sunshine aboard glorious clipper ships evoke memories of a romantic past. Their stories visibly impact Yank and force him to react to them. Hickey's long monologue in the fourth act of *The Iceman Cometh*, about a fifteen minute speech, is possible only because the assembled gang at Hope's saloon anticipates what Hickey has to say and bows their collected heads out of deference to the friend whom they knew and from a desire to shield themselves from the outpouring of truth that he delivers unto them.

An agreement between showing and telling in an O'Neill play blunts its dramatic edge. Performance needs to work against the grain of the text in order to bring those tensions into dramatic relief. When the spoken word and dramatic gesture align perfectly, the visual image amplifies the spoken text and produces a bigger, but often perhaps less powerful, image than if action contradicts or contrasts with the text. In *Shell Shock* (1918), a decorated war hero suffers from the belief that he saved a comrade only in order to get the fallen man's cigarettes. Throughout the play, the hero repeatedly asks his analyst for a cigarette only to discard it immediately after a few puffs and place the butt in his jacket pocket. This recurring gesture signals his guilt which, in the course of his conversation with the analyst, comes to light. The psychiatrist and the audience read the signs of the hero's distress through his recurring gesture with cigarettes. When he cures himself through talking out his past, he no longer desires cigarettes and he's well. The perfect alignment of narrative and dramatic, telling and showing, creates a theatrical, albeit melodramatic moment on stage, when the hero realizes what has happened to him. He throws back his head and emits a scream of horror, recounting the events on the battlefield, and that scream purges him of the demons which have been haunting him. When the spoken and the visual aspects align perfectly the tidiness of the drama wraps up conflicts neatly and conveniently and simplifies visions of events.

Anna's diatribe in *"Anna Christie"* against Mat, Chris and men in general reveals past events which drove her to prostitution, events which justify her histrionic anger. The action onstage amplifies the narrative event and the collusion of showing and telling creates an environment in which melodrama flourishes. Both this play and *Shell Shock* purport to be about something that the drama does not show. The past trauma of the hero and heroine comes to light in a narrative speech in each play. In both instances, O'Neill resorts to melodramatic stage moments as the solution to a formidable obstacle of how to bring the past onstage. In both cases, characters make visible and audible what had been hidden and silent. When the narrative action exerts no contradiction between sight and sound, melodrama is the only possible result.

The exaltation at the end of *Days Without End* in which John Loving enters an old church and keeps a transfixed gaze upon a life-size figure of Christ on the Cross reaches melodramatic ecstasy: "I am John Loving. ... Love lives forever! Death is dead! ... Life laughs with God's love again! Life laughs with love!" (CP3 180). Refrain music from *Lazarus Laughed* returns here as a result of the crushing defeat of John's alter ego, his split personality, Loving, who lies crumpled at his feet. As long as Loving and John coexisted, sustainable tension between the two warring factions endured. Loving's defeat, however, leaves John to integrate both sides of himself into melodramatic wholeness and allows him to utter, "I am John Loving." Suddenly, dramatic gesture and narrative proclamation align themselves. Small wonder, then, that in the closing lines O'Neill resorts to one of his favorite punctuation standards, the exclamation point. The entire action of the play reaches its climax at the very end in which John says his name. All the tension in the play rapidly disappears in the few lines that remain. Father Baird, whom John barely acknowledges, arrives as witness to John's transformation and wraps up the play by assuring him that his wife, who fell ill due to John's cruelty, is now out of danger and will survive.

The need of separate narrative and dramatic functions for speech finds early tentative solutions in O'Neill's two expressionistic dramas, *The Emperor Jones* (1920) and *The Hairy Ape* (1921). That style typically presents the action of the play as if it were seen through the eyes of the protagonist, unlike a naturalistic or realistic play in which the convention maintains that the characters and the audience who watches them share an objective experience. Both plays, too, are dramas of alienation in which Yank Smith and Brutus Jones remain isolated. Yank's recurring pose as "The Thinker" sets him apart from the other stokers who create a chorus effect surrounding Yank with group chants for booze and violence. Yank is not only mentally superior to his cohorts, but he is the strongest among them as well. He reigns as the acknowledged leader in the stokehole, king of that world in which he belongs. Likewise, Brutus Jones is a shrewd manipulator whose ambition and talent vaulted him to the top of an island regime. At the play's outset, he learns from his partner, Smithers, that the native islanders have tired of his tyranny and plan to assassinate him. He voices his contempt for both the natives and for Smithers with assurances that he has always prepared for the moment in which he must now make his escape.

The psychological action in both plays moves from confidence to despair. Yank must persuade his fellow workers, in response to both Long's and Paddy's challenge, that his life in the stokehole remains superior to life on board ship and beyond:

> I gotter talk, see. I belong and he don't. He's dead but I'm livin'. Listen to me! Sure I'm part of de engines! Why de hell not! Dey move, don't dey? Dey're speed, ain't dey! Dey smash trou, don't dey? Twenty-five knots a hour! Dat's goin' some! Dat's new stuff! Dat belongs! But him, he's too old. He gets dizzy. Say, listen. All dat crazy tripe about nights and days; all dat crazy tripe about stars and moons; all dat crazy tripe about suns and winds, fresh air and de rest of it—Aw hell, dat's all a dope dream! Hittin' de pipe of de past, dat's what he's doin'. He's old and don't belong no more. But me, I'm young! I'm in de pink! I move wit it! It, get me! I mean de ting dat's de guts of all dis. It ploughs trou all de tripe he's been sayin'. It blows dat up! It knocks dat dead! It slams dat offen de face of de oith! It, get me! De engines and de coal and de smoke and all de rest of it! [CP2 128].

At the outset, Yank is a part of the mechanical pantheism that he describes. His speech is a gospel sermon to summon the other stokers to his pulpit of manly strength and futurism. The above speech, a fragment from a much longer monologue is less one long speech than it is many short speeches tied together by intervening silences. Yank works the engine room in an attempt to respond to Paddy's vision of the good old days in which men worked in harmony with each other outside on the decks of sailing ships basking in the sunshine. Dramatically speaking, then, the speech must do several things. First, Yank must assert his leadership by putting down a threat to his authority. Secondly, he must rally support for his view which puts his perspective on the world in a most favorable light. He puts himself in the center of the universe. Thirdly, he must articulate to himself why his work is so important. He justifies for himself his importance in the world. Thus, the long narrative speech of Yank's has distinct narrative and dramatic functions.

Brutus Jones' speech in the first scene with Smithers reveals similar disparate uses of narrative and dramatic function. Fed up with Smithers' taunting about his imminent capture, Jones explodes: "Look-a-heah, white man! Does you think I'se a natural bo'n fool? Give me credit fo' havin' some sense, fo' Lawd's sake! Don't you s'pose I'se looked ahead and made sho' of all de chances? I'se gone out in dat big forest, pretendin' to hunt, so many times dat I knows it high an' low like a book. I could go through on dem trails wid my eyes shut. [*with great contempt*] Think dese ign'rent bush niggers dat ain't got brains enuff to know deir own names even can catch Brutus Jones? Huh, I s'pects not!" (CP1 1040). Dramatic resonance in this speech, as well as the excerpt from the one in *The Hairy Ape*, results from the fact that the speaking subject speaks in order to convince the self as well as the other. In both cases, Yank and Jones show their audience that they are in control as a means to prove to themselves that they command their own fates. Very cleverly, dialogue with the self novelizes the drama as characters try to answer internal doubts. Scenically, the audience hears these speeches within a visual context that contradicts the words of the speaker. In *The Hairy Ape*, for instance, the environment for the stokers approximates that of a steel cage. As Yank brags about the fact that he is steel, the audience sees him imprisoned by that steel. Initial directions describe Jones' costume, a get-up of gold, braid, red pants, and pearl-handled as "something not altogether ridiculous" (1033). The discrepancy between the flamboyance of the costume, the flippancy with which Jones regards his predicament, and the ominous portents of the distant tom-toms, undercuts any confidence regarding the success of Jones' escape. As the tumultuous scenes build to a climax in each play, the hero becomes increasingly isolated.

The heroes convince themselves through monologues in each play that they can achieve their goals. Yank attempts to gain revenge on Mildred to recapture the sense of belonging that he had at the start of the play. Jones, as he moves deeper and deeper into the black forest, tries to convince himself that he can escape. Yank confronts the Fifth Avenue crowd who ignores him, faceless voices behind other cells in jail at Blackwells Island, an empty street outside the union office, and a gorilla at the zoo. His audience within the play becomes increasingly inhuman as the action progresses, though, and he has fewer and fewer people with whom to talk. For his part, Jones must address the ghosts from his past. Speech, for him, becomes a matter of maintaining sanity.

The inevitable collapse of confidence into despair that is hinted at in the initial scenes and that steadily erodes in succeeding scenes suggests the limitations of both of these plays. Certainly, both plays exhaust themselves in one act. The most interesting scenes occur early and the conclusion is predictable in both plays. By far the most exciting moment in *The Hairy Ape* is the collision of Mildred and Yank in the third scene, a scene which incites the remaining action and sets Yank into a downward spin. Each successive scene reveals an aspect of his alienation. Similarly, once *The Emperor Jones* establishes the pattern of encountering scenes from the past and Jones begins to peel away his uniform, the final outcome is inevitable. The monologic drama turns monotonous as scenes begin to play out in a station drama on the way to judgment.

In the last period of O'Neill's career, the novelistic desire to tell all begins to collapse. Action in *Days Without End* (1933) literally recaptures wholeness and casts away doubt. John Loving indulges an affair with a friend in order to destroy his marriage and release himself from the constant fear of ever losing what he loves. By damaging the thing he loves, his marriage to Elsa, he does not have to live in fear of losing it. John, a novelist, makes his problem the subject of his new novel and confesses the plot of the novel to his wife and an old family friend, Father Baird. As he narrates the plot, Elsa recognizes the autobiographical implications and leaves the apartment, stays out in the cold, and returns deathly ill, all as a result of the novel's impact upon her. Faced with the possibility of Elsa's death, John searches to resurrect his lost religious faith in order to save her and himself from the torment and doubt that has nearly destroyed their lives.

John's torment throughout the action is that he does not know how to end the novel. His struggle mirrors O'Neill's attempt to find the right ending for his play. O'Neill worked on it longer than he had on any previous play and wrote some seven different endings. In the finished play, John reveals his initial solution to Father Baird at the end of the third act: "He walks out of the church—without love forever now—but daring to face his eternal loss and hopelessness, to accept it as his fate and go on with life" (CP3 161). John's literary and highly romantic version of life solves the quest for certainty that first instigated his despair. This novelistic ending does not bring down the curtain. Instead, John enters the Church in the final act and seems to regain religious faith, an act which miraculously seems to restore Elsa to good health as well. Critics considered the religious ending as O'Neill's own return to the Catholic Church. O'Neill, in fact, did not regain his childhood faith. John's religious conversion rebels against his scripted novel ending because drama demands action. The final scene at the church provides an opportunity for John to face his demons and undergo a spiritual transformation which changes the direction and outcome of the drama. The novelistic posture of the writer stoically facing life's "eternal loss and hopelessness" does not offer

Days Without End, Act II, scene 2 at the Henry Miller Theatre, 1934, directed by Philip Moeller. In this scene, John ponders his plot for a novel as his wife and Father Baird listen apprehensively. John's masked alter ego, Loving, sits next to him. The static quality of the stage picture indicates the weakness of the novel drama reliant upon "talk" rather than "action." Seated (left to right) are Robert Loraine, Selena Royle, Earle Larimore, and Stanley Ridges. Museum of the City of New York. Theater Collection.

comparable theatrical values to an emotional display for a dying loved one, a guilty conscience, and an appeal to God for help and guidance. In *Days Without End*, the melodramatic ending represents an escape from novelistic detachment. The vast territory between those two extremes of behavior remains unexplored in this play and presents the novelized drama as a problem.

Inability to complete the cycle plays of American history in the thirties signals the ultimate failure of the novelistic impulse. When O'Neill started the project, he anticipated only three plays, but at various times the number of plays ballooned from five, to seven, to eight, to nine, and finally to eleven. He confided in letters that he had finished four of the plays, but that they were very long and needed reworking. In an interview in *The New York Times*, he said that in these plays, "I am trying to show the development of psychological characterization in relation to the changing times—what the railroads, what the panics did to change people's lives" ("Nobel Prize"). The story, at that point, chronicled one family's history from 1806 to 1932. Later, O'Neill added three more plays to the cycle and reached back to 1755 as the beginning point of the massive drama. O'Neill intended to reveal generational developments as a means to trace the consciousness of the nation. He subtitled the entire cycle as "A Tale of Possessors, Self-dispossessed." He juxtaposes individual growth, love, and contentedness with the desire for material growth as a result of greed and possessiveness. Simon Harford in *More Stately Mansions*, for example, longs to write books and live in a Thoreau-like cabin in the woods. But he is also a brutal businessman who does not acknowledge the "touch of the poet" within himself and sets a course to accumulate great sums of personal wealth as if such victories were ends in themselves. Here, more than in *Strange Interlude*, time becomes the subject of the plays, a subject which makes the play more novelistic than dramatic. Peter Egri comments in *The Birth of American Tragedy* that "In the Harford saga the novelistic aspect of the dramatic project shattered the framework of the drama sequence" (114). By sequence, Egri confirms an Aristotelian bias and implies the need for the drama to offer a compact form in which one thing follows another and builds to a climactic event. Significantly, the only surviving play among the cycle projects is *A Touch of the Poet*, which features an Aristotelian plot in which the action takes place in a little over a day, the scene does not vary from Melody's tavern, and the action builds to a crisis and climax in which the hero, Cornelius Melody, must finally look in the mirror and see himself for who he is.

The failure of the novelistic impulse, the desire to tell at the expense of seeing, becomes a subject in the best O'Neill plays. He loads *A Touch of the Poet* with many excuses for the hero to narrate a story to suit his purposes. Melody quotes repeatedly from Byron's *Childe Harold*: "I stood among them but not of them." He fashions himself as an aristocrat, high above the rabble who surround him at his tavern. His chronic alcoholism gives him license to speak in long monologues, with or without the presence of an audience. The guilt he suffers when forced to confront his wife and his daughter motivates further speech and rationalization. The action of the play takes place on the anniversary of the great battle at Talavera in which Melody was a hero in service of the Duke of Wellington. The occasion prompts an annual celebration in which Melody dons his old splendid uniform and recalls former days of heroism and glory. These are all means for Melody to fashion a character completely in opposition to the environment in which he is placed, a run-down tavern that has seen better days. The significant detail in the tavern is the door that separates the offstage bar from the room in which Melody greets guests and takes his meals. He confines his rag tag followers, those he would stand among but not of, to that space and never deigns to drink with them there. The entire action of the play depends upon Melody's insistence that he is not one of them, even though the visual signs and comments from his daughter, Sara, suggest the opposite. Melody's speech and persona combat all contrary visible evidence in the play. The collapse of Melody's desire to remain apart from the crowd signifies his failure to author his performance successfully. Novelistic desire crashes against dramatic necessity. Ultimately, Sara Melody, the dramatic realist, the action character who seduces her lover in the upstairs bedroom, wins the day.

Both Tyrone and Edmund attempt to enforce a narrative pattern to the past that explains events in act 4 of *Long Day's Journey Into Night*. After Tyrone tells his son about his frustrations about never becoming a great artist as an actor, Edmund replies: "I'm glad you've told me this, Papa. I know you a lot better now" (CP3 810). Edmund proceeds to tell his father about his adventures at sea. Both of these stories produce the illusion of answering questions in the play, and bring the two men closer together. But the dramatic situation casts doubt upon the truth-telling of this enterprise. The scene occurs late at night and both men are very drunk. Mary, whom they describe as a ghost of herself after a full day injecting morphine, walks the floors above them and neither man wants to confront her, which would require confronting the shared guilt and responsibility regarding Mary's condition. Instead, father and son play cards and tell stories to delay an inevitable march upstairs to bed. Their comments can only be interpreted in the context of the particular dramatic situation. Speech for both means not having to deal with the reality of Mary upstairs. What they say in monologues may be true, but the dramatic impact is that even the truth does not adequately explain how things have come to pass in the Tyrone household: they are drinking themselves into oblivion and Mary, wife and mother, trods the boards upstairs in a drug-induced stupor. Narrative force pales in comparison and in conjunction with the visual image of an intractable situation: static and perpetual.

A Moon for the Misbegotten offers a dynamic variation of the novelistic drama. The irony of this play is that the action achieves the novelistic desire to confess, which, in turn, spurs dramatic possibilities. The entire action builds to the long monologue in which James Tyrone tells the story of his mother's death and his return with the casket aboard the train. He selects Josie Hogan as the one person who could hear his story and forgive him, but the absolution she offers him only brings one night's peace, sad recompense for a lost chance for romance and happiness. The scene of the play, a romantic late night setting with a beautiful full moon, anticipates an inevitable union of kindred spirits. Tyrone's overwhelming guilt, his need for forgiveness and peace, the effects of the booze, his attitude toward women as tarts, and above all else, his desire for this one night to be different from all the rest, doom any chance of a sexual relationship with Josie. That Tyrone kisses her and tells her meaningfully that he loves her at the end before he walks away, makes her final prayer for him to die in peace even more excruciating. Josie tells her father, in the end, that she didn't realize Tyrone was already dead when he came to see her. In a sense, then, the story is already told before the play begins. Tyrone, as the author, waits only for the proper time to tell his story. His novelistic death wish overcomes Phil Hogan's scheming to trap his daughter into marrying him. The dramatic plotting instigated by Hogan reflects an effort and good intention to bring happiness to the "misbegotten" couple. What Tyrone's successful steering of events brings about—regrets, a sense of time passing, the impossibility of change, questions of guilt and missed opportunities—casts him in the role of tragic hero. While he receives his blessing and leaves to die, after the gift of a night of peace, Josie is left to mourn tremendous losses: of a lover, of an opportunity, of a wasted life. Certainly O'Neill wrote the play in memory of his brother, Jamie, who drank himself to death and died horribly after his mother's death in 1922.[17] The play may have assuaged O'Neill's own guilt about the circumstances of Jamie's death, but the desire to give his brother a night of peace victimizes the character of Josie Hogan to the extent that she emerges as the truly dramatic and memorable character. She, after all, must react to Tyrone's story. She is the character who is left standing at the end. The novelistic impulse to confess creates a memorably dramatic and heroic character in the figure of Josie Hogan.

Hughie further exploits novelistic techniques for dramatic purposes, or rather, the failure of the novel drama leads to an exciting play. Given that this 55 minute play marks a return to the one-act form, which O'Neill had abandoned since his early days as a playwright, it hardly approaches the length of a novel. The scope, too, only represents one incident in which stage time equals real time. In more profound ways, however, this little gem of a play, sandwiched between *Long Day's Journey Into Night* and *A Moon for the Misbegotten*, employs radical use of experimental methods from the 1920s and results in mature and dynamic drama. The two character play is almost exclusively a monologue told by "Erie" Smith, a small time gambler returning to his low rent hotel in the Hell's Kitchen area of New York in 1928, who brags about his accomplishments and exploits as a big shot. Charles Hughes, the night clerk behind the hotel desk, is the silent auditor for much of Erie's presentation. His focus throughout much of the play remains outside the hotel doors, absorbing the late night sounds of the city. The opening stage directions, for a start, fold typical description into a psychological profile: "The Night Clerk sits on the stool, facing front, his back to the switchboard. There is nothing to do. He is not thinking. He is not sleepy. He simply droops and stares blankly at nothing. It would be discouraging to glance at the clock. He knows there are several hours to go before his shift is over. Anyway, he does not need to look at clocks. He has been a night clerk in New York hotels so long he can tell time by sounds in the street" (CP3 831). Thought asides from previous plays get a new wrinkle in this play. O'Neill records the silent musings of the clerk but does not have him speak. The text privileges the reader with respect to the fact that the text offers information that the performance necessarily omits. The written monologues of Hughes which are not heard do suggest, if perhaps overtly so, the subtext of the scene for the night clerk. In this play, O'Neill blends the silent monologue with other stage directions such that the two are inseparable: "The Night Clerk shifts his position so he can lean more on the desk. Maybe those shoes he sees advertised for fallen arches—But they cost eight dollars, so that's out— Get a pair when he goes to heaven. Erie is sizing him up with another cynical, friendly glance" (CP3 835). This version of thought asides, unaccompanied by speech, fractures potential dialogue in the scene. Silence, no response from Hughes, intermittently stops Erie from speaking and increases his annoyance and anxiety.

Charles Hughes is not the same "Hughie" to whom the title refers. Hughie was the former night clerk whose death started Erie on a drunk from which he only now returns. This play was only one of several which O'Neill grouped with the joint title, *By Way of Obit*, in which he intended to reveal the character of the deceased, as well as the speaking subject, and the silent listener. There is very little action in the play, just a lot of talk. Erie begins by providing background to the story by recounting his youth spent in a hick town. Stage directions record that "The Night Clerk seems turned into a drooping waxwork, draped along the desk. This is what he used to dread before he perfected his technique of not listening: The Guest's Story of His Life. He fixes his mind on his aching feet" (835). Hughes does not care to listen to another version of the same old thing. For much of the play, Erie tosses his speech into a vacuum. The dynamic onstage is similar to *Desire Under the Elms* in which Ephraim unburdens his soul to his distracted and uncomprehending wife. In that play, Abbie focused upon Eben in an adjacent room. Here, sounds of the city outside the hotel attract the night clerk's attention. Erie tells the new night clerk about his old pal and describes how they first met, how their friendship developed over fifteen years. Erie's account begins to assume a novelistic dimension as he spins his narrative of reminiscence about how Erie impressed Hughie with stories of dames, bangtails at the track, and fast times all along the Big Stem. He revels in old stories in which he played craps with Hughie at the desk, just for fun, with Erie's money, and Erie took him to the cleaners. As told by Erie, Erie was a sport and Hughie was a sucker. He recounts eating at his house, before the missus threw him out, and trying to visit his friend at the hospital before he died.

Emphasis upon narrative throughout the play serves a dramatic function. At the same time that he describes Hughie, Erie reveals information about himself that he would not otherwise divulge. All the talk about the former night clerk reveals something as well about what Erie would like the new clerk to do. Long monologue's ward off silence, loneliness and desperation. Erie's outpourings attempt to restore his former confidence. He confides to the night clerk that he has had no luck since Hughie's death. The long narratives that Erie spins form part of a search for reciprocity, the kind of relationship that he had enjoyed with Hughie for a long time. Erie used to feel good about himself by talking to Hughie. He seeks that same comfort now in Hughie's absence. The fact that Hughes' name is similar emphasizes the fact that Erie needs a substitute for his old friend in order to sustain himself. Throughout much of the action of the play, Erie tries to open up space for dialogue, an offer that Hughes consistently rescinds. Refusal to engage in dialogue constitutes tension in the play. Erie makes first contact with the new clerk by asking for his key, Room 492. The clerk refers to him as 492, the repetition of which throughout the action builds a desperate and lonely picture of Erie's existence. Erie brags about all the women whom he has brought through the corridors up to Room 492. Given the dilapidated condition of the hotel, as well as Erie's physical condition, it is impossible to imagine those trysts as the glamorous episodes Erie describes. Now, he's all alone and he does not want to go up to an empty room, in which he will be trapped alone with his own thoughts. Silence, so effective in Beckett, Chekhov, and Pinter, plays an important role in this play. Speech attempts to break impending silence throughout the play. The layout of the scene creates an existential angst, despite its realistic appearance. The main playing area consists of an empty expanse of a seedy third-rate hotel. On one side of the stage is the door to the street, from which ominous sounds of the urban city emanate: garbage cans; el-trains; footfalls of the beat cop; surface cars; an ambulance; a fire engine. On the other side is the elevator to the rooms upstairs. In between lies the night clerk's desk. As unpleasant and unreceptive as Hughes is to conversation, he remains the only possible human contact with whom Erie can connect.

The desire to grieve for the old Hughie and the need to resurrect a new one (Hughes) motivates Erie's futile attempts to start a conversation. The fact that Erie can't refrain from speaking about Hughie indicates the depth of his feelings and despair. He cannot say enough or the right words to close the subject. He masks the depths of his feelings with a hardened philosophy: "Hell, we all gotta croak. Here today, gone tomorrow, so what's the good of beefin'? When a guy's dead, he's dead. He don't give a damn, so why should anybody else?" (CP3 838). Twice during his ruminations on Hughie, Erie breaks off his narrative due to the fact that Hughes is not listening and makes a false exit toward the elevator. Each time he returns, hopeful of finishing the story and kindling interest in Hughes for his subject. Finally, he gives up trying to get Hughes' attention, as the stage directions read: "Erie begins talking again but this time it is obviously aloud to himself, without hope of a listener" (846). He concludes his long story to himself, simply: "Hughie liked to kid himself he was my pal. [*He adds sadly*] And so he was, at that—even if he was a sucker" (847).

Silence produces the plot reversal that changes the play's course. The sounds outside, by which Hughes marked the passing of time, stop their noise. The pre-dawn morning "vaguely reminds him of death" and he is "vaguely frightened." Struggling to come up with a subject to converse about, realizing that he's heard practically nothing about which Erie has said heretofore, he asks Erie whether or not he knows the gambler Arnold Rothstein. Seizing upon this mythic figure from the underworld of Broadway, Hughes fends off his fears of the silence outside. Irritated at first by Hughes' question, Erie recognizes an opportunity to roll his old dice again in the company of Hughes. At the end of the play, out of mutual need, they arrive at a subject about which they can converse. Hughes wants to pass the time and avoid an oppressive, boring silence. Erie wants to reinvent his old pal in order to shake off his bad luck. He wants to act like a big shot again: "Suddenly his face lights up with a saving revelation" (850). Hughes accepts the role of the new Hughie and the rebirth revitalizes Erie's demeanor: "Say, Charlie, why didn't you put me wise before, you was interested in gambling? Hell, I got you all wrong, Pal. I been tellin' myself, this guy ain't like old Hughie. He ain't got no sportin' blood. He's just a dope. [*generously*] Now I see you're a right guy. Shake" (850). The two men agree upon the rules for a relationship.

Dialogue restores the familiar pattern to the game in which each man plays a role. Erie gives Hughes a glimpse of the big shot gambler's universe, a world in which there are wise guys and suckers. Erie gets to play the role of the wise guy, Hughes the sucker. Erie, after all, has come from the outside. He fears that other gangsters will hurt him because he owes them money. He certainly doesn't run with Arnold Rothstein, although he's seen him, and has run errands for him occasionally. Beaten down by the world outside, Erie needs to feel like a big shot when he talks to Hughes. Hughes, the inside guy, trapped behind a desk, agrees to play the part of Hughie as a means to experience a life beyond the desk and as a way to pass the time of a lonely night. Erie says of the former night clerk: "Yeah, Hughie lapped up my stories like they was duck soup, or a beakful of heroin" (845). Hughes accepts the old role as a means of creating an illusion of a life that is more exciting than the one he leads.

The play ends with the two men playing craps at the clerk's desk, just as Erie formerly played with Hughie. He demands that they use real money in order for the game to look real. The action of the game restores Erie's confidence in himself, a feeling he gets by seeing himself in Hughes' eyes. Earlier, Erie recalls the mirror image that Hughie provided for him as he spun his stories: "I'd get to seein' myself like he seen me. Some nights I'd come back here without a buck, feeling lower than a snake's belly, and first thing you know I'd be lousy with jack, bettin' a grand a race. Oh, I was wise I was kiddin' myself. I ain't a sap. But what the hell, Hughie loved it, and it didn't cost nobody nothin', and if every guy along Broadway who kids himself was to drop dead there wouldn't be nobody left. Ain't it the truth, Charlie?" (845–846). When Hughie died, Erie could no longer see his reflection in Hughie's eyes. Initially, Erie says that he lost his luck when Hughie died. Toward the end, he says something quite different. He lost his confidence. Faced with seeing himself as others saw him, or even as he saw himself in Room 492, Erie feels desperate and alone. Right before the night clerk pleads with him finally to enter a conversation, right before Erie makes another move for the elevator, he concludes: "But now I got a lousy hunch when I lost Hughie I lost my luck—I mean, I've lost the old confidence. He used to give me confidence" (849). Erie transforms into his old self once Hughes agrees to play with him. Getting back to the old familiar game of craps, Erie resumes his old colorful banter and seems to get his luck back as well. He says: "I just want to show you how I'll take you to the cleaners. It'll give me confidence" (851). In other words, if they were really playing for money, Erie wants to act like the man whom Hughes imagines him to be. Neither one has to face the other as he really is. The principle of reciprocity rescues both of them. Dialogue, playing the game, is a matter of reflecting back to the other one what he wants to see. Erie, throwing the dice again at the end, re-energizes and restores his former persona by playing the old game. This action expiates grief for Hughie. His last lines echo his first regarding his old pal, but this time they do not carry lament, but joy that the moment of crisis has passed: "Y'know, it's time I quit carryin' the torch for Hughie. Hell, what's the use? It don't do him no good. He's gone. Like we all gotta go. Him yesterday, me or you tomorrow, and who cares, and what's the difference? It's all in the racket, huh?" (851). Dialogue, reciprocity, staves off silence and the fear of death and loneliness. Erie's ability to play the game and renew an old pattern with Hughes, the new Hughie, keeps him from going up to Room 492 alone and facing himself. In the reflected glory of Hughes' eyes, he can be Erie Smith, Broadway sport, "a teller of tales." Even his name is a made up concoction, made up to sound good and fit in with the gambling crowd with whom he associates. By the end of the play, it's clear that very few of his tales are actually true. Even his affection for Hughie he tries to mask as best he can. The monologues that he tells give way to a dialogue which reassures him that he is the person who he sees reflected in the others' eyes.

Two characters, one setting, a short play comprised almost exclusively of a single monologue does not hold much promise for an exciting theatrical event. *Hughie* represents, on the one hand, O'Neill's most didactic work. There seem to be no open questions in the text. Yet, the prescriptive nature of this play actually increases dynamic flexibility for the theatre. Despite the realistic detail of the seedy hotel lobby, the scene is truly O'Neill's most sparse and Beckettian. The text suggests a frightening void outside the hotel doors. An urban soundscape creates rich production opportunities and challenges. The only requirement for the set is a desk for the night clerk and a clock. Spatial references to an outside door, an elevator, and Room 492 upstairs create a provocative and minimal groundplan within which all the action takes place. The silent monologues beg the most obvious question: how will they be produced in the theatre? Ignore them by using them as the actor's subtext? Speak them? Broadcast them through speakers? Use a live microphone? Project the text on a screen? It is possible to imagine a successful production using any of these methods. Erie's stories, too, provide tremendous latitude in terms of interpretation. He spins stories that ultimately can be neither confirmed nor rejected. He tells them in order to combat loneliness, ease desperation, and stave off death. These stories also represent defiant acts of self-fashioning in which he creates himself within a universe that lies beyond comprehension. Such acts of will require support from others to bolster

Hughie at the Long Wharf Theatre, 1996, before moving to the Circle in the Square Theatre later that year, with Paul Benedict (seated) as the Night Clerk and Al Pacino as Erie Smith. The open space of a seedy hotel lobby and the prominence of the clock give this ostensibly realist play an existential dimension. Photograph by T. Charles Erickson. Billy Rose Theatre Collection. The New York Public Library for the Performing Arts. Astor, Lenox and Tilden Foundations.

the conceived illusion. Theatre, the medium of illusion, the Show Shop, carries this illusion.

In O'Neill's most novelistic play, dialogue emerges in the end as a hope for negotiation in a hostile world. The purely novelistic drama, seeking to dictate every aspect of performance, is a dead end of loneliness and despair, best represented in the stories of Tyrone in *A Moon for the Misbegotten* and throughout much of *Hughie.* O'Neill's plays resist performance as if the written play were self-contained and self-explanatory. But the more descriptions, stage directions, and monologues present in the text, the more questions arise about the ability of the written text to have the last word. The more novelistic the play, the more theatrical it becomes. The failure of the novel drama, the inability to say everything and answer all questions and contain all meanings, results in a constant state of exciting uncertainty that opens performance opportunities and possibilities. In *Hughie*, absence of dialogue demonstrates the need and desire for it. "Who needs dialogue?" the play seems to ask. Depth of feeling attending this question in all of O'Neill's late masterpieces makes them truly novel dramas.

Chapter 2

Masks and Mirrors

"Oh, Father, why can't you ever be the thing you can seem to be?"

— Sara Melody in A Touch of the Poet

Despite O'Neill's antitheatrical prejudice, the need for illusion, or the pipe dream or the hopeless hope, figures as his dominant theme in early plays such as *Beyond the Horizon* (1918) and *The Straw* (1919), as well as mature plays such as *A Touch of the Poet, Long Day's Journey Into Night*, and most emphatically of all, *The Iceman Cometh*. Virginia Floyd defines the message in that play as one applicable to all of the plays: "humanity's desperate need for a life-sustaining illusion to lessen the despair of soul-destroying reality" (*Plays of Eugene O'Neill* 512). Action in *Gold* (1920), an expanded and unsuccessful retooling of an earlier play, *Where the Cross Is Made* (1918), seems to articulate this need explicitly. Captain Bartlett commits murder to obtain a treasure which he subsequently never looks at again for fear that it is brass instead of gold. He justifies his barbarism by maintaining that the treasure is real and that the victims attempted to steal it from him. For years, he stubbornly awaits the return of his ship with his former accomplices and the rest of the booty. A doctor observes his behavior and diagnoses his condition to Bartlett's daughter: "No, your father won't let himself look the facts in the face. If he did, probably the shock of it would kill him. That darn dream of his has become his life" (CP1 941). Obsession with an illusion of great riches allows him to live. Without a dream, an illusion, life is not worth living. Indeed, Bartlett dies after finally acknowledging the truth that his few tokens are worthless junk.

The captain's need for illusion is analogous to O'Neill's ambivalent need for the theatre: it may be worthless junk, but it's all that there is. Theatrical trappings give him material form for his illusion/reality theme. O'Neill, however, twists this rather hackneyed theme into an original shape which challenges a pat understanding of his plays. He doesn't oppose the two terms so much as claim them as identical. For O'Neill, everything is an inevitable illusion, and the theatre becomes the perfect medium for his expression. Seen in this light, the binary opposition breaks down and leaves only layers of illusion to explore. In a 1922 interview with Oliver Sayler, O'Neill claimed that "The theatre to me *is* life—the substance and interpretation of life" (Cargill 107). Theatre serves as metaphor and medium to embody life. In *Lazarus Laughed*, the title character mocks Caligula: "Tragic is the plight of the tragedian whose only audience is himself! Life is for each man a solitary cell whose walls are mirrors" (CP2 572). O'Neill's notebook for *Marco Millions*, researched and detailed by Virginia Floyd in *O'Neill at Work*, records further identification of theatre with life: "Our lives are theatre—in the worst sense—the history of Man the forced posturing of an actor to empty benches. The Gods laughed once—then grew ashamed and went away" (67). The *Lazarus* notebook highlights still another theatrical image that posits life as a theatrical performance: "He [Man] thinks of himself as a hero fighting the dragons of evil. Alas, this dragon is a grave worm born in himself and he is a feeble actor making brave faces into a mirror and saying 'I am a warrior!' If he could see what applause his audience would give to his last gesture how happily would he die, acting the hero!" (*O'Neill at Work* 103).

Recurring motifs in these theatrical images require further unpacking in order to see clearly how O'Neill views life as theatre. First, O'Neill portrays life as an unconvincing performance played by feeble actors posturing before an empty house. The physical theatre provides the means for O'Neill to project his vision of the world. Lee Simonson, O'Neill's frequent designer at the Theatre Guild, reverses Shakespeare's phrase to make an acute point about great dramatists, including O'Neill: "All the world's a stage. But to the playwright, as he writes, any stage is all the world" (41). Existential crisis deepens the theatrical metaphor by virtue of the fact that no one watches the performance. The actor performs the role of life in a "solitary cell" and to "empty benches." In a Nietzschean universe, gods have vanished. O'Neill suggests that if there were an audience to applaud, the actor could finish his performance. Instead, actors perform for themselves and watch their show in a mirror. Their solo efforts try to convince themselves that they are who they pretend to be. In the absence of anyone watching them, they must convince themselves of the authenticity of their performance by making "brave faces into a mirror."

Too often, the second-rate ham actor fails to do so. O'Neill characters ⅄ struggle to be that whom they seem to be by casting themselves as heroes "fighting the dragons of evil." This projected melodrama of external events shades an internal struggle where the real dragon, according to O'Neill, is "a grave worm" born within the individual.

How to see this "grave worm" remains O'Neill's dramatic problem to solve. How does he access the hidden recesses of character where the real drama lies? O'Neill published his only contribution to dramatic theory in a series of short essays for George Jean Nathan's and H. L. Mencken's *American Spectator* magazine in late 1932 and early 1933 called *Memoranda on Masks*. In it, he advocated extensive use of masks in theatre to convey the inner truths of existence: "…the use of masks will be discovered eventually to be the freest solution of the modern dramatist's problem as to how—with the greatest possible dramatic clarity and economy of means— he can express those profound hidden conflicts of the mind which the probings of psychology continue to disclose to us" (Cargill 116). While the mask forces a fixed representation upon the actor's face, it simultaneously shields what is underneath the mask. The introduction of masks always begs the question: who and what is behind the mask? The presence of a mask seems to perpetuate the illusion and reality theme. What I hope to show in the following pages is not the reality beneath the mask so much as the frightening possibility that yet another illusion, another version of the self lies under the exterior presentation. For O'Neill, character is not a question of appearance and essence, but a matter of compatibility between multiple versions of the self.

Reflective surfaces such as mirrors play a key role in mask maintenance. The mirror allows characters, first of all, to see themselves. Certainly, the mirror in *A Touch of the Poet* is a most striking example, in which Cornelius Melody repeatedly observes himself striking Byronic poses, and into which he recites *Childe Harold*. Melody essentially plays the part of Byronic hero for himself in order to convince himself of his own aristocratic nobility. Equally important as an actual mirror, however, is the reflection that characters see of themselves in the eyes of another character. To see themselves in the unflattering light of how others see them proves a devastating blow in *The Hairy Ape*, *Mourning Becomes Electra*, and *Hughie*. O'Neill frequently mirrors characters as well: Andrew and Robert Mayo in *Beyond the Horizon*; Dion Anthony and Billy Brown in *The Great God Brown*; Jamie and Edmund in *Long Day's Journey Into Night*; Oedipal and Electra complexes in *Mourning Becomes Electra*; two sets of parents and a split stage in *Dynamo*; a split protagonist in *Days Without End*; Hickey and Parritt in *The Iceman Cometh*. Mirrors both distort and reveal

The Tyrone family in the 1956 production of *Long Day's Journey Into Night*, directed by José Quintero. Seated are Florence Eldridge and Fredric March. Standing are Bradford Dillman (left) as Edmund and Jason Robards, Jr., as Jamie. The two brothers are foils for each other in a love/hate relationship. Jamie, like Dion Anthony in *The Great God Brown*, is described as Mephistophelian. The perspicuous bottle in the foreground both assists and hinders the unmasking action. Billy Rose Theatre Collection. The New York Public Library for the Performing Arts. Astor, Lenox and Tilden Foundations.

character by showing one character in terms of another or in terms of an opposite. Pairing characters is a visual means to demonstrate fractured identity.

Use of masks in the plays varies from literary description to expressionistic economy to metaphorical pretense. Initially, masks appear only in stage directions in which O'Neill tries to indicate the surface and depth of emotion. Later, when actual masks appear on stage, they function variously as symbols of inhumanity, as representative types of people, or as protective skin. O'Neill dispenses with masks altogether in his final plays. Paradoxically, however, pretense in these plays functions as a kind of mask and the process of unmasking in each play comprises the dramatic action. The mask transforms in these plays from a static image or a visual sign to a dynamic process that unveils in time. Plays end at the point when characters expose themselves fully to the spectator's, including the audience's, view. This marks the point of desire beyond which nothing more can be seen. The mask, then, is a means of survival for the characters and for the life of the play as well. Unmasking produces emotional tumult which precipitates the ending. Dramatic tension breaks when the barrier between the outside and the inside comes down. It is not so much that the world cannot be faced as it is; facing it as it is exacts a level of human courage that is impossible to sustain. At its best, O'Neill's drama celebrates and dramatizes the cost of vulnerability.

One of the first references to masks comes in the stage directions of *Diff'rent* (1920) describing Caleb Williams in Act 2: "His face wears its set expression of an emotionless mask but his eyes cannot conceal an inward struggle..." (CP2 41–42). The fact that the audience cannot actually see his "inward struggle" in his eyes highlights the literary aspect of the description. Indeed, Caleb's lack of visible emotion marks a severe deficiency in the play. The action takes place in a New England whaling town over a thirty year interval during which Caleb arrives at Emma Crosby's annually to ask her hand in marriage. Each year she refuses on account of one affair Caleb had before they were supposed to marry. Ideals prevent them from marrying, despite the fact that they suit each other perfectly. Emma wears an "expressionless mask" as well. Action fails to convey the depth of emotion and feeling that each character has for the other. The mask in *Diff'rent* never comes off because it is identical to the face.

Similarly, Eleanor's face in *Welded* (1923) twice becomes mask-like when she tries to seek revenge against her husband Michael Cape by throwing herself into the arms of another lover. The mask represents her determination to act according to her cognitive will. Nervous twitching reflects conflict between external presentation and internal turbulence. O'Neill takes pains in stage directions to show the physical burden that the mask exerts (e.g., rage, twitching, mad expressions, rigidity). Urge to show everything enhances the playwright's ability to communicate a message, but it detracts from the possibility to create an artistic experience. The idea of the mask registers psychological conflict within characters unambiguously and denotatively. The mask also serves as a protective shield for Eleanor. When John, her suitor, kisses her, he notices that he's not really kissing her, but only her shell: "Under his kisses her face again becomes mask-like, her body rigid, her eyes closed. John suddenly grows aware of this" (CP2 254). He exclaims that her body feels like a corpse. Ultimately, Eleanor almost collapses under the strain of her stated desire to exact revenge and her emotional feeling for her husband. She constructs a new mask, one of pride instead of revenge, and rushes back home to her husband. The "exultant pride" (258) of the stage directions indicates a similar feeling shared by Mrs. Royleston in *Servitude* and later Nora in *A Touch of the Poet*. Pride, too, functions as a kind of mask, which both projects character and protects vulnerability.

The literary use of masks reaches its most pervasive expression in *Mourning Becomes Electra*. The mask as shield ensures privacy, but it's also associated with death in this play. Christine describes the Mannon house as a kind of tomb, a whited sepulcher: "pagan temple front stuck like a mask on Puritan gray ugliness!" (CP2 903–904). Character descriptions in the text portray all the Mannon characters, including Christine, Lavinia, and Adam Brant as wearing a life-like mask. This mask functions as a kind of death mask, as if the Mannons were not quite alive, as Eleanor is not alive sexually in *Welded*, but able to give the impression of being alive. One of the town chorus remarks to the onlookers: "That's the Mannon look. They all has it. They grow it on their wives. Seth's growed it on too, didn't you notice—from bein' with 'em all his life. They don't want folks to guess their secrets" (896). Portraits of the Mannon family, too, all possess the same mask-like quality that suggests death and lifelessness. It is the curse of inheritance. Christine, the only non–Mannon by birth, has "growed it on" and she, understandably, is the character who resents the burden most of all and most wants to shake it off. Her husband's homecoming incites the action. Returning from the Civil War as a hero, General Ezra Mannon speaks as one who has seen too much of death in his lifetime. He describes the meeting house of worship among the Mannons as a temple of death. Clean-scrubbed and whitewashed, it, too, is a whited sepulcher, like the Mannon facade. He describes the repetition and meaninglessness of death in the war: "But in this war I've seen too many white walls splattered with blood that counted no more than dirty water. I've seen dead men scattered about, no more important than rubbish to be got rid of. That made the white meeting-house seem meaningless—making so much solemn fuss over death!" (938). Ezra returns home determined to live, having survived the war. He tells his wife that there has always been a barrier between them, "a wall hiding us from each other!" (938). Ezra regrets that he has not been able to show his love before: "Something queer in me keeps me mum about the things I'd like most to say— keeps me hiding the things I'd like to show. Something keeps me sitting numb in my own heart—like a statue of a dead man in a town square" (939). Mannon tries to tear off the mask of death that separates him from his wife.

After Mannon's murder, Orin, the son, returns home and sees his father laid out in the study. His address to the corpse echoes Mannon's own words earlier regarding his death in life posture: "Death sits so naturally on you! Death becomes the Mannons! You were always like the statue of an eminent dead man—sitting on a chair in a park or straddling a horse in a town square—looking over the head of life without a sign of recognition—cutting it dead for the impropriety of living! [*He chuckles to himself with a queer affectionate amusement.*] You never cared to know me in life—but I really think we might be friends now you are dead!" (CP2 975). The death-like mask that the corpse wears becomes the character in the play. Passed down from generation to generation, this mask marks the Mannon inheritance. O'Neill punned with the title of his play on two counts. First, he uses "becomes" in the sense that mourning befits Lavinia. She looks good in black; it is her best color; in black, she is most herself. But he also chooses "becomes" in the sense that mourning is her fate. Lavinia, in time, becomes mourning. She buries her father, mother, and brother in the course of the trilogy. She is the last to grieve for the Mannon dead. The mask of mourning, of black, of a funereal and military posture, is one that she cannot ultimately avoid. All the Mannons try to tear off the mask but they inevitably fail. They clutch for life and that struggle defines the dramatic action. Certainly, Lavinia's struggle is the most compelling of all. Lavinia rebels against her fate but, in the end, she submits and dons, once again, the mask of the Mannons.

The first actual use of masks in an O'Neill play occurred in the production of *The Hairy Ape* (1921).[1] The Fifth Avenue crowd of men and women, exiting from churches, stroll past Yank and Long without even noticing them. Although the published version of the play did not call for using masks, descriptions of the crowd make masks a reasonable choice in performance, emphasizing the inhuman quality of the crowd, as opposed to the very human Yank: "The crowd from church enter from the right, sauntering slowly and affectedly, their heads held stiffly up, looking neither to right nor left, talking in toneless, simpering voices. The women are rouged, calcimined, dyed, overdressed to the nth degree. The men are in Prince Alberts, high hats, spats, canes, etc. A procession of gaudy marionettes, yet with something of the relentless horror of Frankensteins in their detached, mechanical unawareness" (CP2 147). Despite Yank's oral and later physical assault against them, they do not react to his presence. The masks differentiate the crowd from Yank along class lines. They exist in a much different world than the world of Yank. This expressionistic moment, visualizing the protagonist's subjectivity, demonstrates Yank's impotence in the world.

All God's Chillun Got Wings (1923) features the marriage between a black man, Jim Harris, and a white woman. Race, itself, functions as a kind of mask in this play. Civic authorities at the time seldom saw past the masks, viewing the play as a treatise about miscegenation which featured the audacious image of a white woman kissing a black man's hand.[2] In the second act, an authentic Congo mask appears in the couple's apartment, a wedding present from Jim's sister, a reminder of his cultural heritage. Stage directions preceding the scene describe the mask: "a grotesque face, inspiring obscure, dim connotations in one's mind, but beautifully done, conceived in a true religious spirit" (CP2 297). Ella's hostility toward the mask increases as the action proceeds. The first half of the play concerns Jim's pursuit of Ella and their marriage. The last half of the play details Jim's recurring efforts to pass the bar exam and enter the white world as a lawyer. While he needs to pass the bar exam in order to feel worthy of her, she needs him to fail in order to feel superior to him and to punish herself for marrying a black man. At the end, after learning that Jim has failed to pass the exam once again, Ella plunges a knife through the mask and pins it to the table. She justifies her actions to Jim by arguing that she saved his life: "It's all right, Jim! It's dead. The devil's dead. See! It couldn't live—unless you passed. If you'd passed it would have lived in you. Then I'd have had to kill you, Jim, don't you see?—or it would have killed me. But now I've killed it" (314). Passing the bar exam would signal cross-over into the white world, and if Jim did so he would be able to integrate his cultural past as well, symbolized by the Congo mask. Ella can only love and accept Jim if he fails. Stabbing the mask kills any chance of true union between the couple. After this climactic moment, Ella relies upon Jim to play the role of old kind Uncle Jim, or the boy who used to play marbles with Ella. O'Neill graphically presents his theme of fractured identity in this play by working schematically on an oppositional basis. Black and white are juxtaposed not so much as a study of race relations, but as a visual study of opposites. The wedding scene is visually spectacular as the couple emerges from a church, blacks lining one side of the stage, whites the other. The Congo mask clearly symbolizes Jim's cultural past and heritage. When Ella drives a knife through it the irreconciliability of the relationship is clear along with Jim's failure to integrate all aspects of himself. The binary pull in the play simplifies a reading and eliminates ambiguity. Later works show the same concerns, but O'Neill's technique appears both more subtle and more emotionally powerful and convincing in the final plays.

Use of masks in the above plays remains incidental compared to their widespread use in *The Great God Brown* (1925). The action creates a love triangle between two friends, William Brown and Dion Anthony, and one woman, Margaret. Architect Billy Brown steals the identity of his artistic and romantic rival, Dion Anthony, but the weight of his friend's mask destroys him. In the prologue, only Dion and Margaret wear masks. Dion's is "a fixed forcing of his own face—dark, spiritual, poetic, passionately supersensitive, helplessly unprotected in its childlike, religious faith in life—into the expression of a mocking, reckless, defiant, gayly scoffing and sensual young Pan" (CP2 475). The description of the mask and the face underneath visually details the two aspects of Dion's character and name. He is a combination of ascetic St. Anthony and sensual Dionysus. The mask operates as a protective barrier between the character and the outside world. As the play unfolds, characters repeatedly put on and take off their masks. Early in the first act, Dion precedes his first major speech, a monologue, by removing his mask when he observes that no one is around:

> Why am I afraid to dance, I who love music and rhythm and grace and song and laughter? Why am I afraid to live, I who love life and the beauty of flesh and the living colors of earth and sky and sea? Why am I afraid of love, I who love love? Why am I afraid, I who am not afraid? Why must I pretend to scorn in order to pity? Why must I hide myself in self-contempt in order to understand? Why must I be so ashamed of my strength, so proud of my weakness? Why must I live in a cage like a criminal, defying and hating, I who love peace and friendship? [*clasping his hands above in supplication*] Why was I born without a skin, O God, that I must wear armor in order to touch or to be touched? [479–480].

The alternation between masked and unmasked face fashions the entire character of Dion. The action indicates that the masks are necessary for protection in a hostile world, a disguise, the cost of which becomes evident at the outset of Act 1, in which Dion's mask hangs from a strap around his neck, giving him the appearance of having two faces. His real face seems older, more ravaged and more selfless than before. His masked face has become Mephistophelian. During the course of the action, Margaret can only accept and love the masked face. She does not recognize him with his mask off. Only in the company of the prostitute, Cybel, can Dion reveal himself as he is and relax. In another excellent speech, Dion recalls his father, reminiscent of one by Orin about his father in *Mourning Becomes Electra*: "What aliens we were to each other! When he lay dead, his face looked so familiar that I wondered where I had met that man before. Only at the second of my conception. After that, we grew hostile with concealed shame" (495–6). The masks visually embody the problem of how much to reveal and how much to conceal from others. Removal and replacement of the masks create tension in the work as well as show character through contrast of the masked with the unmasked face. The fact that Margaret can only remove her mask when Dion is wearing his makes the issue of intimacy and identity clear. Dion's despair over the necessity of wearing the mask, revealed in both of the examples above, shows the tenderness of his character that is hidden beneath the exterior drunken cynic.

Over the length of the drama, however, the use of the masks assumes other functions that obscure meaning in the play. Dion is an artist whose innate talent provokes William Brown's jealousy. After Dion dies, Brown hides the body, steals Dion's mask, and poses as his friend in order to take Margaret and her children as his own. Brown wants more than Margaret, however; he wants to be an artist himself. A rift between the two halves of Dion's personality, ascetic and Dionysiac, causes his demise. His artistic spirit, the exterior mask, leads him to the debauched pursuit of women and booze which kills him. Brown, as his stolid name seems to indicate, has none of the artistic spirit about him. O'Neill makes it clear that this character is incapable of creating or even understanding another creative and artistic spirit. Once Brown assumes Dion's mask, he shoulders a tremendous strain similar to Dion's, as though the artistic mask cannot fit properly on his head. The mask, which initially seems to represent only the barrier that separates characters from each other and from themselves, assumes the mantle of artistic sensibility. Why Brown cannot wear it comfortably remains a mystery. The mask literally becomes a character in the end. When Brown announces that Dion is dead, several policemen carry out his mask as if it were a body. The literal representation of this action reaches ritualistic levels.

The changing functions of masks (e.g., shield, symbol, ritual) confused

Robert Lansing (center) as William Brown in the Phoenix Theatre revival of *The Great God Brown* in 1959, directed by Stuart Vaughan. The masks graphically represent the "dualism of man's soul," in accord with the illusion/reality theme. In his better plays, O'Neill discarded a literal use of masks and probed identity as a changing multiplicity of possibilities as opposed to a fixed face. Photograph by Friedman/Abeles. Billy Rose Theatre Collection. The New York Public Library for the Performing Arts. Astor, Lenox and Tilden Foundations.

audiences very much in performance, but they flocked to the production anyway (Wainscott 194). O'Neill argued that the confusion lay in the execution of the masks, not in the way they were conceived. His letter to Benjamin De Casseres thanks him for reading the play, an opportunity that afforded an interpretation that production completely wiped out. About the actual masks in production, O'Neill concluded: "They suggested only the bromidic, hypocritical & defensive double-personality of people in their personal relationships—a thing I never would have needed masks to convey" (SL 246). Protestations aside, the best parts of the play detail frustrations of integrating the mask with what lies beneath it. Dion's two monologues, parts of which are quoted above, represent the best language in the play. The masks are, as O'Neill admits, completely dispensable in these scenes to the extent that they are redundant. In fact, the idea of the mask worn by Dion would be a much more powerful image if it were not represented literally. O'Neill apologized, in a way, for his unsuccessful use of masks, in a letter to critic John Mason Brown in 1934: "Perhaps I have sometimes been off the track, possibly my use of masks and asides is artifice and bombast—... But I fully believe that my long absorption in the dualism of man's mortal soul has been worth while" (SL 440). *The Great God Brown* attempts to show the dualism of Dionysus and St. Anthony within a character, as well as the dualism between characters, Dion Anthony and William Brown, the familiar collision between the artist and the man of business. Absorption with dualism ends up showing only that and nothing more. Brown sums up the tragic condition resting upon such dualism by uttering the following banal pronouncement in the final act: "Man is born broken. He lives by mending. The grace of God is glue!" (528). Final moments manage to surpass everything previous in terms of straining the obvious and the mundane. After Brown dies, Margaret kisses the mask of Dion as if it were him: "Good-by. Thank you for happiness! And you're not dead, sweetheart! You can never die till my heart dies! You will live forever! You will sleep under my heart! I will feel you stirring in your sleep, forever under my heart! (532–533). When asked the name of the body on the floor, the prostitute Cybel looks at the body of Brown and says simply, "Man!" (533). The strain for a symbolic ending results in a grossly simplified ending that makes the subject of dualism obvious and thoroughly uninteresting. If audiences were confused by this play, they were confused by the opaqueness of its construction and not any ideas emanating from it.

Stripped to its essentials, the use of masks in *The Great God Brown* does not add anything that is not evident in an earlier play such as *Beyond the Horizon*. In the early play, the love triangle pits two brothers, Robert and Andrew Mayo, against one another. The former has "a touch of the poet" about him, while the latter is a successful farmer. The woman who is the focus of their desires, Ruth Atkins, chooses to marry the artist because he's different. Robert gives up his dream of travel in order to settle down on the farm with Ruth. Andrew, who loves Ruth deeply, betrays his own nature, too, by taking Robert's place at sea. Domestic life on the farm literally kills Robert, just as the mundane requirements of making a living and rearing children seem to destroy Dion Anthony. William Brown, who loves Margaret and wishes to be a family man, destroys himself through his jealousy of Dion. Similarly, Andrew Mayo pursues a get-rich-quick scheme as a ruthless grain speculator in foreign markets and removes himself from the life he formerly loved. Although patently mechanical in construction, *Beyond the Horizon*, as creaky as it is, aspires to the same heights as *The Great God Brown*. Without resorting to masks or explanations about the "dualism of man's immortal soul," this play, which precedes *Brown* by seven years, effectively shows the split nature of human identity which threatens to cancel the best ambitions.

Lazarus Laughed (1926) requires the most elaborate use of masks found in any play. Stage directions specify masks for all except the title character.[3] The subtitle reads: *A Play for an Imaginative Theatre.* Apparently no such theatre exists.[4] There has never been a professional production of this play, although it always remained one of O'Neill's favorites.[5] His stage directions ask for masks to represent seven age groups and seven personality types. Instead of showing the dualism within an individual as in *The Great God Brown*, or the symbolic death mask in *Mourning Becomes Electra*, the masks erase individuality in an attempt to represent all of humanity. Permutations of masks according to period and type, in addition to oversized and half-masks, contribute to the bombast of the entire production scheme which completely overwhelms the significance of the play. Without the masks, though, without the huge ensemble and immense spectacle, no production seems warranted. Excess as a principal virtue makes production plans scarce.

Days Without End (1933), the last O'Neill play to use masks, does so in a limited fashion. It portrays the dualism of John Loving by splitting the character into two personas played by two actors. Frederic Carpenter notes that John and Loving are divided along melodramatic lines: "The one is wholly kind and good, the other, wholly malicious and bad" (140). The former is unmasked, while the evil one wears a half mask that resembles John's face. Loving's face "is a mask whose features reproduce exactly the features of John's face—the death mask of a John who has died with a sneer of scornful mockery on his lips. And this mocking scorn is repeated in the expression of the eyes which stare bleakly from behind the mask" (CP3 113). This trick enables the two characters to conduct dialogue with each other throughout the play until the good one finally vanquishes his evil twin at the foot of the cross at play's end. Visual representation of the two characters simplifies the play despite adding a veneer of technical sophistication. Religious content certainly contributed to the play's failure in production, but the form of the play destroyed any sense of mystery and intrigue that could have complicated the message and outcome.

The mask, in the above examples, is the means to represent character, but the idea of the mask functions more importantly as a dynamic process in the essential dramatic action of the drama. O'Neill asks in *Memoranda on Masks*: "For what, at bottom, is the new psychological insight into human cause and effect but a study in masks, an exercise in unmasking?" (Cargill 116). Critic Eugene Waith points out that the mask is a primary dramaturgical device even in the many plays in which no literal mask appears: "The mask was a way of getting at the inner reality of character. In fact, it may be said that for O'Neill it was *the* way, for even in the many plays where actual masks are not used, we find the same preoccupation with concealment and discovery" (30). Visually, the mask externalizes the unseen forces at work in the mind. It works as a tool to reveal the loneliness and sensitivity of existence as well as the dividedness and multiplicity of human identity. The plays exhibit a pattern of movement from protection (concealment) to vulnerability (discovery). Addressing the early plays in particular, Ralf Remshardt observes that "Conflict arises out of being rather than action, while a character's actions and his nature are either completely synchronous or diametrically opposed" (131).

The mask of bravado that Yank wears in *Bound East for Cardiff* shields fear of death that can't be completely hidden. The degree to which he and his friend Driscoll avoid the inevitability of Yank's death creates the drama. In *The Moon of the Caribbees*, Smitty assumes a superior role to that of his drunk and coarse shipmates. Yet in the context of the beautiful landscape and hedonistic pleasure, Smitty's aloofness produces signs of his insecurity and weakness. Writer Stephen Murray in *The Straw* treats his loyal confidante and typist Eileen Carmody with professional respect and distance. When she drops her mask and admits her love for him, he retreats, but he can no longer write. When he meets her again, when she is on her deathbed, he agrees to play the part of a lover in order to help her get well. When he commits to the role of lover, however, he discovers that the mask no longer comes off. He discovers by throwing himself into a part and trying to save a friend, that he does love her. And, at that point, he realizes that he loves someone who is fated to die soon, a discovery which leads to the adoption of the hopeless hope, in which the probability of impending death negates any dreams of future happiness. As long as Murray remains disinterested, he lives in no danger. The moment at which he professes his love for another, he risks the pain of suffering which death will bring. In this play, Murray's projection of a mask becomes the character; he undergoes a transformation. The play ends once that transformation occurs, and stops with a question: what is the nature of love? How does Murray's play-acting become real? What this early play tentatively suggests, I believe, is that the dualism implied by the masks is much more complicated than the illusion/reality scheme allows. There are masks under masks and there is no question about which one is real and which one is not. It becomes a question of accessing or promoting a given mask to the surface. It's about seeing more masks.

Even in O'Neill's best plays, however, a metaphoric unmasking action fosters the illusion of dualism. Con Melody swaggers as an aristocratic gentleman, but ends up as an Irish drunk keeping bar at a third-rate tavern; Larry Slade thinks of himself as a wise philosopher in the game of life, but stares straight ahead at the end, fully aware of the hollowness of the game he formerly played; Josie Hogan pretends to be the town whore, but she remains a virgin; the Tyrones appear to be a happy family in the morning, but late night discovers them drunk, silent, and stoned to the world; "Erie" Smith plays the role of Broadway sport, but that game is a ruse to keep him from trudging up to his room alone. These examples show characters whose actions, in Remshardt's vocabulary, diametrically oppose their natures. Action in the plays always moves toward an unmasking in which oppositions become synchronous. Such synchronicity precipitates the end of the drama. All of the characters in *The Iceman Cometh* pretend to be one thing, but are truly something else. The characters exist in contented drunkenness as long as they collude in each others' fantasies. The game the bums play determines that Harry Hope is a popular local politician even though he hasn't ventured outside the bar in twenty years; Jimmy Tomorrow is a journalist; Willie Oban a brilliant lawyer; Joe Mott, owner of his own gambling house; Rocky is a bartender, not a pimp; Larry Slade a wizened philosopher; Piet Wetjoen and Cecil Lewis are Boer War heroes; Ed Mosher is a circus man, and Pat McGloin is a police lieutenant. The dramatis personae carefully introduces characters in terms of what they once were. Hickey unmasks each of them and forces them to see themselves as they are and face the truth. All the inhabitants of Hope's saloon, save two, restore their illusions about themselves and their actions at play's end. Of the two who do not restore a mask, one commits suicide, and the other, Larry, after pining for death theatrically throughout the play, longs for it to come in earnest. The mask keeps the illusion of dualism alive.

The unmasking action in *The Iceman Cometh* transforms a comic structure into a tragic one. In classical comedies, protagonists often appear as something other than who they are. The comic response recognizes the gap between pretense and reality and such plays usually end with the elimination of that gap and a new proclamation of moral order. O'Neill does something similar in *The Iceman Cometh*, but for different purposes than moral instruction. According to him, the play begins as a comedy before the tragedy comes on. He wrote to Lawrence Langner in 1940 that "there are moments in it that suddenly strip the secret soul of a man stark naked, not in cruelty or moral superiority, but with an understanding compassion which sees him as a victim of the ironies of life and of himself" (SL 511). By contrast, *Ah, Wilderness!* (1933), O'Neill's lone comedy, features a protagonist whose mask remains in place from beginning to end. Both plays adhere to a comic structure insofar as characters project a mask that shows one image and hides another. In tragedy, however, the characters glimpse the underside of their own masks, while comic characters seldom have to confront an unmasked image of themselves.

O'Neill wrote *Ah, Wilderness!* very quickly while he was struggling to find the right conclusion for *Days Without End*.[6] While he could not bear to bill it as a comedy, it plays as one. Without a doubt, it stands apart from all of his other plays. It hails the transition from examining the big, conceptual themes of the world, as in *Lazarus Laughed*, *The Great God Brown*, *Days Without End*, *Dynamo*, and *Strange Interlude*, to domestic themes and settings. Set in 1906, it also signals a preoccupation with the past that unites all of the final plays. *Ah, Wilderness!* reflects the flip side or mirror image of the later tragedy, *Long Day's Journey Into Night*. Too often, the earlier play is viewed as a light foray into the deeper and more painful truths of the later and greater play. A typical view recognizes the Tyrones as the true representation of O'Neill's family life, while the Miller family represents a fantasy. O'Neill, himself, once said in an interview: "That's the way I would have *liked* my boyhood to have been. It was a sort of wishing out loud" (Basso 48).[7] Removing the former play from the latter's shadow, seeing it on its own terms, the comedy loses none of its luster when sober implications of its action come to light. The dark side of this lovely play does not reside in the depiction of Uncle Sid's alcoholism, sexual politics, prostitution, or even the patriarchal relationships that dominate the Miller home, but in the mask of Richard Miller, the comic young hero of the play.[8]

Comedy in the play centers around the characterization of Richard. From the beginning, he spouts quotations from all sorts of worldly literature: Ibsen, Swinburne, Fitzgerald's translation of *The Rubáiyát of Omar Khayyám*, Shaw's *Candida*, Oscar Wilde, Kipling. His mother worries that he's having an affair with Hedda Gabler. Richard swings the plot of the play, what there is of it, in motion by sending Swinburne's poetry to his girlfriend. The girl's father intercepts the verses and visits the Miller household to voice his disapproval. The offending lines read as follows:

> That I could drink thy veins as wine, and eat
> Thy breasts like honey, that from face to feet

Thy body were abolished and consumed,
And in my flesh thy very flesh entombed! [CP3 23].

The comedy flourishes with the acknowledgment that Richard quotes poetry that he's read and admired in books but that he does not fully understand. He is not the person whom he pretends to be. If he really were like Eilert Lovborg in *Hedda Gabler*, a character whom he professes to admire, then the play would not be nearly as funny. Indeed, Richard visits a bar, flirts with a kind prostitute, and gets drunk for the first time. That's a far cry from Lovborg's nocturnal trip to Mademoiselle Diana's boudoir where he inadvertently shoots himself in the bowels. Richard stays a sweet kid who doesn't have the least intention of fulfilling his prophesies of literary licentiousness. When he does meet Muriel for a clandestine rendezvous at the beach, one chaste kiss quiets his beating passion. An integration of Richard's outside mask with his inner consciousness never occurs. While the audience perceives the difference between Richard's affectations and his essential nature, Richard never has to remove his mask and examine himself in the mirror. Nat Miller, his father, justifies his refusal to explain the facts of life to his son: "You feel, in spite of all his bold talk out of books, that he's so darned innocent inside" (79). Innocence remains intact at the end. The pain in comedy never hurts for long. Mr. Miller finally punishes Richard by insisting that he must attend college at Yale and graduate, too.

Glare from this sunny view of family life hides the foreboding portent of the play. Richard's mother believes that her son is destined for some kind of greatness and mentions the possibility of Richard becoming a great writer. If that were to occur, Richard would have to embrace the sort of attitudes and values that would be unacceptable in the Miller household and in the town in which he lives. Swinburne and Ibsen would be no laughing matters. O'Neill parodies *Hedda Gabler* in *Now I Ask You* (1916), an early unproduced play. In that play, the regular businessman humors the artistic hypocrisies of his young wife and tames her in marriage. In so doing, O'Neill seems to betray his own values and sensibilities regarding the artist in society. *Ah, Wilderness!* presents a nostalgic and flattering view of small town America and delights with warm humor, rich characters, and all the satisfactions of bourgeois life. If Richard Miller were to become an artist, he could no longer pose as one and still retreat to the safety of benign and loving parents. *Ah, Wilderness!* portrays the rewards of not pursuing an artistic life. The dark side of the play travels in the shadows of the road not taken.

Ah, Wilderness! is a play without pain precisely because Richard Miller never has to confront his mask. Everyone within the play protects him and his mask stays in place. In most O'Neill plays, though, characters recognize another identity under the mask which seems to be the real face. How do characters see themselves when the mask comes off? These moments of recognition indicate something much more profound than the illusion/reality opposition can supply. For example, the contest between Ezra and Christine Mannon in *Mourning Becomes Electra* resolves in the darkness of their bedroom in early morning. Playing the part of dutiful wife, Christine allows Mannon to make love to her. Much like Eleanor when she endures John's kisses in *Welded*, Christine only gives Mannon her body and not her spirit. The barrier, the mask, remains up between them and Mannon accuses her of not being his wife: "You were only pretending love! You let me take you as if you were a nigger slave I'd bought at auction! You made me appear a lustful beast in my own eyes!—as you've always done since our first marriage night!" (CP2 944). Pushed to the brink of what she can tolerate, Christine responds finally: "I loved you when I married you! I wanted to give myself! But you made me so I couldn't give! You filled me with disgust!" (944). New England Puritanism that regards sexuality as sinful pollutes Ezra's relations with his wife and contributes to his deviant behavior. Christine confronts her husband, admits her affair with Adam Brant, and boasts that he is her lover and not Ezra. When Christine reflects her feelings for Ezra back to him, he does not see himself as he is, necessarily, but he does see himself as Christine sees him. The image of a "lustful beast" proves intolerable to him, but it reflects the legacy of the Mannon family. When the mask drops, Christine resolves as a mirror and shows Mannon someone whom he cannot accept. Struggling with his anger, Mannon suffers an apparent heart attack, brought on by Christine's disclosures.

The Emperor Jones works by peeling away slowly the mask of civilization and superiority from the hero, but *The Hairy Ape* rips Yank's mask away in a single moment. He subsequently tries to avenge his honor and find his rightful place in the world. The third scene of the play, in which the rich and ghost-like Mildred descends from the deck above ship to see how the other half lives, produces the inciting moment. Her invasion of the stokehole surprises Yank and when he turns to see her, he frightens her with his dirty, brawny, sweaty appearance. "Oh, the filthy beast!" she exclaims, fainting (CP2 137). Her words are similar to the accusations that Christine Mannon levels at her husband in *Mourning Becomes Electra*, but in this case, Yank endures public humiliation that changes his view of the world and his place in it forever. Prior to this moment, Yank considered himself as the prime mover in the world and the one who most belongs in it as king of the stokers. O'Neill's opening directions name Yank as the stokers' "most highly developed individual" (CP2 121). In the modern world of speed, power, and reliance upon the machine, Yank reigns in his glory. He refutes easily romantic tales of the past spun by his mate Paddy which threaten the primacy of the stokers feeding coal to the engines. At the end of the first scene, he rebuts Paddy in front of his shipmates: "Tinkin' and dreamin', what'll that get yuh? What's tinkin' got to do wit it? We move, don't we? Speed, ain't it? Fog, dat's all you stand for. But we drive trou dat, don't we? We split dat up and smash trou—twenty-five knots a hour!" (130). Before Yank encounters Mildred, he rests secure in his power and confident of his position of dominance in the world. After enduring her slight against him and the laughter from his comrades, Yank assumes the pose of "The Thinker" in each subsequent scene. The shock of his collision with his exact opposite forces him to re-evaluate his view of the world.

Reflection creates crisis in the play. Yank tries to avenge his honor, an attempt to reassert his will on the world. He ends up at the zoo, staring in the face of a gorilla. Looking at the ape, Yank acknowledges that "yuh're what she seen when she looked at me, de white-faced tart!" (161). Yank finally sees what Mildred saw, he sees himself from her perspective, an image that destroys him. The stokehole in which he formerly worked was nothing more than a kind of steel cage in which ape-like men slaved to shovel coal into the ship's furnaces. At the end of the play, the image of Yank in a steel cage at the zoo echoes the initial image of the ship's stokehole. O'Neill's literary postscript, "And, perhaps, the Hairy Ape at last belongs" is ironic in the sense that Yank's position has unchanged (163). He belongs to the monkey cage in exactly the same way that he belongs to the ship's stokehole. The dualism of his character (the best among men/ a filthy beast) is really an illusion. Only the perspective changes from how he envisions himself, initially, and how his friends see him, to how others see him, particularly Mildred and her ilk. Yank's refusal to recognize himself in that light constitutes the action of the play. To the extent that he rebels against the image that others have of him, Yank wears a mask of himself. Action in the play rips off that mask and Yank struggles mightily to put it back on again to restore his own self-conception of his role in the world. He's unable to accept a non-flattering version of his character. The irony of the ending points out that Yank fails to recognize and integrate all aspects of his character.

An impressive military uniform, a full-length mirror, vast quantities of alcohol and cultured speech are all means Cornelius Melody employs to promote one version of identity in *A Touch of the Poet* (1935). Even his nickname, Con, suggests the character who pretends to be one thing, but is truly another. In this play, however, all the other characters know him to be exactly who he is. Accoutrements that adorn his character do not convince others or the audience that Melody is other than a shebeen keeper in Ireland. All Melody's efforts to disguise his nature are attempts to hide himself from himself. Even the no account drunks who hang on his coattails only to drink his liquor see through Melody's pretenses. One of them, O'Dowd, remarks: "Ain't he the lunatic, sittin' like a play-actor in his red coat, lyin' about his battles with the French!" (234). In the same scene, Melody responds in such a way to indicate that he is not unaware of what goes on around him: "So you may go on fooling yourselves that I am fooled in you" (235). Melody constructs his game of pretense in the face of present circumstance. Despite the poverty in which he lives, Melody self-fashions his identity as an aristocrat and gentleman. The uniform recalls former days of valor. Melody constantly looks at himself in the mirror in order to see the image that he wants to see. Repeatedly, O'Neill directs the character to sag at first sight of the reflection before asserting control over the figure. It is as though Melody sees himself all too clearly with all his imperfections, as though he is completely aware of the disparity between who he is and who he aspires to be. Only through an act of will does he assume a military bearing which strikes regal comportment. He exerts discipline to maintain a mask that no longer fits. In the most poignant moment of the play, his daughter, Sara, who embodies the same split between peasant and aristocrat as her father and who will be the legacy figure in the cycle plays, pleads with him: "Oh, Father, why can't you ever be the thing you can seem to be?" (228). Characters enter rooms on three occasions to interrupt Melody's view of himself in the mirror. In short succession, scenes reveal who Melody is, who he wants to be, and how he presents himself to other characters. The action resolves with Melody's failure to embody the role that he fashions for himself and his inability to live without that part as well. By consuming alcohol in enormous quantities, Melody attempts to make the mask fit, to live with the knowledge that it doesn't. Final recognition that others see him for who he is finishes his attempt to hold onto the mask. After riding off to the Harford mansion to avenge the family honor, Melody returns to his tavern beaten and bloody, his once sparkling uniform torn and frayed. Mrs. Harford, an attractive woman who had rebuked his flirtation earlier, punctuated Melody's humiliation by witnessing the drunken street brawl. In the midst of the fight, Melody looked up and saw her: "that pale Yankee bitch watching from a window, sneering with disgust!" (267). She effectively rips off Melody's mask. The action sustains as long as all characters allow Melody to play his part. But in one look, Melody realizes that the game is up. He can no longer flatter himself once he sees his reflection in Deborah Harford's condescending eyes.

The pretender, Con Melody, finally sees himself as he truly is and reverts to form. Stage directions at the end describe Melody as a "loutish, grinning clown" (277). When he speaks, the brogue which he demonstrably mastered with perfect diction, returns. All pretense of grandeur vanishes, and Melody adopts a new role to play. Strangely, Sara, who had argued throughout the play that her father should see himself as he is, reverses herself at the end and implores: "Won't you be yourself again?" (277). She tries to rouse the old Melody, but he protests vehemently: "For the love of God, stop—let me go—!" (279). He cannot live without the illusion that he created for himself. Sara watches her father exit and offers a benediction: "May the hero of Talavera rest in peace!" (280). After the street brawl, his friend Creegan comments on Melody's ravings: "It's the same crazy blather he's talked every once in a while since they brought him to—about the Harford woman—and speakin' av the pigs and his father one minute, and his pride and his honor and his mare the next" (267). Melody fails to integrate two dominant strains of his character. He can no longer reconcile who he is and what he's become with who he used to be and who he'd like to be. When Sara asks herself, "Why do I mourn for him?" she halts at the contradictions in Con's personality (281). Michael Manheim astutely observes: "She panics at the realization that Con is caught between two irreconcilable natures—both genuine yet at the same time both poses" ("O'Neill's Transcendence of Melodrama in *A Moon for the Misbegotten*" 152). Throughout the play, there has been an insistence that Melody pretends to be a gentleman but that he's really just a tavern keeper. This division between illusion and reality is, as it turns out, another illusion.

Melody's "performance" at the end is no more authentic than his performance as Major Melody of Wellington's dragoons. Sara begins to realize only at the end that her father is neither one nor the other but, at least, both. Her own dividedness and multiplicity forms the subject in O'Neill's next play, *More Stately Mansions*, in which she battles to balance her love for Simon Harford and her lust for money and power. For his part in that play, Simon tries to integrate his desire to write books with a competing desire to build more stately mansions as a captain of industry. The mask, then, does not shield the essence of character so much as other aspects of character. In the recognition scenes I've outlined in *Mourning Becomes Electra*, *The Hairy Ape*, and *A Touch of the Poet*, characters glimpse other parts of themselves which they would rather not see. Their inability to integrate these aspects leads to their downfall. The mask is a strategy that above all else, simplifies an approach to character. It allows characters to see themselves as they would like to be seen. Mannon is a sensitive lover; Yank is a powerful leader; Melody is a brave aristocrat. These readings of respective characters are true but incomplete. Characters in O'Neill can never be the thing that they can sometimes seem to be. They can never accept less than that either, even as they can never see more of themselves.

A Moon for the Misbegotten culminates O'Neill's conception of character as mask and acting as necessary pretense. O'Neill juxtaposes the sham of theatre with a painful unmasking of human vulnerability. Very little happens in this play. A dying man confesses his sins on the altar of a virgin's breast. That summarizes the dramatic action and emphasizes the unmasking that occurs between James Tyrone and Josie Hogan. Action strips away all pretense, an ironic pattern in a play that builds itself around acting and scheming. Phil Hogan, Josie's father, operates as a playwright within the play who designs schemes within schemes to bring the two reluctant lovers together. Ultimately, such scheming results in heart-breaking failure, but it also forces a transvaluation of values as it confers a state of grace upon the three principal figures. Religious imagery, blasphemed early and often in the play, emerges in a fresh new context at the end of the play. Despite the fact that the two lovers do not end up together for a happy ending, love remains the positive value as it has in no previous O'Neill play. Hogan and Josie reach new levels of understanding and intimacy. Romantic love transforms into love as sacrifice, the same value championed first in O'Neill's unproduced *Servitude*. While the message remains the same, the medium in which O'Neill conveys his theme achieves tremendous emotional richness in his last play.

The three principal characters are all actors who mask interior thoughts and feelings with a very different exterior presentation. Josie is the greatest actor of all. She plays the part of the village wanton, who has been with so many men that none will marry her and make a decent woman of her. In truth, she is a virgin. She concocts her elaborate charade as a defense system against her own conception of herself as ugly and unworthy. Rather than feel the shame of being scorned by men, she invents a scheme in which she pretends to have slept with the entire town. When Hogan raises the possibility that she might catch Tyrone for a husband, a man whom she does love and admire, she responds: "Och, Father, don't play the jackass with me. You know, and I know, I'm an ugly overgrown lump of a woman, and the men that want me are no better than stupid bulls" (CP3 870). Josie pretends that her appearance prevents Tyrone from loving her: "If I was a dainty, pretty tart he'd be proud I'd raise a rumpus about him. But when it's a big, ugly hulk like me—[*She falters and forces herself to go on.*] If he ever was tempted to want me, he'd be ashamed of it" (903). Josie refuses to see herself as desirable, although both Tyrone and her father love her deeply. Josie plays the part of the wanton precisely because she fears that men perceive her as sexually unattractive. She protects herself from ever having to realize her worst fears.

Her father, Phil Hogan, delights in his role as a combative Irish curmudgeon. He presents himself as cynical and hard-hearted, but he remains the most sentimental character in the play. His rough talk belies a loving father who tries to get what's best for his daughter. As an act of kindness, Hogan props up Josie's story of herself as a promiscuous woman. Knowing that Josie will never accept a compliment directly from him, Hogan conveys affection in third person reference to Tyrone: "You're a pure virgin to him, but all the same there's things besides your beautiful soul he feels drawn to, like your beautiful hair and eyes, and—" (901). From the outset, Hogan sees his daughter clearly and knows why she plays the game of the wanton. He does not destroy her illusion out of great pity, understanding and love. To make her face the facts would be too harsh for her. Hogan proceeds with his elaborate schemes to marry his daughter to Tyrone on the basis of his knowing precisely who Josie is and the nature of the mask she wears. He plays the matchmaker in the play in order to give her a shot at happiness.

Even before James Tyrone enters at the end of Act 1, his character precedes him onstage by way of description. Hogan and Josie spy him down the road on his approach to their farm, and Josie announces him: "Look at him when he thinks no one is watching, with his eyes on the ground. Like a dead man walking slow behind his own coffin. [*then roughly*] Faith, he must have a hangover. He sees us now. Look at the bluff he puts up, straightening himself and grinning. [*resentfully*] I don't want to meet him. Let him make jokes with you and play the old game about a drink you both think is such fun. That's all he comes for, anyway" [*She starts off again.*] (874). Tyrone plays the part of the Broadway sport who revels in the gambling life of hotel bars and prostitutes. His demeanor and wardrobe suggest, according to O'Neill's stage directions, "that he follows a style set by well-groomed Broadway gamblers who would like to be mistaken for Wall Street brokers" (875). Yet the description of him as a "dead man walking" aptly characterizes his true nature beneath the jovial and joking exterior. Tyrone harbors a secret that the action of the play will reveal. When Josie surprises Jim with a friendly kiss later in the first act, she reacts: "Och, there's no spirit in you! It's like kissing a corpse" (882). Like Eleanor Cape in *Welded*, Tyrone is dead on the inside. At the very end of the play, Josie laments the fact that her would-be lover has gone:

"I didn't know he'd died already—that it was a damned soul coming to me in the moonlight, to confess and be forgiven and find peace for a night—" (937). Tyrone is dead before he enters the action of the play. His mask, the opposite of the Mannon mask, provides the illusion that he's alive. He performs his role when he comes onstage and an audience watches him. Just as Josie reveals herself in the course of the action, Tyrone unburdens himself of his secrets and the mutual unmasking of the two concludes the play.

Characters play games to establish bonds of affection between them. Since they all wear masks, they agree upon certain games to play that have rules which allow them to act roles without fear of exposure. These games communicate affection without having to reveal intimate thoughts and secrets. The games spark rituals of good feeling. Invective and blarney are two means to hide inner feelings among the principals. Tyrone and Hogan good-naturedly trade insults about the condition of the farm, their relationship of landlord and tenant, and proceed to engage in a match of wits in which Tyrone begs for a hospitable drink and Hogan cheerfully refuses. Josie, listening to the entire charade, finally interrupts: "Ain't you the fools, playing that old game between you, and both of you pleased as punch!" (879). Father and daughter play similar games with each other. Hogan makes his entrance calling his only daughter a "great slut" and an "overgrown cow" (862). Josie counters these jibes by insulting her father as a "bad-tempered old hornet" and an "ugly little buck goat" (862), and then flattering him as a fighter: "Sure, you could give Jack Dempsey himself a run for his money" (863). The initial confrontation ends with Hogan threatening to beat his daughter, calmed only by the fact that she wields a club: "A fine curse God put on me when he gave me a daughter as big and strong as a bull, and as vicious and disrespectful. [*Suddenly his eyes twinkle and he grins admiringly.*] Be God, look at you standing there with the club! If you ain't the damnedest daughter in Connecticut, who is?" (863–4). Banter, in the form of insult or compliment, establishes a bond between characters and communicates affection. Each character agrees to sustain the others' illusion. They engage the mask of each other, but politely leave the private face alone.

Tyrone and Josie, too, combine compliments and complaints to keep each other at a respectful distance. Tyrone, from the outset, knows that Josie is not whom she pretends to be, and welcomes her with an appropriate, yet satirical address: "and how's my Virgin Queen of Ireland?" (877). Josie, in turn, needles Tyrone by suggesting that he would feel more at home in the arms of some of his tarts on Broadway than on the Connecticut farm of his tenants. Tyrone forces her to blush with his new admission:

"I like them tall and strong and voluptuous, now, with beautiful big breasts" (878). With her, Tyrone tries to drop his role as a Broadway sport and prove himself a gentleman. Josie reluctantly drops her guard, fearful that she will make herself vulnerable if she admits her love for Tyrone. She repeatedly, in the first two acts, tries to play the familiar part of the promiscuous woman, but Tyrone won't let her play the game. At the end of Act 2, he says: "Lay off that line, for tonight at least. [*He adds slowly*] I'd like tonight to be different" (910). Tyrone instinctively knows that the games interfere with what he wants to say. The irritation that Tyrone expresses when Josie attempts to resume the ritual of play indicates that something unusual will happen between them. Absence of play indicates a change in Tyrone's character. He appears differently than he has on previous occasions, a fact attributed to two things. Josie believes that his inability to play the usual games results from his decision to sell the farm to the rich neighbor, T. Stedman Harder. When Tyrone arrives late for his moonlight date with Josie in Act 2, Josie suggests that he has a bad conscience, implying that he feels guilty about what he has done to sell the farm which he had promised to the Hogans. Tyrone responds by staring at her guiltily and asking: "What put that in your head? Conscience about what?" (909). Tyrone is guilty, but not about selling the farm. Both characters misunderstand each other at this point and only in the final act does Tyrone unveil his secret. His guilt stems from the death of his mother and his behavior surrounding it. The issue around the sale of the farm supplies only the overt melodrama that provides suspense. "Some viewers of the play," according to Michael Manheim, "never do get the point that melodramatic intrigue is not finally the central interest of this play" ("O'Neill's Transcendence of Melodrama in *A Moon for the Misbegotten*" 154). The real drama, however, takes place before the action of the play begins. The plot, in this case, is an excuse for something revelatory to happen. That event discloses Tyrone's haunted past and his desperate plea for forgiveness (Manheim 153–157).

Scheming within the play makes up the plot. Hogan, of course, invents the scheme that Josie falls for in which Tyrone sells the farm for quick cash in order to return to his high rolling life of New York. But even before Hogan appears, the importance of scheming manifests itself in the opening scene between Josie and her brother, Mike. The scene is a leave-taking, in which Mike follows the pattern of his other brothers, Thomas and John, and leaves the farm for the city. Josie helps Mike escape from Hogan by preparing his bags, distracting Hogan, and even stealing a little of the old man's money to support Mike's trip. When Hogan discovers that Mike has left, he feigns outrage and blusters against his daughter. The initial scene of Mike's departure establishes Josie's tenderness and goodness toward her brother, whom she does not like, and feigned hostility toward her father, whom she does like. Scheming binds father and daughter together in fun and affection. Hogan and Josie revel in the memory of tricking their neighbors, the Crowleys, on the sale of a lame horse, and Josie's flirtations as a young girl with Tyrone's father in order to stave off paying the rent. Hogan tells Josie, admiringly, "You should have gone on the stage" (869). Josie's analysis of her father hints at the structure of the entire play: "You old divil, you've always a trick hidden behind your tricks, so no one can tell at times what you're after" (869). The play works as artifice packed within artifice, scheme within scheme, in order to unpack human truths at the center. What the play's after and what Hogan is after is withheld until the end of the action.

The arrival of T. Stedman Harder, the Standard Oil millionaire whose fence borders the Hogan's land, provides the opportunity to put acting and trickery on full display. Apparently, Hogan repeatedly breaks down the fence in order for his pigs to wallow on the banks of Harder's ice pond. Harder arrives in Act 1 to make his complaint in person and to demand restitution. O'Neill's long description of Harder puts him at a decided disadvantage against the likes of Hogan. The initial description begins: "Harder is in his late thirties but looks younger because his face is unmarked by worry, ambition, or any of the common hazards of life. No matter how long he lives, his four undergraduate years will always be for him the most significant in his life, and the moment of his highest achievement the time he was tapped for an exclusive Senior Society at the Ivy university to which his father had given millions" (884). The college boy, for O'Neill, always represents an individual who cannot master a situation. Bounded by institutional thinking and an easy life, the college educated character lacks the ability to act, to perform a role, and he cannot fool others. Despite all Harder's money, he proves no match for Hogan and Josie in a battle of wits. Hogan seizes the offensive quickly by accusing Harder of breaking down the fence and encouraging the pigs to risk pneumonia in the winter at the ice pond!

The duplicitous nature of the Hogans on display against Harder amplifies the main scheme of the action. While the audience watches the confrontation between Hogans and Harder, Tyrone listens and laughs behind the wall of the Hogan farmhouse. The Hogans act for the benefit of Tyrone. His presence as an auditor heightens enjoyment of the performance and creates a play within a play. This scene also stimulates an impetus for Hogan's grand improvisation that follows. The squabble provides a motive for Tyrone to sell his farm to Harder. After Harder rides away in defeat, Tyrone refers to the farm as a gold mine on three separate occasions. He confides that Harder wants to buy the farm in order to throw Hogan off the property. Jim predicts that Harder's humiliation at the hands of Hogan will triple the value of the farm and that he will make a lot of money on the sale. Of course, he's kidding, he would never actually sell the farm to Harder. He loves the Hogans. But Hogan, ever scheming, uses Tyrone's words to hatch his matchmaking plot upon his unsuspecting daughter.

Hogan improvises and modulates his scheme as the action progresses. It begins as a question of how to get a rich man to marry Josie. Honest son Mike, no match for Hogan either, actually first breathes life into the scheme for Josie to catch Tyrone for a husband. Reasoning that she cannot marry a decent man, Mike figures Tyrone for a possible mark: "I know it's crazy, but maybe you're hoping if you got hold of him alone when he's mad drunk—Anyway, talk all you please to put me off, I'll bet my last penny you've cooked up some scheme to hook him, and the Old Man put you up to it. Maybe he thinks if he caught you with Jim and had witnesses to prove it, and his shotgun to scare him—" (860). When Josie discloses Mike's plot to Hogan, the father allows that it might just work. To calm Josie's outrage, Hogan intimates that the future of the farm would be settled if Josie were to marry Tyrone, the landlord of the property. Hogan's scheme, hiding a good hearted desire inside a pecuniary motive, elaborates in Act 2. He feigns heavy drunkenness in order to proclaim his profound sadness that Tyrone has, in fact, promised to sell the farm to Harder. He manipulates Josie into accepting a revenge plot for an act of betrayal. She agrees to lure Tyrone into bed in order for Hogan to bring witnesses to catch them there in the morning. They employ the time honored bed trick to ensure that she marries him and that they save the farm. Hogan stages his departure from the farm in front of the approaching Tyrone, assuring Josie and Tyrone that he will not return again until morning.

Prior to leaving, however, Hogan reveals his true motivation. After Hogan goads Josie into collusion with him, she exits to her bedroom, ostensibly to freshen up and re-apply her makeup. Alone on stage, Hogan's demeanor changes. O'Neill's directions read: "Abruptly he ceases to look like a drunk who, by an effort, is keeping himself half-sober. He is a man who has been drinking a lot but is still clear-headed and has complete control of himself" (906). He observes that Josie's room remains dark. She cannot even look at herself in the mirror and face the task for which she has set herself. Hogan speaks: "God forgive me, it's bitter medicine. But it's the only way I can see that has a chance now" (906). In an instant, the mask drops to show the scheme within the scheme. Such a moment reveals the loving father beneath the feisty curmudgeon. Later, after having been found out, Hogan vents his full motivation for his devious conniving: "All you said about my lying and scheming, and what I hoped would happen, is true. But it wasn't his money, Josie. I did see it was the last chance—the only one left to bring the two of you to stop your damned pretending, and face the truth that you loved each other. I wanted you to find happiness—by hook or crook, one way or another, what did I care how? I wanted to save him, and I hoped he'd see that only your love could—It was his talk of the beauty he saw in you that made me hope— And I knew he'd never go to bed with you even if you'd let him unless he married you" (944).

Tyrone's own counter scheme makes marriage impossible and thwarts Hogan's plot. He arrives at the farmhouse late for his moonlight date with Josie and not noticeably drunk, a significant sign for the occasion. In the following act, Act 3, Josie brings him her father's liquor and he accepts it gratefully, acknowledging that "The booze at the Inn didn't work tonight" (910). Alcohol does not provide refuge for him on this night from haunting memories of the past. Typically, the alcoholic mask shields a character from bitter self-knowledge. O'Neill's description of Tyrone's entrance for his date with Josie reads in part: "…his eyes have a peculiar fixed, glazed look, and there is a certain vague quality in his manner and speech, as if he were a bit hazy and absent-minded" (907). That the alcohol doesn't work leads to Tyrone's desperation. When the bums in *The Iceman Cometh* return from the streets to Hope's saloon, fresh from realizing the vacuity of their pipe dreams, they complain in unison that the booze doesn't work. They can get drunk only when they restore their life illusions. Tyrone, unlike the characters in *Iceman*, possesses no illusions, but the booze helps him to numb the pain of his guilty past deeds. Before his first entrance, Hogan and Josie discuss the mask-like function of alcohol on Jim's character:

JOSIE: He only acts like he's hard and shameless to get back at life when it's tormenting him—and who doesn't?

HOGAN: Or take the other kind of queer drunk he gets on sometimes when, without any reason you can see, he'll suddenly turn strange, and look sad, and stare at nothing as if he was mourning over some ghost inside him, and—

JOSIE: I think I know what comes over him when he's like that. It's the memory of his mother comes back and his grief for her death [872–873].

The action of *A Moon for the Misbegotten* picks up at the precise moment at which Jim can no longer erase memory of his performance surrounding his mother's death. The inability of alcohol to do its work motivates him to visit Josie, although the real reason remains a mystery at this point: "Had to get out of the damned Inn. I was going batty alone there. The old heebie-jeebies. So I came to you. [*He pauses—then adds with strange, wondering sincerity*] I've really begun to love you a lot, Josie" (908–909). Debauched to the core, Tyrone sees through the hollow pretenses of Josie. Her purity and simple goodness attract him. While Josie masks her innocence, Tyrone fears that his fine dress, good manners, and college education cover up a rotten soul and dirty secrets. Aware of the polarity between them, Tyrone fears that he will ruin Josie. Alone at the end of Act 2, after Josie goes in search of another bottle, Tyrone reviles himself for his need to see Josie. "You rotten bastard!" he says, failing miserably to light a match with a trembling hand as the curtain falls (911).

Physical desire for Josie leads to self-loathing and the threat of violence in the first part of the third act. Josie continues to assume her role as a wanton, but Tyrone threatens her: "If you don't look out, I'll call you on that bluff, Josie. [*He stares at her with a deliberate sensualist's look that undresses her.*] I'd like to. You know that, don't you?" (913). Jim assures her that he's over his case of heebie-jeebies, and adds: "Let the dead past bury its dead" (914). But as the scene unwinds, Tyrone, filled with memories and booze, begins to confuse Josie with the blonde woman whom he met on the train while taking his mother's body back East for burial. And as they converse, he also begins to force an intimate conversation with Josie in order for them both to drop their masks and see each other: "You can take the truth, Josie—from me. Because you and I belong to the same club. We can kid the world but we can't fool ourselves, like most people, no matter what we do—nor escape ourselves no matter where we run away. Whether it's the bottom of a bottle, or a South Sea Island, we'd find our own ghosts there waiting to greet us—'sleepless with pale commemorative eyes,' as Rossetti wrote" (923).

The allusion to the South Sea Islands usually refers to a libidinous zone of health and sexual freedom, a counterpoint to the Puritanism of New England, in plays such as *Beyond the Horizon*, *Diff'rent*, and *Mourning Becomes Electra*. Here, Tyrone argues that sexuality only excites ghosts of the past. Josie misreads Tyrone's intentions when she finally admits that she is a virgin. She follows this painful admission with a plea for love and a longing to take Tyrone to her bed. He, however, can only accept sexual relations in terms of sordid transactions. His demeanor changes and his language reflects the fact that he sees Josie now as the blonde woman on the train: "Sure thing, Kiddo. What the hell else do you suppose I came for? I've been kidding myself. [*He steps up beside her and puts his arm around her and presses his body to hers.*] You're the goods, Kid. I've wanted you all along. Love, nuts! I'll show you what love is. I know what you want, Bright Eyes" (925). Tyrone's transformation into a hustling john kills any possibility of romance between the two. Sex, for Tyrone, satisfies his self-hatred and the conviction that he destroys everyone whom he touches. "...when I poison them, they stay poisoned!" (926). His performance for Josie allows her to view him as he sees himself. She responds as he wishes and reacts with fear and disgust.

About to walk away, Tyrone adds a final plea: "I came here asking for love—just for this one night, because I thought you loved me" (926). The love Tyrone needs is not sexual. His desire for this night to be different than all the others is now clear. He doesn't want to defile or poison Josie like all the other whores he's bedded. Tyrone wants this night to be different in order for him to tell, finally, the story about the blonde woman on the train. He wants to confess his sins that make him hateful to himself. Josie welcomes him back to her arms and allows him to lie down with his head back against her breast. He tells about how his mother's death angered him by leaving him all alone. Unable to cry at her funeral, he remembers feeling obliged to act the part of the bereaved: "So I put on an act. I flopped on my knees and hid my face in my hands and faked some sobs and cried, 'Mama! Mama! My dear mother!' But all the time I kept saying to myself, 'You lousy ham! You God-damned lousy ham!'" (931). He goes on to describe how he slept with the "blonde pig" on the train for fifty bucks a night while his mother lay in a coffin in the baggage car. He remembers lines from a tear-jerker song, voiced out of context at the start of the act, but which now, given the situation, reveal the depth of Tyrone's pursuit of self-defilement:

> "And baby's cries can't waken her
> In the baggage coach ahead" [932].

The connotations of the above dramatic situation strike a grotesque image. Tyrone constructs the entire story theatrically as though he were a performer. He describes his revenge against his mother as an actor in a play: "It was like some plot I had to carry out. The blonde—she didn't matter. She was only something that belonged in the plot" (931–932). Tyrone sleeps with the prostitute on the train in order to express his anger against his mother for leaving him all alone. He asks Josie, for one night, to play the part of his mother in order to hear his confession. That she

A Moon for the Misbegotten, directed by Daniel Sullivan, at the Goodman The-atre in 1999, later transferred to the Walter Kerr Theatre on Broadway in April, 2000. In this penultimate scene, James Tyrone, Jr., played by Gabriel Byrne, tells Josie Hogan, played by Cherry Jones, about his mother's death. Tyrone's confession forces Josie to assume a new role as a Madonna figure and the scene achieves tragic pathos by staging an ironic pietà. Photograph by Eric Y. Exit. Courtesy of the Goodman Theatre, Chicago, Illinois.

agrees attests to the power and strength of her love for him. After con-fessing all, Josie hugs Tyrone to her. She wanted to take Tyrone as a lover, but she ends up in the role of his mother. The act ends with Tyrone sob-bing against Josie's breast, later falling asleep, and Josie staring into the moonlight: "You're a fine one, wanting to leave me when the night I promised I'd give you has just begun, our night that'll be different from all the others, with a dawn that won't creep over dirty windowpanes but will wake in the sky like a promise of God's peace in the soul's dark sad-ness" (933). What began with the prospects of romance, ends with a scene of wish fulfillment enacting the past: a son asking for and receiving for-giveness from his mother.

When Hogan reappears to find Josie still clutching a sleeping Tyrone to her breast in the pre-dawn hours of Act 4, Josie speaks of a miracle: "A virgin who bears a dead child in the night, and the dawn finds her still a virgin. If that isn't a miracle, what is?" (936). The wanton woman transforms into the Madonna. Josie sacrifices her own physical desire for Tyrone as a supreme gift of love. Whereas themes of sacrifice receive rhetoric in early plays such as *Servitude, The Personal Equation, Welded,* and a mature play such as *Days Without End, A Moon for the Misbegotten* dramatically represents sacrifice through Josie's enduring pose of cradling Tyrone. As she accepts him into her arms at the end of the preceding act she recognizes the trade she makes for Tyrone's love: "It's easy enough, too, for I have all kinds of love for you—and maybe this is the greatest of all—because it costs so much" (927). Josie sacrifices her one chance for romantic love in exchange for giving Tyrone one night of peace. The dawn which rises is beautiful, not another gray dawn creeping over dirty windowpanes, but Tyrone first tries to cover up his response to the scene with customary cynicism: "God seems to be putting on quite a display. I like Belasco better. Rise of curtain, Act-Four stuff" (942). Tyrone distances himself from the immediate experience by casting the sunrise in theatrical terms. He seems unaware of what transpired during the night. After imbibing an eye-opener, the flood of the night's memories rush back to him and he tries to leave quickly. Josie stops him, though, and he finally confesses that he does remember what happened and what Josie did for him: "I'm glad I remember! I'll never forget your love! [*He kisses her on the lips.*] Never! [*kissing her again*] Never, do you hear! I'll always love you, Josie. [*He kisses her again.*] Good-bye—and God bless you!" (944). Tyrone exits for the last time immediately after this farewell, certain never to return. Josie offers the final benediction of grace: "May you have your wish and die in your sleep soon, Jim, darling. May you rest forever in forgiveness and peace" (946).

The tragedy of *A Moon for the Misbegotten,* a love story, is that the two lovers cannot come together. As Josie says to her father, she didn't know that Tyrone was dead already when he came to see her. The moon provides the perfect atmosphere for romance. Josie dresses up in anticipation of the event. When Tyrone reveals, too, that he has no intention to sell the farm to anyone except the Hogans, no obstacles seem to stand between the two lovers. Sexuality, itself, becomes the final hurdle. Tyrone didn't come to meet a lover, he came to ask forgiveness from the one person who could best represent his mother's memory. The action of the play strips Josie naked and sets up an expectation, at least a hope that she will get Tyrone as a reward. The painful realization comes when Tyrone doesn't accept what Josie first offers and she has to transform herself completely from a wanting and willing lover to a forgiving mother. Josie first masquerades as a promiscuous woman, but Tyrone sees through her performance. But when she tries to give herself to him as a woman, he rebuffs her. His encounter with her in which he pretends that she's a whore is disgusting. But Josie is not a willing virgin, either. It is a part she's forced to play. The tragedy lies in the fact that she is forced to play first one role and then the other. Only at the end do the two lovers embrace in a way that reveals the depth of their sexual passion for each other. Only after eliminating the possibility for romance do they come together. The two would-be lovers finally see each other completely and honestly but the moment is fleeting. Once they face each other without masks, there is nothing left in the drama.

At the end of the play, Hogan begins a curse, but apologizes quickly to Josie in deference to her love for Tyrone: "I didn't mean it. I know whatever happened he meant no harm to you. It was life I was cursing—[*with a trace of his natural manner*] And, be God, that's a waste of breath, if it does deserve it" (945). The curse faintly echoes the curse of old Chris looking out to sea, in the wake of his daughter's marriage proposal from Burke, at the end of *"Anna Christie."* Hogan, the observer in the play and the matchmaker, fails to write the happy ending that he intended. Surprisingly, though, absence of a lifetime romance makes the love story more moving. The brief final contact between the two lovers conveys an enduring intensity of feeling. Josie forgives her father for all his scheming and the end of the play marks a return to the beginning. After all the masks of the characters have been removed in the course of the action, daughter and father agree to put them back on and resume their old games of friendly antagonisms. They fit comfortably back into their old roles and restore bonds between them. The performative mode in which they lead daily life once again girds the underpinnings of love, familiarity and respect which sustain their relationship. Everything is the same, but unspeakably different.

The action in *A Moon for the Misbegotten* seems to unmask character in a fairly straightforward way. The town whore is revealed as a virgin. The virgin/whore dualism that governs Tyrone's behavior prevents him from accepting all the love that Josie wants to give him. As she says to Tyrone, "I have all kinds of love for you...." The painful realization in the play is that she can only give one aspect of her love to Tyrone. Just at the point when Josie stands unmasked, naked before him, and is ready to take him as a lover, Tyrone demands that she limit her love to only one role. He can only accept her innocence and purity and love as a substitute mother, but he cannot tolerate her sexuality. The dualism of *this* or *that* simplifies an approach to character as well as a response to the world. Josie is not this or that, necessarily, but this *and* that, a crucial distinction. Unmasking is ultimately an illusion in O'Neill. It promises through time to reveal the essence of character and provide an easy answer. But in fact, the process of unmasking doesn't reveal an essence so much as show more masks, the unknown sum of which make up the range and depth of human feeling and experience. Failure to embrace the totality of identity, in oneself and in others, accounts for a tragic response to this play. In Tyrone's and Josie's final embrace, it is finally clear that he loves her passionately and wants her as a lover. Their final kisses at last simultaneously fulfill and frustrate audience expectations. But to paraphrase from *The Great God Brown*, the characters remain broken and unable to mend each other. Nevertheless, the effort that they put forth to try and heal each other, given their limitations, inspires awe and compassion and confers a state of grace upon them.

Chapter 3

Beyond the Proscenium

"What d'yuh tink dis dump is, a dump?"
—*Rocky the Bartender to a patron in* The Iceman Cometh

At the end of *Beyond the Horizon,* Robert Mayo stumbles back to the section of country highway upon which the play began. Stage directions indicate that the fallow fields reflect Robert's lack of farming ability, a marked contrast to the healthy environment in the first act. Robert, too, is dying, but determined to see the rising dawn one last time, a symbol of his former hopes and dreams. He speaks to allay the despair of his brother and wife who have come to find him:

> [*in a voice which is suddenly ringing with the happiness of hope*] You mustn't feel sorry for me. Don't you see I'm happy at last—free—free!—freed from the farm—free to wander on and on—eternally! [*He raises himself on his elbow, his face radiant, and points to the horizon.*] Look! Isn't it beautiful beyond the hills? I can hear the old voices calling me to come—[*exultantly*] And this time I'm going! It isn't the end. It's a free beginning—the start of my voyage! I've won to my trip—the right of release—beyond the horizon! Oh, you ought to be glad—glad—for my sake! [*He collapses weakly.*] [CP1 652]

The clarity of expression, the tubercular victim watching his last sunset, the grieving brother cursing fate, the defeated wife averting her head from the dying spectacle, casts the scene in melodramatic hues and wrings full dramatic value out of suffering. Still, this early play, written in 1918 and produced in 1920, winner of O'Neill's first Pulitzer Prize, reflects O'Neill's tragic theme of triumph through defeat and the value of struggle to determine human worth. Characters attempt to transcend their physical surroundings and escape their material bodies, and, similarly, O'Neill's plays attempt to transcend the theatre.

Melodramatic excess in this closing scene of a landmark play prominently displays O'Neill's manipulation of scenic space. Robert's body literally stretches toward the audience in the final scene. Desire to see something, to touch something, beyond the frame of the proscenium transgresses the fourth wall and breaks through the apparent realism of the text. Such distant points remain unrealized and unrepresented in the drama. The reach exceeds the grasp and thus exerts dramatic tension throughout the action. The desire to have what is not readily or visually apparent or available enlarges the drama. If what is desired does not lie within the frame of the representation, characters must then look outside, a bodily gesture which opens the drama for an audience. My focus in this chapter examines scenic space as a manipulation of what is visible to the eye and what is not. Visual patterns oscillate between absence and presence, here and there, inside and outside the proscenium frame. Identifying textual struggles to escape from the field of representation, a battle between the seen and unseen, alters the perception and evaluation of O'Neill's realism.

O'Neill's final masterpieces all belong to a recognizable and realistic style. *Ah, Wilderness!* is a domestic comedy set in the Miller family home in Connecticut. *Days Without End* features all realistic interiors as well. *A Touch of the Poet*, set in a tavern, is the first full-length O'Neill drama to require only one setting. O'Neill created movement in earlier plays, in part, by shifting locales in every act. *The Iceman Cometh* occurs in a single setting with minor variations in each act. *Long Day's Journey Into Night* and the one-act *Hughie* have only one set. All of *A Moon for the Misbegotten* takes place on the Hogan farm, although the second act makes use of an interior space inside the house. Absence of any marked theatricality in description or design especially distinguishes these late plays from earlier ones. There are no cut-away rooms, no dream sequences, no special lighting effects, seemingly no opportunities for simultaneous staging. In dramatizing interior spaces in the last plays, O'Neill seems to narrow his focus and place a microscope upon scenic detail. Depicted scenes appear to be genuine locale rather than theatrical space. Memories of Jimmy the Priest's, The Hell Hole, and the Garden Hotel taproom inform O'Neill's conception of Harry Hope's saloon in *The Iceman Cometh*.[1] Likewise, the house in *Long Day's Journey Into Night* is obviously Monte Cristo Cottage, O'Neill's summer home, a museum today, which one can still visit and test for its veracity.[2] References to real places diminish the plays as novel works for the stage.

Realism as a style tries to hide its artifice. If the purpose of art, in the words of the formalists, is to make the familiar strange, the purpose of realism is to make the familiar more familiar. Linguistically, realism is tautological, a point emphasized by Rocky the Bartender's appraisal of Harry Hope's saloon to a patron in *The Iceman Cometh*: "What d'yuh tink dis dump is, a dump?" (CP3 587). Recognizing on stage a replica of things from the mundane world often proves thrilling. "Yes, that's exactly how it is!" responds the audience. Realism, according to Roland Barthes, is "any discourse which accepts statements whose only justification is their referent" (15). Realism tries to reduce the symbolic function of language to denotative meanings only. This is, of course, an illusion, and it makes sense to consider realism as a strategy to seduce an audience. The best way to rid a picture of symbolic value is to put a lot of stuff in it, enough to deflect attention away from any one object. Consider the opening stage description of *Ah, Wilderness!*:

> The room is fairly large, homely looking and cheerful in the morning sunlight, furnished with scrupulous medium-priced tastelessness of the period. Beneath the two windows at left, front, a sofa with silk and satin cushions stands against the wall. At rear of sofa, a bookcase with glass doors, filled with cheap sets, extends along the remaining length of wall. In the rear wall, left, is a double doorway with sliding doors and portieres, leading into a dark, windowless, back parlor. At right of this doorway, another bookcase, this time a small, open one, crammed with boys' and girls' books and the best-selling novels of many past years— books the family really have read.... [CP3 5]

These stage directions say a lot about the social and economic standing of the Miller household, and descriptions of tastelessness and details about books for show and books to read also speak volumes about the attitude of the playwright toward his subjects. Furnishings of the house place the Millers in a familiar environment and one the audience recognizes as decidedly middle class. Nothing theatrical tips off the audience that it sees anything other than a typical room in a middle class family home.

Excess of detail in the represented scene camouflages the fact that missing elements exist outside the picture plane. Brenda Murphy puts it this way in *American Realism and American Drama, 1880–1940*: "Whereas the traditional forms of tragedy, comedy and melodrama tend to emphasize, to exaggerate, to inflate the piece of human experience being represented, the impulse of realism is to deflate it by emphasizing its context, the larger rhythms of human life within which it occurs" (114). Scenic excess robs the stage of symbolic value and deflates human experience. At

The original production of *Ah, Wilderness!* (1933), Act I, scene 2, directed by Philip Moeller. Recognizable details and a domestic gathering around the dinner table try to convince the audience that the scene is not staged for its benefit. Seated (clockwise from the head of the table) are George M. Cohan as Nat Miller, Eda Heinemann as Lily, Elisha Cook, Jr., as Richard, Gene Lockhart as Sid Davis, Marjorie Marquis as Essie Miller, Walter Vonnegut, Jr., as Tommy and Adelaide Bean as Mildred Miller. Photograph by Vandamm. Museum of the City of New York. Theater Collection.

the same time, the realistic emphasis inflates the unseen presence of offstage things and events. Murphy's definition of realism suggests a radical change in the development of modern drama. In classical drama, emphasis remains upon the characters as they work out their problems before the audience. By the late nineteenth century, melodrama dominated the stage by inflating human experience and making the drama larger and more visible. Realism, and the wave of modern drama that followed in its wake, paints a smaller picture, but with more detail. As a result, in order to gain in size, the drama enlists what's not seen as an important element. The fog, the sea, the sounds of the urban city, three examples in O'Neill of the larger rhythm of life to which Murphy refers, function as unseen presences in the plays. O'Neill slides drama into the wings of the theatre to make a dynamic and visually appealing rival of melodramatic appeal. The realistic detail of the Tyrone house in *Long Day's Journey Into Night* pales against the opaque background of the enveloping fog outside the house. Edmund's alienation regarding family life contrasts with his story of freedom and escape and sense of belonging at sea. The beauty of the moon and rising dawn on the Hogan farm in the final act of *A Moon for the Misbegotten* offers visual relief from Tyrone's bitter complaint about cheap nights spent on Broadway followed by gray dawns seen through dirty window panes.

Understanding realism's motives are steps toward seeing how O'Neill approaches "real realism." He voiced his frustration with the question of style and terminology in a letter to Nathan on May 7, 1923: "Damn that word, 'realism!' When I first spoke to you of the play [*Welded*] as a 'last word in realism,' I meant something 'really real,' in the sense of being spiritually true, not meticulously life-like—an interpretation of actuality by a distillation, an elimination of most realistic trappings, an intensification of human lives into clear symbols of truth" (SL 175). O'Neill wrote all his drama for a proscenium theatre in which clear separation exists between performer and audience. Everything that he describes in his copious stage directions forms part of the visual field of his drama. He fills up the stage space with objects, but also introduces elements which cannot be seen. No wonder, then, that entrances and exits, which pass through the boundaries of what's visible, demarcating the seen and unseen, shape scenes and dramatic development. The limits of the stage, the walls of an interior, delineate space into what can be seen and what cannot. The drama alludes to outside forces and creates an illusion of an offstage world that remains unseen and poses a constant threat to the onstage world. To draw an analogy from biology, the stage represents a kind of cell and the border of what can be seen, the line between the seen and unseen, functions as a kind of membrane. Tension builds up between the seen and the unseen and through a process of diffusion, the offstage world permeates the stage representation. Resistance to diffusion sustains the dramatic action, but once it occurs, the elements of the inside representation diffuse outward to points beyond the field of representation.

Despite innovations among the experimental plays in the 1920s, for all the attention they receive in terms of daring subject matter and new staging techniques, lack of tension between the "inside" and the "outside" flaws many of them. Of the plays written after *"Anna Christie"* and before *Mourning Becomes Electra*, fourteen plays in all, only three remain as important contributions to the O'Neill repertory: *The Emperor Jones, The Hairy Ape*, and *Desire Under the Elms*. Except for the eighth of nine acts in *Strange Interlude*, that play, even with the thought asides, remains visually dull. The thought asides try to show the split between the "inside" and "outside" of a character, but the stage picture itself remains relatively lifeless. The stage picture easily contains the action through a lot of talk. According to Ronald Wainscott, Jo Mielziner's design for *Strange Interlude* remained largely uninteresting except for the possibility of simultaneous action afforded by the boat race scene in act 8 (Wainscott 236–237).[3] In that scene, on one side of the stage, Sam Evans and Madeline, his prospective daughter-in-law, look over the stern of a cruiser anchored in position to watch the finish line for Gordon, Jr.'s, championship crew race. The offstage and unseen action of the race animates the entire scene. On the other side of the stage, Nina, Darrell, and Marsden quietly recap events that have led them to the present. Cheers for Gordon, the eventual winner in the race, contrast with tones of regret and sadness that capture the competing focus of the scene.

Lee Simonson's design for *Dynamo* (1928) recreated the doll house effect of *Desire Under the Elms*, but by stripping away all the exterior walls he made it more skeletal in nature and positioned not one but two houses on stage, the Fife house and neighboring Light house. This design, too, allowed for the possibility of simultaneous action in both houses and allowed for the focus to shift, not only from room to room, but from house to house. O'Neill's conception of the scene showed the religious Lights pitted against the atheist and electrical engineer, Mr. Fife. The separation of the two houses in the first two acts melds together in the last one. Religion and science, in separate houses initially, merge in the last act at the hydroelectric plant in the quasi-religious image of the dynamo. Thematic and visual dualism and a final reduction or synthesis to God as the dynamo helps to account for this play's reception as one of O'Neill's worst failures.[4] While *Dynamo* crudely displays its oppositions between science and religion, two houses, old and new gods, O'Neill's historical pageants, including *The Fountain, Marco Millions*, and *Lazarus Laughed* resort to centrifugal settings, according to Timo Tiusanen in *O'Neill's Scenic Images*, in which all the detail is described on the outside of the representation, creating a vacuous bubble onstage with no core (147–148). Imbalance between the inside and outside eliminates tension along the edges of shared space. An aging Ponce de Leon searches for the Fountain of Youth in *The Fountain* in order to win the love of Beatriz, the daughter of a woman who once loved him passionately. Repetition and renewal thus play dominant thematic and structural roles in the play. Nietzsche's concept of eternal

Act 8 in *Strange Interlude* with Jane Fonda as Madeline and Pat Hingle as Sam Evans in the 1963 Actors Studio production, directed by José Quintero, at the Hudson Theatre. The focus on the exciting offstage boat race on one side of the stage contrasts with a private conversation between Nina and Marsden on the other side. Attention to offstage events enlarges the drama and turns the actors out to the audience. Photograph by Friedman/Abeles. Billy Rose Theatre Collection. The New York Public Library for the Performing Arts. Astor, Lenox and Tilden Foundations.

recurrence finds banal expression in the fountain song, which reprises throughout the play:

> Love is a flower
> Forever blooming
> Beauty a fountain
> Forever flowing
> Upward into the source of sunshine,
> Upward into the azure heaven;
> One with God but
> Ever returning
> To kiss the earth that the flower may live [CP2 230–231].

Sprawling over twenty years of time and multiple locales, no opposing forces ground the play from its lyrical flight. The woman who loves Juan observes his split nature between romantic dreamer and ambitious thinker, and soldier of iron. She tells him, "God pity you if those two selves should ever clash!" (173). If this battle were ever seen in the action of the play, visual possibilities would arise from the perspectives of the dreamer looking beyond the frame of the representation to that which cannot be seen, and the soldier who conquers all that he does see. Instead, only the dreamer seems to dominate the action. As a result, tension relaxes over the course of the action.

Marco Millions sets up an opposition between East and West. By dramatizing Marco Polo in the East, tension develops between western dualism and eastern monism, between desire as assertion of individual will, particularly in terms of business and pursuit of capital, and non-desire and the search for oneness. James Robinson posits in *Eugene O'Neill and Oriental Thought: A Divided Vision* that O'Neill longs himself to adopt an Eastern vision but cannot ultimately escape from Western attitudes. This same division, even if it is true, however, does not find its way into the play. *Marco Millions*, a satire on the American businessman and the American way of life in the tradition of Sinclair Lewis' *Babbitt*, does not repeat the internal split within the author in the character of Marco Polo. Marco never deviates from his initial decision to travel to the East and to make money and return home a wealthy man. He remains completely indifferent to the values he encounters in the East and shuns the love of the Princess who adores him. Unwittingly, he causes her death. In the action, Marco appears insensitive, smug, and scarcely human. Eastern values appear, on the other hand, to hold integrity, emotional richness, and wisdom. One is bad, the other good. Failure to mix adequately these values destroys dramatic tension.

Finally, *Lazarus Laughed* repetitively states its mantra that "Death is dead." Despite recurring motifs of laughter, use of masks, and ritual structure, there is nothing visually compelling in this spectacle. It reads as a thesis play and demonstrates the dangers of slavish adherence to philosophy. As the nearest O'Neill play to embodying Nietzschean principles, one that quotes Nietzsche within the text, *Lazarus Laughed* states repeatedly what it is about, and in this "play for an imaginative theatre," no imaginary forces lurk outside the border of the stage picture; no unseen pressures force what's visible and inside to the outside.

The shifting dynamic between the inside and the outside, absence and presence, here and there, distinguishes O'Neill's more realistic plays from his experimental ones. The details of realism present a confining style against which the action in the plays rebels. In Act 1 of *Welded*, Michael Cape begins thinking aloud to himself (the first vestige of O'Neill's thought asides) as follows: "More and more frequently. There's always some knock at the door, some reminder of the life outside which calls you away from me" (CP2 243). The action of the play concerns the idealism of love and the desire of the two lovers to possess each other exclusively. Intrusion from the outside, a knock at the door, breaks them apart at the moment of their embrace and trip up the stairs to the bedroom. Figuratively, if not literally, a knock at the door serves as an organizing principle in all of the O'Neill plays. The door separates the visible from the invisible space and makes transition and access to that space possible. O'Neill's use of doors and references to offstage and unseen places and characters, create a seamless illusion of a represented area. At the same time, this technique enlarges his drama by directing the attention of characters away from each other (i.e., sharing a scene) to the periphery of the stage boundaries (i.e., turning the actors out).

A young black killer in *The Dreamy Kid* (1918), holed up in an apartment, must choose between staying with his dying grandmother or making his own escape in advance of the approaching police. O'Neill enlarges the scenic space by having the character of Dreamy constantly look out the window and listen to sounds on the other side of the door. The fact that no one ever appears outside the door, except Dreamy's girlfriend, Irene, who comes to warn Dreamy, adds suspense (who else is out there?) to the action. The turning point in the play occurs when Dreamy decides that he must not leave his grandmother because she'll curse him if he abandons her. He foregoes the possibility of escape and recognizes the inevitability of his defeat. He instructs Irene to "get the gang," a tactic designed to save her by getting her out of the room. O'Neill creates suspense by not allowing any escape from the inside/outside tension. The play ends with Dreamy looking at the door, just at the moment when forces from the outside (the police) poise to break into the room. The drama ends at the precipitous moment when the outside must meet the inside. The outside has been closing in throughout the action. The inside, too, has been struggling for a way out. Reconciled to defeat at the end, Dreamy vows that they won't take him alive.

The door possesses literal and metaphorical significance in *More Stately Mansions*. In Act 3, Simon recalls a story which his mother used to tell him about a king who wandered the earth in search of a magical door. An enchantress told him that he would regain his kingdom if he walked through it. Just when he was about to do so, the enchantress warned him that she might have lied, and that if he opened the door he might find that his kingdom had been transformed into a horrible desert. Unable to face this possibility yet eager to reclaim his kingdom, the king froze, unable to act, and ultimately died a beggar never having crossed the threshold through the door. The impasse of desire, mixed with fear, reveals the inside/outside dynamic in this "tale of possessors, self-dispossessed." Throughout the play, Deborah threatens to open the door to her summerhouse and step into the madness of her fantasy that she is Napoleon's Josephine. While so much of the play concerns the future and the desire for greater and greater acquisitions, the summerhouse represents flight into the past and insanity. The desire to go, and the fear of doing so, creates the static movement that sustains tension. Deborah, at the end of the play, finally steps through the threshold, after several false exits in the course of the action, and releases her son in the custody of Sara. As long as Deborah does not go through the door, tension between the three principal characters sustains the action. Once Deborah goes through the door, tension breaks, Sara takes Simon back to their cabin, and the action concludes in an epilogue.

Dynamics between the seen and the unseen, the inside and outside, receive eloquent expression in the scenic description of *A Touch of the Poet*. O'Neill's opening stage directions separate the dining room in Melody's Tavern from the barroom: "The dining room and barroom were once a single spacious room, low-ceilinged, with heavy oak beams and painted walls—the tap-room of the tavern in its prosperous days, now divided into two rooms by a flimsy partition, the barroom being off left. The partition is painted to imitate the old paneled walls but this only makes it more of an eyesore" (CP3 183). This description of the place does much more than present a realistic interior that grounds the scene in a recognizable context. Melody does not set foot in the barroom until his final exit. He claims identity as an aristocrat who does not drink with commoners.

Throughout the play, the chorus of town drunks—Dan Roche, Paddy O'Dowd, and Patch Riley—careen and cavort offstage in the tavern. Their slovenly commonness contrasts with Melody's refined manners. Yet such behavior, representative of Melody's own heritage, carries the day at the end when Melody resumes his brogue, denies his former illusions of grandeur, and stumbles through the door to the bar. The "flimsy partition" that divides the playing space separates visually one aspect of Melody's character from another. Melody's denial of his base roots comprises the entire action. The offstage bar, the adjoining space, unseen, represents defeat for Melody. The fact that the painted partition looks like a paneled wall calls attention to the construction of Melody's divided character. Two spaces, one seen, one unseen, reveal the genius of O'Neill's spatial design.

Sounds of urban mid-town New York, the elevator door, and Room 492 upstairs are perimeter spaces, on either side of the stage, and above, which oppress Erie Smith and night clerk Hughes in *Hughie*. Once again, the scene layout opposes what's visible with what's offstage and invisible. The desperation of Erie not to go upstairs alone forces him to try to strike up a conversation with the new night clerk and to fill silence with a series of monologues in order to postpone an inevitable solitude. Hughes, on the other hand, measures night's progress by the repetitive nocturnal movements in the city: trains, ambulances, garbage haulers, cops. The silence that falls when those noises recede drives him to pick up conversation with Erie. The rituals of conversation, a meeting point between them, a shared dialogue, defends against the outside forces pressing in upon two helpless victims. Despite the realistic nature of the dialogue, the action functions to ward off oppression by forces which can be felt but cannot be seen. The effect of this dynamic creates the illusion of Erie and Hughes as the last two inhabitants in the world. O'Neill creates a cosmic drama on a small scale by extending lateral space (e.g., the street, the elevator) and by fashioning an illusion of vertical space (e.g., Room 492 upstairs).

An early one-act, *Where the Cross Is Made* (1918), determines the tensile strength of the boundary between the inside and the outside, between the seen and unseen. *The Dreamy Kid*, the play immediately preceding it, ends at the precise moment when the police must become visible. The outside forces actually break into the interior room in *Where the Cross Is Made*. O'Neill considered this play an experiment in which he tried to make the audience as mad as Captain Bartlett.[5] He attempted to bring ghosts from the outside onstage: "All are in their bare feet. Water drips from their soaked and rotten clothes. Their hair is matted, intertwined with slimy strands of seaweed. Their eyes, as they glide silently into the room, stare frightfully wide at nothing. Their flesh in the green light has the suggestion of decomposition. Their bodies sway limply, nervelessly, rhythmically as if to the pulse of long swells of the deep sea" (CP1 710). By bringing the outside in, O'Neill violates the rigorous separation between the inside and the outside. Seeing the ghosts onstage kills the illusion of their existence. As long as they remain offstage, out of sight, they retain terrifying potential. Once onstage, though, they become a melodramatic joke.[6] Their visibility and corporeality make it impossible to view them as apparitions. The presence of "ghosts" onstage in the form of actors whom the audience recognizes as such kills the illusion. When the illusion breaks, the play ends.

Whereas the inside/outside paradigm concerns the contiguity and diffusion of adjoining spaces, seen and unseen, onstage and off, a second visual paradigm, here and there, concerns distant points of reference best expressed in terms of land and sea, in which characters express dissatisfactions with present positions and long for salvation at an unseen place. *"Anna Christie"* offers an excellent example of this model. Anna, who has been defiled on a farm in Minnesota and who has turned to a life of prostitution, transforms when she travels on her father's barge. She believes in the redemptive powers of the sea to transform her and make her clean. The enveloping fog, she says, bathes her, and cleanses her past sins. Chris, her father, on the other hand, has devoted his life to the sea and hates it. All his family, save Anna, have died at sea and he refers to the sea as "dat ole davil." For him, the sea represents evil fate. He sent Anna to live on a farm with relatives because he thought that would be a healthy environment in which to raise a young girl. Both Anna and Chris idealize what is foreign to them. Stephen Murray sums up the here and there rhythm succinctly at the end of *The Straw* with his lament: "When you've got it, you find you don't want it" (CP1 783). The reverse of this statement also proves true: when you want something, you find you can't have it. Constant yearning for what is not present directs appeal to points outside the frame of the representation. What is immediately and visually available never satisfies desire. Edmund even flaunts a Chekhovian note in *Long Day's Journey Into Night*: "It was a great mistake, my being born a man, I would have been much more successful as a sea gull or a fish. As it is, I will always be a stranger who never feels at home, who does not really want and is not really wanted, who can never belong, who must always be a little in love with death!" (CP3 812). There's great humor in the melodrama of youthful angst, to be sure, but the theme of belonging is one of O'Neill's principal concerns. The here and there model suggests that an O'Neill character is never at home on stage, that he or she always fights to be somewhere else, somewhere beyond the scope of the representation. The desire to be elsewhere and the corporeal reality of the visual scene creates dynamic tension.

Another early sea play, *Ile* (1917), illustrates perfectly the land and sea dilemma. The captain of a whaling ship must decide between returning home to save his wife's sanity or pursue his mission in order to defend his honor. Mrs. Keeney left her home to be with her husband because she thought that it would be romantic and much better than being left behind. The reality of life at sea does not correspond to her imaginings of that life. Once at sea, she preoccupies herself with thoughts of her beautiful house which she left behind. Mrs. Keeney's decision to join her husband, and the disillusionment that follows, leads to disaster: "I used to dream of sailing on the great, wide, glorious ocean. I wanted to be by your side in the danger and vigorous life of it all. I wanted to see you the hero they make you out to be in Homeport. And instead—[*Her voice grows tremulous.*] All I find is ice and cold—and brutality!" [*Her voice breaks.*] (CP1 500). The action picks up after the ship has already been at sea two years, expository information which further motivates the crew to threaten mutiny and Mrs. Keeney to plead with her husband to return home. Swayed by his wife's pleadings to go home with only a fraction of the whale oil that he usually gets, Captain Keeney finally orders his ship to turn back. A reversal follows in which news of the ice breaking up, which had kept the ships from pursuing the whales, erupts. Keeney, intent upon getting the oil, abruptly changes his mind and directs the ships to pursue the whales. As a result of his decision, Mrs. Keeney lapses into insanity. Desire to be with her husband brought her on board, but that same desire brought madness upon her. The here/there model of desire represents an escape for the audience as well as the characters from the oppressive theatrical reality of the represented scene. An imagined life somewhere else is always better than the visible realized life. Scenically, what's not real, present, or visible is always more grand than the depressing visual scene of the dramatic situation. Desire to escape from the material conditions of wood, plaster, and canvas plants an alternative space elsewhere in the minds of the audience that is always superior to what it sees on stage before it. The audience does not see the conditions under which the ship operates. The entire action takes place in the captain's room, an enclosed space below deck with only a skylight that exposes part of the poop deck above. The decision to go forward or to go backward is played out within claustrophobic quarters that spur the desire for escape that holds true equally for Captain Keeney, his wife, and the audience as well.

In most of the plays, however, the sea, or sea islands, or the Blessed

Isles as they are mostly called, a reference to Nietzsche, represent escape
and freedom from oppression of life on land. In the first act of *Chris Christophersen*, two old sailors, Mickey and Devlin, recall the old days of sailing and its superiority to modern steamships. Mickey expresses their
dream to travel to the warm climates of South America: "We'll find a tall,
smart daisy of a full-rigged ship with skys'ls—a beautiful, swift hooker
that'll take us flyin' south through the Trades" (CP1 811). The romance
of this picture is not altogether different from Mrs. Keeney's fantasies
concerning life at sea with her husband. This same nostalgia for the past
sailing life is expressed by Paddy in the first scene of *The Hairy Ape* (1921):
"Oh, to be scudding south again wid the power of the Trade Wind driving her on steady through the nights and the days! Full sail on her! Nights
and days! Nights when the foam of the wake would be flaming wid fire,
when the sky'd be blazing and winking wid stars" (CP2 126–127). The
brutality of modern life, epitomized by life in a dark hole shoveling coal
into steam engines, and Yank's subsequent alienation from such an existence, comprise the action of that play. The expanse of sailing above board
in clean air directly contrasts with the stokers' lives in cramped conditions in dark quarters feeding infernal machines. Shortly after the start
of the play, the following stage direction indicates the visceral quality of
the scene: "There is a tumult of noise—the brazen clang of furnace doors
as they are flung open or slammed shut, the grating, teeth-gritting grind
of steel against steel, of crunching coal" (135). Bright light and terrific heat
pour out of the open furnace doors. The opening image finds men at work
in the stokehole and O'Neill's stage directions read: "The treatment of
this scene, or of any other scene in the play, should by no means be naturalistic" (CP2 121). O'Neill's directions on style are a bit deceptive.

What does an audience see? Regardless of whether the scene is played
as expressionism or realism, the audience encounters a graphically brutal
male world. The men are sweaty, dirty, cursing, drinking (many are drunk),
singing, half-naked, crammed into the bowels of the ship, "imprisoned by
white steel." The low ceiling of the stokehole forces them to stoop like
Neanderthals; the hard labor of shoveling coal has overdeveloped their
shoulder muscles; coal dust settles in their eye sockets and gives them a
simian quality. The point of all this is not to achieve either expressionism or realism. O'Neill devotes a lot of space and energy to a description
of this scene in order to involve all the senses: the sight of the men; the
sound of the men and the rhythmic pattern of their heavy work; the contrast between the fiery furnaces and the dark quarters. The mechanical
rhythmic shoveling of coal into the engines is a representation of power
and the visceral quality of the scene reminds the audience of the power

of bodies in motion. Against this reminder, Paddy talks about the past when men stood up above board and sailed on glorious clipper ships.[7] The image of sunlight and men standing up contrasts with the visual images in the play. It is the first crack in Yank's picture of himself as the center of power. Certainly, Paddy hints at the kind of gross exploitation that leads Long, the other outspoken shipmate, to speak of a future of political revolt, class solidarity and socialism. Alternative points of view which speak of a world at a remove in time and place from the represented scene force an audience to see the stokehole from different perspectives, as, in fact, Yank does as the action progresses. The action of the play tosses Yank from the ship to Fifth Avenue to the union office to jail and finally dumps him back home at the gorilla cage. Yank grows increasingly powerless as the play drags through its eight scenes. His immense physical strength begins to be seen in service not only of the engines, but the officers who control them, and finally those who own the ships. Yank can never see these forces who have control over him. Similarly, the effect of the visual images in this play of alienation asks the audience to consider who controls their lives.

The sexuality of the South Sea Islands in both *Diff'rent* (1920) and *Mourning Becomes Electra* (1931) reverses the energy flow found in *The Hairy Ape*. The scene in both plays is a joyless one of New England Puritanism, and the distant, unrepresented islands function as a sexual escape and release. In the former play, Emma Crosby refuses to marry whaling captain Caleb Williams because of his single indiscretion with a native islander woman. He tries to justify what happened by convincing her that life down there is not governed by the same rules as in New England whaling towns: "I wish you could see them Islands, Emmer, and be there for a time. Then you might see—It's hard 's hell to explain, and you havin' never seen 'em. Everything is diff'rent down there—the weather—and the trees an water. You git lookin' at it all, and you git to feel diff'rent from what you do to home here. It's purty here-abouts sometimes—like now, in spring—but it's purty there all the time—and down there you notice it and you git feelin'—diff'rent" (CP2 23). Emma's idealism prevents her from accepting Caleb's rationale. Her struggle to have only what is "diff'rent" from the rest sets her against everyone in her town. Even her mother tells her in the opening scene: "...it'd be jest like goin' agen an act of Nature for you not to marry him" (20). Nature refers in this case not only to the natural attraction between Emma and Caleb, but to the rules of society that condone marriage. Invoking nature in this way also hints at the repercussions of Emma's resolute stand and the personal cost of her rigid idealism.[8] The rigidity of Emma's moral stance has a physical dimension as well. Both she and Caleb adopt a formal tone with each other. The scene is a parlor room which enforces another layer of formality. As in *The Hairy Ape*, O'Neill describes the room as "small and low-ceilinged" (3). The closed in environment of the little house constrains the physical action and dampens emotional expression as well. The stiffness of courting and the mating ritual as seen on stage contrast with Caleb's description of things in the warm islands. He hints at relations with women down there as being more relaxed. His implication of what's natural opens yet another perspective on that term, different from Mrs. Crosby's, and suggests following instinctual behavior. References to the South Sea Islands critique New England society by asking what is natural and what is cultural, but Emma Crosby actually holds neither standard up to Caleb. "Diff'rent" to her, is always something other than what is. The play doesn't turn on a moral question so much as the nature of ideals themselves as being not real. Emma cherishes ideals that are profoundly different from the real. The play's title is repeated endlessly in the play. Early on, Emma says to Caleb: "I mean I just look at things diff'rent from what they do—getting married, for example, and other things, too. And so I've got it fixed in my head that you and me ought to make a married couple—diff'rent from the rest—not that they ain't all right in their own way" (5). Different, in the action of the play, is always whatever is *not* present. The ideal is always something not represented and out of reach. The action of the play revolts against realism at the same time that it shows the problems of not accepting the way things are.

Action in *Mourning Becomes Electra* attempts to escape the oppressiveness of the Mannon mansion and flee to the beauty and freedom of the South Sea Islands. Adam Brant explains the attraction of the distant land: "Unless you've seen it, you can't picture the green beauty of their land set in the blue of the sea! The clouds like down on the mountain tops, the sun drowsing in your blood, and always the surf on the barrier reef singing a croon in your ears like a lullaby! The Blessed Isles, I'd call them! You can forget there all men's dirty dreams of greed and power!" (CP2 909–910). Of course, no one does see the islands in the play. As an image, they counterpoint the murders and machinations and revenge plots carried out on the Mannon estate. Whereas the islands in *Diff'rent* contrast with the austerity and social formality of a New England whaling town, the islands in *Mourning Becomes Electra* are a kind of utopian society of free love, which contrasts with the represented scene of violence, lust, and sexual deviance. The action in *Mourning Becomes Electra* produces a revolting picture of sexual manipulations, adultery, aberrant sexuality, jealousy, and incest. The one sexual act that is in the play, the homecoming of Ezra Mannon, is depicted as a near rape in which Mannon is seen as a bestial figure.[9] The bodies on the stage present a repulsive carnality. The other (island) space, unseen, is a gentle alternative and loving place. Orin asks his mother at one point if she has read Melville's *Typee*, about the South Sea Islands. A returning Civil War hero, Orin equates the islands with everything that represents "peace and warmth and security" (972). To him, the islands represent his ideal relationship with his mother. The only scene set in a locale other than the Mannon house is Brant's clipper ship, set to sail for the South Sea Islands and escape from the repressive land of guilt and shame. This scene comes at about the midpoint of the entire trilogy and visually represents the near success of Christine and Brant to break free of the death-in-life Mannon grip. Orin's murder of Brant stops those plans short, and when Christine commits suicide in the wake of that revelation, Orin's hope to find the peace of those islands vanishes too. In *The Haunted*, the last play of the trilogy, Orin and Lavinia, return from an extended trip that included a stay at the South Sea Islands. Lavinia tried to escape from New England and transform herself into her mother's image, a woman of freedom and sexuality. This visual cloning appears at a juncture in the play in which Lavinia departs from the traditional Mannon mold. What is "here" almost, but not quite, becomes "there." These recurring surges of escape stretch the drama to the breaking point. Ultimately, Lavinia rejects her mother's garments and dons her mourning again. There is no escape from the secrecy and restraint of the Mannon legacy. The desire to escape the represented confines and the failure to do so receives its final hammer-strokes with Lavinia's self-entombment within the house. *Mourning Becomes Electra* dramatizes the "dirty dreams of greed and power" and puts them on display in all their gross materiality. The dream world of peace, love, and harmony, represented by the South Sea Islands, remains always unseen and offstage.

A contingent offstage and unseen space govern the visible action in *A Touch of the Poet* (1935). While the marriage of Simon Harford and Sara Melody incites much of O'Neill's unfinished cycle plays and is the subject of the only other extant play of that cycle, *More Stately Mansions*, their romance occurs entirely in the wings of *Poet*. Nevertheless, Simon Harford remains integral to that play even though he never appears. Throughout the play, he convalesces in an upstairs bedroom of the Melody tavern. His prolonged presence there allows for a romance between Sara Melody and him to develop as she makes frequent trips to nurse him back to health. News of his extended stay at the Tavern brings his mother Deborah to pay a visit and later Nicholas Gadsby, the Harford family lawyer, calls and attempts to buy Melody's assurance that his daughter will not marry the young Harford. This affront to Melody's honor leads him to seek out the elder Harford for a duel, which leads to his final disgrace and transformation. The unseen presence of Simon provides the necessary plotting for the play to develop, an excuse for the tragicomic unmasking of Cornelius Melody to happen. O'Neill hides his plot, which allows him to maintain focus on the character of Melody without forcing his "hero" to do anything. All the events in the play occur elsewhere: the battle of Talavera, the romance between Sara and Simon, the fight at the Harfords' and the killing of the mare. O'Neill displaces action on the inside and transfers it to the outside. The lack of visible action onstage accentuates Melody's impotence. Sara criticizes him for not helping his wife tend the bar. O'Neill's structuring of the plot with all the action on the outside further sets Melody's indolence and powerlessness in relief. At the same time, the occasion of Melody's defeat is also Sara's biggest victory. During the nocturnal streetfight, Sara confides to her mother that she seduced Simon and accepted his proposal for marriage. Father and daughter, at odds during the course of the entire play, rival each other in their struggles with the Harfords. Sara emerges as the winner and her marriage carries her father's fight against the aristocracy into the next play of the cycle.

The spare room in *Long Day's Journey Into Night*, Eugene's, the dead baby's, plays a key part in the action of that play. The death of that baby years ago represents one of the events in the past that damns each member of the family to endless torment. It is also the unseen space upstairs to which Mary habitually retreats to inject herself with morphine. The Tyrone men, as well as the audience, project visions of what happens in that haunted space. The entire last act anticipates Mary's entrance at play's end. While killing time below, the men listen to her movements with hope that she will go to bed and that they will not have to face her ghostly image again. The sound of Mary's footfall, the rhythm of her distracted to and fro movements above, expands the scene and prevents the dialogue between father and son from becoming too conversational. Mary's unseen presence directs their attention to the outer boundaries of the represented scene. At one point, the men hear Mary coming down the stairs, but when Edmund goes to check, he reports that she must have gone back up (CP3 801). This transitional moment, a false alarm, ends just at the point at which Mary must become visible. Certainly, it is part of the build to her final entrance at the end of the act. But it is also a strategy to make sure that Mary's presence in the house never leaves the consciousness of her family, and the audience. Unlike the male Tyrones, Mary is the only one who never leaves the house. Her footfall and false entrance, as well as the conversation about her, keeps her unseen presence in mind at all times. The dynamic between the small talk that the men make downstairs while drinking and playing cards contrasts with the awful scene of Mary's unseen hallucinatory private hell upstairs. That the Tyrones refer to Eugene's room as "spare" raises connotations of aridity and barrenness. Instead of a young man's room, it is the site where a middle aged woman goes to escape from her family and drift back to childhood memories in a drug induced stupor.

Emphasis upon unseen characters or locales, near or far, in all of the preceding examples, enlarges and expands the drama. Pictorially, this tactic turns the drama outward. Instead of characters sharing a scene, the desire to see things and go places outside the immediate and visible field of representation (the stage) forces characters to transcend material presence. In the final act of *Long Day's Journey Into Night*, Edmund tells one of his sea stories to his father, an apocryphal tale for the kind of spatial tension that I've described as an oscillation between here and there:

> When I was on the Squarehead square rigger, bound for Buenos Aires. Full moon in the Trades. The old hooker driving fourteen knots. I lay on the bowsprit, facing astern, with the water foaming into spume under me, the masts with every sail white in the moonlight, towering high above me. I became drunk with the beauty and singing rhythm of it, and for a moment I lost myself—actually lost my life. I was set free! I dissolved in the sea, became white sails and flying spray, became beauty and rhythm, became moonlight and the ship and the high dim-starred sky! I belonged, without past or future, within peace and unity and a wild joy, within something greater than my own life, or the life of Man, to Life itself! To God, if you want to put it that way [811–812].

The belonging to which Edmund aspires bridges the distance between here and there, but the only medium that can transport him is via language. He describes a scene "out there," but his physical presence remains stuck on stage. This account is a kind of religious epiphany for him, but it also describes the kind of exaltation that an audience might experience during a performance of this play, or any play. What happens on the stage, the visible action, is only the means to achieve a certain kind of exalted experience among the audience. The real drama, or "really real" drama, to invoke O'Neill, takes place internally within the viewer. A unified group response from the audience amplifies a personal response and enlarges the entire experience. The "belonging" that Edmund experiences translates in the theatre to the shared feelings among the audience. The theatre has the power to transform an audience individually and collectively. The real action doesn't happen on stage, then. Audiences want to go beyond the proscenium as much as characters do. Realism, as a style, fosters the illusion that the represented scene is actually where the action takes place. The style, though, the means in which the play is presented, is merely the necessary excuse for something revelatory to happen for the audience.

As many of the preceding examples have shown, O'Neill's work relies upon unreachable and unrepresented destinations to create dramatic tension. Unseen space is to scene what illusions are to characters. The "hopeless hope" that remains out of reach sustains life among O'Neill's various heroes; images of things not represented visually in the plays allow them to function. One of O'Neill's masterpieces, *The Iceman Cometh* (1940), critiques realism and O'Neill's spatial dualism in the figure of the protagonist Theodore Hickman, who questions the value of aspirations that remain always unseen and out of reach. Anne Fleche sees Hickey's intrusion as an attempt to destroy theatrical illusion: "We are now, therefore, confronted with a drama in which what is at stake is our own capacity for illusion. The power and efficacy of the imagining self are put on trial by the play, threatened with obsolescence. We are at a theater that threatens to 'save' us from theater" (52). For Edwin Engel, *The Iceman Cometh*, the first play to be produced by O'Neill in twelve years since the failed *Days Without End*, is another diatribe against the theatre and disavows O'Neill's career as a playwright: "In so doing, he repudiated not only love, faith and truth but also, by implication, that to which he had dedicated his life: the theatre itself dependent as it is upon the willing acceptance of illusion" (295). The ultimate success of Hickey's assault against the theatre and illusion and pipe dreams meets defeat, but it does puncture the structural solidarity of O'Neill's scenic dualism (seen/unseen, illusion/reality, realism/non-realism) by displacing these convenient pairings. This is an initial strategy to transfer the action of the play from the stage to the mental constructs in the minds of the audience.

In the opening dialogue, Larry Slade shows up the pretenses of all who lie passed out around him in the early morning hours at Harry Hope's saloon: "To hell with the truth! As the history of the world proves, the truth has no bearing on anything. It's irrelevant and immaterial, as the lawyers say. The lie of a pipe dream is what gives life to the whole misbegotten mad lot of us, drunk or sober" (569–570). The necessity for the pipe dream surfaces as a dominant theme even in the dramatis personae which introduces characters in terms of former professions: one-time circus man; one-time police lieutenant; Harvard Law School alumnus; one-time proprietor of a Negro gambling house; one-time leader of a Boer commando; etc., etc. Each man believes that his past occupations and exploits are still readily attainable and can be reclaimed at any moment.

Kevin Spacey (standing on chair) as Hickey and the cast of *The Iceman Cometh* **in the 1999 production directed by Howard Davies at the Brooks Atkinson Theatre, New York City. As staged above, Hickey plays this merry scene directly to the audience in a moment of overt theatricality which contradicts his later stated intentions to put an end to all illusions. Such a moment questions the supposed realism of the play. Photograph by Joan Marcus. Courtesy of Ms. Marcus.**

James Cameron, or "Jimmy Tomorrow," a former war correspondent, exemplifies this trait shared by all the spongers at Hope's saloon. Always prepared to get his old job back tomorrow, he begins each day with more drink. O'Neill suggests that these men cannot face the truth of their lives, and that pipe dreams make life tolerable for them. The pervasive and repetitive theme has justifiably prompted comparisons between O'Neill's play and Ibsen's *The Wild Duck*.[10] To Dr. Relling, the seeming raisonneur of that play, Ibsen ascribes the thematic line in the final act: "Deprive the average man of his life-lie and you've robbed him of happiness as well" (Ibsen 477). Superficial resemblance between the two plays fades with the discovery of crucial differences in spatial design and character function which lead to very different interpretations.

Whereas Ibsen creates two spaces, a realistic photographer's studio and a hidden, symbolic place, the loft, O'Neill's saloon, his metaphoric loft, occupies the entire theatrical space in his pipe dream play. He creates the world in a bar and populates it with the dregs of society. A group of mostly men build a community apart from the daily activity of the outside world. Harry Hope's saloon spawns the mutual pipe dreams of all the inhabitants. Two aspects of the scene deserve special notice. First, the design hermetically seals the interior space. Stage directions read: "Two windows, so glazed with grime one cannot see through them, are in the left wall, looking out on a backyard" (CP3 565). The window between the inside space and the outside remains opaque. Secondly, O'Neill's design of the space presents two different parts of the saloon, a back room and a section of the bar. The audience looks at the room as though it were a cross section. Only a dirty curtain separates the two spaces, but never evenly. The first act exposes the back room and section of the bar. The bartender pulls back the curtain to move between the two spaces. Act 2 presents the back room exclusively, then the following act shows mostly the bar, and only a section of the back room. The final act repeats the same first act configuration. Although all of the action occurs within Hope's bar, each scene shifts slightly. The scene oscillates from side to side creating a sense of movement. Within the proscenium, the design of *The Iceman Cometh* always shows a box within a box to the extent that the pressure of the outside upon the inside is visually apparent. Breaking the proscenium space into two unequal spaces crowds the stage and helps to create the illusion of a refuge in the back room space. By hinting at the contiguous spaces in *The Iceman Cometh* O'Neill plants the visual concept of the outside permeating the inside space which defines dramatic action precisely in the play.

Rarely venturing outside, the menagerie of characters survive on alcohol that fuels dreams of tomorrow which they never have to fulfill. When asked about the bar, Larry replies: "It's the No Chance Saloon. It's Bedrock Bar, The End of the Line Café, The Bottom of the Sea Rathskeller! Don't you notice the beautiful calm in the atmosphere? That's because it's the last harbor. No one here has to worry about where they're going next, because there is no farther they can go" (577–578). Slade adds that he has never known more contented men. Edmund says something similar in *Long Day's Journey Into Night* when he talks of beatitude on the high seas: "Then the moment of ecstatic freedom came. The peace, the end of the quest, the last harbor, the joy of belonging to a fulfillment beyond men's lousy, pitiful, greedy fears and hopes and dreams!" (CP3 812) The peaceful image of a "last harbor" in each speech about the sea indicates a state of physical transcendence in which all the material problems of the world have been left behind. This place of rest to which Edmund aspires at the end of *Long Day's Journey Into Night* is precisely where the bums reside at the opening of O'Neill's preceding play. The first act of *The Iceman Cometh* is sleepy, tranquil, and congenial.

The entrance of Hickey at the end of the first act, anticipated by preparations for Harry's annual birthday bash, brings the outside world onstage. In no other O'Neill play is the protagonist's entrance delayed ("Waiting for Hickey"), and Hickey's arrival changes the direction of the drama. Before he enters, comedy rules in the dark and sleepy world of the saloon. Hickey wakes up the inhabitants to the light of a new day, peddling salvation. Religious imagery has not escaped critics' eyes.[11] The title brilliantly evokes the double meanings of the play, a combination of biblical reference and dirty joke.[12] Hickey's regimen for happiness requires that the inhabitants at Hope's saloon give up their pipe dreams. Unlike Gregers Werle in *The Wild Duck*, who wants to free Hjalmar Ekdal by dredging up the past, Hickey plans to rob Hope's denizens of their future and always out of reach dreams. Werle, evoking the image of the wild duck, tries to drag Hjalmar to the surface of light and truth. Hickey, on the other hand, wants to cut loose the ties to a better tomorrow. He wants his friends to reach a level of peace which, if what Larry says is true at the beginning, they have already found: "You can let go of yourself at last. Let yourself sink down to the bottom of the sea. Rest in peace. There's no farther you have to go" (613). Unwinding after a long speech, Hickey falls asleep immediately after finishing the above. Getting rid of dreams, this gesture implies, equals a kind of death. Indeed, the only peace that Hickey offers is the kind that the Big Sleep, death, provides. Larry recognizes him as the iceman who brings the cold touch of death with him. Hickey argues in Act 2 that real peace is possible only after all the pipe dreams have been dismissed: "Then you'll know what real peace means, Larry, because you won't be scared of either life or death any more. You simply won't give a damn! Any more than I do!" (629) Later in the act, he preaches his doctrine of peace with even more fervor to the assembled group: "I swear I'd never act like I have if I wasn't absolutely sure it will be worth it to you in the end, after you're rid of the damned guilt that makes you lie to yourselves you're something you're not, and the remorse that nags at you and makes you hide behind lousy pipe dreams about tomorrow. You'll be in a today where there is no yesterday or tomorrow to worry you. You won't give a damn what you are any more" (647–648).

Hickey is the ultimate realist. Earlier, I called realism a strategy to make the familiar more familiar. Hickey wants the bums at Harry's really to see themselves as bums. He fancies that such clarified visions will release them from the need for their dreams and allow them to stagnate happily forever as bottom feeders at the saloon. Hickey is unlike any other O'Neill protagonist. His typical hero is a dreamer who desires to transgress the limits of his own capabilities. In innumerable examples, ranging from Robert Mayo to Yank to Con Melody, this serves as a standard tragic formula. *The Iceman Cometh* negates such action and shows what happens when dreams die. While Gregers Werle argues that there is a lot of the wild duck in Hjalmar, referring to his friend's propensity to dive under the water and bite fast to the weeds on the bottom, Hickey's advice to save his friends is for them to "swallow the anchor" and content themselves with no hope of ever rising. Werle and Hickey work in opposite directions in their respective plays.

Hickey's peace doctrine actually surfaces first in a much earlier play, *Chris Christophersen* (1919), an unsuccessful play that later developed into *"Anna Christie."* The undramatic and uncharacteristic theme, in fact, led to the play's failure. When O'Neill re-wrote the play, that theme largely disappeared and emphasis shifted from Old Chris to his daughter. That shift became necessary because Chris was essentially a passive character and Anna an active, hence dramatic, one. In the first play, Chris and young Paul Andersen have "swallowed the anchor," a thematic which signifies that they refuse to engage in the struggle of life. Chris works as a barge captain to avoid a seaman's life and the fate of the ol' davil sea. Andersen, an underachiever, coasts in his position as Second Mate in order to avoid responsibility. In the second act, he explains his philosophy of life to Anna: "Working, slaving, sweating to get something which only disgusts you when you've got it! That's ambition for you! But is it living? Not to me! Freedom—that's life! No ties, no responsibilities—no guilty feelings. Like the sea—always moving, never staying, never held by anything, never giving a damn..." (CP1 859). Once again, sea imagery connects this speech to much later ones by Slade, Hickey, and Edmund. Andersen's ideal of "never giving a damn" is one Hickey quotes virtually verbatim. Andersen explicitly defines "swallowing the anchor" for Anna in the third act: "To loose your grip, to whine and blame something outside of yourself for your misfortunes, to quit and refuse to fight back any more, to be afraid to take any more chances because you're sure you're no longer strong enough to make things come out right, to shrink from any more effort and be content to anchor fast in the thing you are!" (880–881). Again, Hickey says something quite similar when he urges his friends to let go of their pipe dreams: "You won't give a damn what you are any more." Ultimately, Chris goes back to sea and Andersen determines to strive for a captain's chair, but the play fails to embrace this struggle within the action. Absence of struggle makes this play uncharacteristic of O'Neill and dooms it to relative lifelessness.

The stage picture becomes lifeless in *The Iceman Cometh* once Hickey's plan goes into full effect. The end of pipe dreams forces characters outside. The structure of the play, organized around Hickey, is as follows: Hickey's arrival; Hickey's challenge of the bums to go outside; the rush out the door in the third act; the return of the bums from the outside at the beginning of Act 4; Hickey's arrest and final exit in the last act. The entire third act consists of a series of exits, as one by one, and two by two, characters walk through the exterior door to the streets outside. All of the characters leave with a challenge to prove Hickey wrong. Harry's departure defines the pivotal moment in the act. Formerly a ward politician, Harry, who hasn't been out of the bar in twenty years, says that he's going to walk around the old district to see friends. Rocky the bartender describes Hickey's exit in suspenseful terms in hopes of proving Hickey wrong: "Jees, Harry's startin' across de street! He's goin' to fool yuh, Hickey, yuh bastard! [*He pauses, watching—then worriedly.*] What de hell's he stoppin' for? Right in de middle of de street! Yuh'd tink he was paralyzed or somethin'! [*disgustedly*] Aw, he's quittin'! He's turned back! Jees, look at de old bastard travel! Here he comes!" (CP3 675). Hope's attempt to leave expands the stage space. The elaborate set-up for his move outside, and Rocky's play-by-play announcing of it, dramatizes in one moment the action of the play. Hickey forces Hope to admit that what's outside is not real. He reduces the world to only that which is visible. Hope returns and insists, comically and pathetically, that an automobile almost ran over him. He looks to Rocky and Larry for support of his story, which Larry grants reluctantly. Only Hickey forces Harry to admit the truth: "All a lie! No automobile. But, bejees, something ran over me! Must have been myself, I guess" (676–677). Hope's identity begins to erode once he hears the hollowness of his own pipe dreams. He tries to console himself with booze, but complains that it has no kick in it and that he can't get drunk. Having confronted himself, having been "run over by himself," he no longer finds peace in the bottle. All of the bums return in failure by the start of the final act. Hope accuses Hickey of doing something to the booze: "There's no life in it now. I want to get drunk and pass out. Let's all pass out. Who the hell cares?" (678). The fact that the booze no longer works, that the men cannot get drunk, indicates the failure of Hickey's plan to deliver peace by forcing characters to face the truth. Hickey predicted that the truth would set them free with themselves. Booze not working indicates trouble insofar as characters cannot face themselves without illusions of that identity. Hickey rips away the pipe dreams that the men hold among themselves. The inhabitants of Hope's saloon grumble and become unpleasant when deprived of their pipe dreams. The booze is another illusion to comfort them.

Hickey's gambit fails to bring peace for a number of reasons. First of all, the men are already at peace prior to his arrival. What gives them peace is the illusion that they can go outside and pursue their dreams. The force of Hickey's program dissolves the "here and there" relationship. A world of tomorrow or yesterday no longer exists and the inhabitants of Hope's saloon must deal with each other as they are once they return to the bar after their brief forays in the outside world. Driving the men outside establishes the bar as an existential place of death. As long as the pipe dream goes unchallenged, an illusion of freedom regarding the lives of the characters persists. By exposing the lie, Hickey's plan cuts off an avenue of escape. The men stay content as long as they don't go outside. As soon as they do, they run up against their own limitations. This is analogous to the many O'Neill characters who romanticize the sea while standing at dry dock, or vice versa. From a structural standpoint, the action of the play sustains itself because of the here/there opposition. When the illusion of the outside world peels away, the action ends.

Two policemen, Lieb and Moran, arrive to arrest Hickey for the murder of his wife, an act which draws the play to its conclusion. Hickey's confession unravels in a long monologue in which he insists that he killed his wife as an act of kindness so she would be put out of the misery of living with an habitually unfaithful husband. The long confessional life story speech reaches a surprising climax at the moment of the murder, when Hickey blurts: "'Well, you know what you can do with your pipe dream now, you damned bitch!'" (700). Recognition of his true motive for murder, hate of her pipe dream which he has failed to fulfill (the iceman cometh ... not?), as opposed to love, leads to a quick reversal. Hickey, unable to face the truth of his actions, claims insanity, and Harry Hope and the rest of the gang, eager to discredit Hickey and to preserve their own illusions, support his plea. The police take Hickey away in handcuffs and the men, pipe dreams restored, can finally get drunk again. They celebrate and break into song, capped by Hugo Kalmar's rendition of the French Revolution's "Carmagnole." Hickey, the voice who demands that characters see themselves and accept themselves as they are, reveals himself as having bought the biggest pipe dream of all: that he has no, and needs no illusions. The loss of illusions creates an anxiety that even booze can't cut. Hickey finally adopts a new pipe dream in order to maintain the illusion that he loved his wife. The return of the pipe dream at the end, made even stronger now with Hickey's defeat and subsequent rally behind the pipe dream gospel, reaffirms the notion that life is not livable without the dream. At this level, the play refutes the desire of realism to present things as they are. As *Chris Christophersen* fails as a play, Hickey's program to swallow the anchor fails in *The Iceman Cometh*. Without aspiring to go beyond where one is, life is impossible and not worth living. And, just as Gregers Werle's actions in *The Wild Duck* are seen as foolish, Hickey's plan to save the bums at Harry's appears completely unnecessary.

Hickey drives the play, but his arrest and final exit does not end the play. If it did, then his revelation and reversal regarding illusions, what's unseen, would wrap the play up conclusively. O'Neill critiques the need for pipe dreams through Hickey, but Hickey's ultimate confession asserts even more strongly the need for illusions. This reading of the play goes a long route only to prove Slade's opening remarks that the truth is "irrelevant and immaterial," and "has no bearing on anything." In fact, the drama balances the need for the pipe dream to sustain life with the need for action in order to live in the world. This dilemma is embodied not in the action figure of Hickey, but in the passive body of his nemesis, Larry Slade. This creates a problem for the drama insofar as Larry is clearly not the most interesting dramatic character in the play. Judith Barlow states the case elegantly: "Larry is the only genuinely tragic figure in this complex dramatic work, yet he is also less histrionic than many of the others. Compassion and understanding, Larry's primary attributes, are not always theatrically arresting qualities—a dilemma O'Neill would face again with Edmund Tyrone in *Long Day's Journey Into Night*" (62). Larry is the moral center of the play. He was a former member of the Movement, an anarchist and idealistic group of revolutionaries dedicated to overthrowing the government and creating a utopian, free society. He quit when he became disenchanted with the direction that this movement was headed. He rationalizes his choice in the opening scene: "I saw men didn't want to be saved from themselves, for that would mean they'd have to give up greed, and they'll never pay that price for liberty. So I said to the world, God bless all here, and may the best man win and die of gluttony! And I took a seat in the grandstand of philosophical detachment to fall asleep observing the cannibals do their death dance." (570) Slade reveals an idealism very similar to that voiced by Adam Brant and Orin Mannon in *Mourning Becomes Electra* and Richard Miller in *Ah, Wilderness!* and Edmund Tyrone in *Long Day's Journey Into Night*, especially when he speaks against greed and gluttony. The fact that Slade appears to echo a young innocent such as Richard suggests that Slade, too, is playing a role, the part of the world weary sage. Yet, his similarity to Richard also focuses the action around his sensibilities. The opening speeches identify him as the most important character of the play, insofar as the audience will experience the play through him. Later on in the first act, Larry further justifies his decision to quit the Movement, to which he had dedicated over thirty years of his life: "I was born condemned to be one of those who has to see all sides of a question. When you're damned like that, the questions multiply for you until in the end it's all question and no answer. As history proves, to be a worldly success at anything, especially revolution, you have to wear blinders like a horse and see only straight in front of you. You have to see, too, that this is all black, and that is all white" (580–581). Hickey, of course, carries all the zeal of a revolutionary. Larry, the articulate boarder at Harry's who insists that he's "never known more contented men," is the antagonistic force against Hickey (584). Formerly a political revolutionary, Slade has traded action for the reflective pose of the philosopher. He no longer espouses beliefs about going out and changing the world. Instead, he ministers to the group at Harry's by feeding their illusions beneficently. Hickey accuses Larry of having the wrong kind of pity because it "lets itself off easy by encouraging some poor guy to go on kidding himself with a lie" (629). Regarding the young stranger, Don Parritt, Hickey adds: "He's licked, Larry. I think there is only one possible way out you can help him to take. That is, if you have the right kind of pity for him" (630). The play turns on what the right kind of pity is, and surprisingly, on this count, Hickey is exactly right. Hickey succeeds in goading Larry into taking action, the single event in the play that produces a transformation within Larry. Hickey draws Larry out and forces him finally to drop his pose of ironic detachment.

Don Parritt, as his name suggests, functions as a mirror to Hickey. He is an outsider, too, having only recently arrived at Harry Hope's from the West Coast. While all of the characters regard Hickey as an old and dear friend, they all despise Parritt. As the action transpires, fondness for Hickey turns cold as well. This is due to the similar projects of both Parritt and Hickey. Both of them harbor terrible secrets and guilt. Hickey recognizes himself in Parritt from their first encounter although he professes not to know the significance of the encounter: "In my game, to be a shark at it, you teach yourself never to forget a name or a face. But still I know damned well I recognized something about you. We're members of the same lodge—in some way" (612). Both Hickey and Parritt target Larry to make their strongest appeals. Parritt, the son of Larry's former lover, attempts to engage Slade about the circumstances of his mother's capture and arrest as a leader of the Movement. Parritt seeks to confess his involvement in her arrest. He first tells Larry that he turned his mother in because of his growing patriotism to the democratic American way. Next, he changes his story and says that he needed money to support a couple of whores he was seeing. This confession comes out slowly, not because Parritt doesn't want to tell, but because Larry refuses to listen. He does not want to know anything about what Parritt's done. Both Hickey and Parritt demand that the inhabitants of Hope's saloon do something. Hickey wants them to take collective action to face the emptiness of their pipe dreams and accept themselves for who they are. Parritt wants Larry to take action by listening to his confession and by directing his punishment. Larry's position, as the grandstand foolosopher, assumes no action. He insists that he's only waiting for death. Goaded by Parritt and Hickey, Larry resists action and turns on the young man: "All I know is I'm sick of life! I'm through! I've forgotten myself! I'm drowned and contented on the bottom of a bottle. Honor or dishonor, faith or treachery are nothing to me but the opposites of the same stupidity which is ruler and king of life, and in the end they rot into dust in the same grave. All things are the same meaningless joke to me, for they grin at me from the one skull of death. So go away. You're wasting breath. I've forgotten your mother" (636–637). Larry's pipe dream, like Hickey's, maintains that he hasn't any dream left. He's resigned from life. and sits in the grandstand, now, to watch fools go by. Larry insists that he has no convictions other than that he is waiting to die. Ironically, that's the outcome of the drama. In the end, Larry undergoes a revelation in which he finally truly believes what he has always said as mere pretense. Action unmasks fraudulence and reveals it as the truth.

While Hickey reaches his personal climax, Parritt makes a confession of his own to Larry in which he claims that he turned in his mother, not for money, but because he hated her. Thus, the two plots, public and personal, remain parallel. After the policemen take Hickey away, Parritt continues to apply pressure on Larry to respond to his confession. He eggs him into a response by emphasizing how much his mother must be suffering and how guilty he is for her situation. He finally breaks through Larry's defenses as the older man finally turns on him: "Go! Get the hell out of life, God damn you, before I choke it out of you! Go up—!" (704). Parritt forces Larry to betray his pose as the grandstand foolosopher who sits outside of life with one foot in the grave. Larry abandons his cool detachment and finally makes the judgment that Parritt goaded him into making. Parritt's confession expiates his guilt and satisfies his desire for punishment. Parritt's suicide, a jump from the back fire escape, not Hickey's confession, ends the play.

While the others at Harry Hope's sing wildly and get very drunk, a return to a former peaceful state, Larry alone undergoes a transformation. The final image finds the group in renewed drunken bliss on one side of the stage. Larry sits alone on the other side, mulling the ramifications of his actions which sent Parritt to his death. In a speech to himself, Larry startles himself with the implications of his self-discovery: "Be God, there's no hope! I'll never be a success in the grandstand—or anywhere else! Life is too much for me! I'll be a weak fool looking with pity at the two sides of everything till the day I die! [*with an intense bitter sincerity*] May that day come soon! [*He pauses startledly, surprised at himself—then with a sardonic grin.*] Be God, I'm the only real convert to death Hickey made here. From the bottom of my coward's heart I mean that now!" (710). Unable to face the consequences of his own actions, Larry prays for the peace of death. He, in the face of his contact with Parritt, cannot restore his former illusions.

The parallel plots driven by Hickey and Parritt merge at the end with the subtle transformation of Larry. Hickey, who professes his great love for his wife Evelyn throughout the play, admits in one line that he hated her. Hope makes a similar admission about his wife when the booze stops working in Act 3. Larry, on the other hand, judges Parritt, finally, because the young man awakens his former feelings of love for Parritt's mother, Rosa. By lashing out in anger, Larry gives away the fact that he, in spite of all his protestations, still cares very much about Rosa. His entire pose of not giving a damn about anything protects him from the pains of love. He left the political movement, not because he became disillusioned with it as much as the fact that Rosa, in spite of loving him best, would not stay with him exclusively. Larry finally responded by leaving her. Edwin Engel unequivocally states that love is the subject of the play: "That the unmasking of love is the main intention of the play is borne out not only by the fact that the individual tragedies of all the principal characters achieve that end, but also by the title of the drama itself" (294). Rosamind Gilder took up the theme of love in her review of the 1946 production: "The greatest illusion of all is to believe that disillusionment—the unaided processes of the intellect—can solve man's dilemma. There is a force that, like the love that Hickey's wife bore him, is made of understanding and forgiveness. Man finds such love intolerable" (Cargill 205). Hickey and Parritt collectively awaken Slade's emotional feelings for his former lover. Slade attacks Parritt violently and in utter hatred and contempt.

Hickey's wife, Evelyn, is one of three primary female characters who remains absent and offstage, yet critical in the action. The other two are Bessie Hope and Rosa Parritt. As a group, they are the "three bitches" of *The Iceman Cometh*. Harry Hope maintains that his wife was saintly throughout much of the action. Yet by the end of Act 3, after he's taken his walk around the ward that didn't last as far as across the street, he refers to his dead wife as a "nagging bitch" (678). Echoing Hickey's confession, Parritt voices a similar motive for squealing on his mother to the police: "'You know what you can do with your freedom pipe dream now, don't you, you damned old bitch!'" (704). Collectively, the three absent women represent a range of wifely types: the sainted woman, the nag, and the independent woman. They come alive in the play only insofar as male characters create them. Of the three, Bessie is known by many of the spongers at Harry's, including her brother Ed Mosher and his friend Pat McGloin. Together, their portrait of Bessie Hope as a mean woman is perhaps more accurate than the kindly woman whom Hope remembers. Still, there's no reason that a self respecting person would appreciate two moochers like the circus man and the corrupt cop. Hickey modifies the picture as he corrects Hope's memories of her: "You never did want to go to church or any place else with her. She was always on your neck, making you have ambition and go out and do things, when all you wanted was to get drunk in peace" (674). Hickey's view from the outside paints her as neither a "bitch" nor a "saint" but a woman who demanded an equal partner in life. Hope's relationship with his wife, given Hickey's credible analysis, is not unlike Jimmy Tomorrow's marriage to his former wife, Marjorie, yet another unseen woman in the play. In the fourth act, Jimmy suddenly discloses that he left his wife long before she left him: "Why Marjorie married me, God knows. It's impossible to believe she loved me. She soon found I much preferred drinking all night with my pals to being in bed with her. So, naturally, she was unfaithful. I didn't blame her. I really didn't care. I was glad to be free—even grateful to her, I think, for giving me such a good tragic excuse to drink as much as I damned well pleased" (692). Bessie and Marjorie are not nearly as unsympathetic as they might first appear. Similarly, Parritt disparages his mother throughout the play as a means to justify his actions. At the same time he directs these attacks against her at Larry as an attempt to get under his skin and force a confrontation with him. The vehemence of his hatred finally prompts Larry to demand his suicide. Even under all the outward hatred, Parritt ultimately seems like a little boy who has been abandoned by his mother and cannot control his anger against her. His anger against his mother is not unlike James Tyrone's in *A Moon for the Misbegotten*. He hates her so much because he loves her so much. He visits Larry because he thinks of him as a father figure. As a surrogate parent for Parritt, he is the only one capable of giving him the punishment he desires or deserves.

The most elusive woman of the three is Evelyn Hickman, who is only known by Hickey, himself. He describes her as a perfect woman dating back to when they were high school sweethearts. His long fourth act monologue portrays her as a loving and forgiving and pitying spouse in spite of all his transgressions. Yet, as he goes on, her relentless forgiving turns into a weapon against him: "I even caught myself hating her for making me hate myself so much. There's a limit to the guilt you can feel and the forgiveness and the pity you can take! You have to begin blaming someone else, too. I got so sometimes when she'd kiss me it was like she did it on purpose to humiliate me, as if she'd spit in my face!" (699). Hickey explains his attraction to Harry's place that kept him away from his home with Evelyn in Astoria: "I'd get so damned lonely. I'd get thinking how peaceful it was here, sitting around with the old gang, getting drunk and forgetting love, joking and laughing and singing and swapping lies" (699). The bar is a male sanctuary and women are clearly outsiders. The force of the play is not to show that love is an illusion, but to demonstrate the awesome responsibility and burden of achieving intimacy. In *The Wild Duck*, Relling, too, although a doctor, is hardly a trustworthy character. He is clearly an alcoholic. More interesting, however, is the fact that previous to the action of the play, he had a relationship with a woman, Mrs. Sørby, who, speaking of her choice to marry another man, emphasizes: "At least he hasn't wasted the best that's in him. Any man who does *that* has to take the consequences" (462). Like Larry Slade, Theodore Hickman, Harry Hope, Jimmy Tomorrow, Relling could not maintain an intimate relationship. Instead, he chose to comfort himself with a bottle. The life lie or the pipe dream justifies human weakness and the failure of courage to live life. The action in *The Iceman Cometh* details the terrors of love and the demands of love and the failures to meet those demands. Hope's bar welcomes those people who are unable to live in the world and accept love's offerings. The drunks in the bar struggle as best as they can to survive without it.

The right kind of pity is neither Hickey's nor Slade's. It does not force people to confront the truth about themselves, even if one knows what the truth is. Nor does it require one to validate everyone's experience. Instead it asks for an understanding and compassion of how difficult life truly is and ministers to the needs and answers the cries for help when they are voiced. Michael Hinden defines the tragic experience in *The Iceman Cometh* and applies it to *Long Day's Journey Into Night* in a non-tendentious and humane way as follows: "The right kind of pity demands a creative widening of our capacity to extend ourselves, to experience the suffering of those who are partly guilty as well as partly innocent so that we may come to terms with our own complicity in life" (89). Complicity in life demands action and involvement. Action in *The Iceman Cometh* draws Larry out of his grandstand onto the playing field to condemn Parritt to death, an act which fascinates and horrifies Larry and from which he recoils in his final speech. Significantly, Parritt commits suicide just offstage; he jumps off the fire escape from above. This final dynamic between the inside and the outside demonstrates the possibilities of action. On one side of the stage, a drunk group celebrates their newly minted brotherhood based upon mutual "willing suspension of disbelief." They agree once again to collude in each other's fantasies. On the other side of the stage, Slade sits alone waiting for verification that he executed a man. The simultaneous drunken revelry, solemn apprehension, and suspense surrounding the unseen suicide produces a moment which asks the audience to consider what they would do in a similar situation. Beyond the mimetic situation, the moment dramatizes the ramifications of action. Significantly, Larry sits at his table staring directly at the audience as if to project his moral dilemma immediately upon the audience. Larry's role in Parritt's suicide causes him great agony: "It's the only way out for him! For the peace of all concerned, as Hickey said! [*snapping*] God damn his yellow soul, if he doesn't soon, I'll go up and throw him off!—like a dog with its guts ripped out you'd put out of misery!" (710). Larry's fury at Parritt is colored by his own remembrance of his love for Rosa; at the same time, he answers the genuine needs of Parritt to be punished. Larry's involvement in the case forces him to act and make a fateful decision. Set in relief against the rest of the bums getting drunk again, the final scene demonstrates life's awesome choices. Who among us has the courage to greet the bridegroom?

Chapter 4

Plays Without End

"If you would not feel the horrible burden of Time weighing
on your shoulders and crushing you to the earth, be drunken
continually."

—Edmund Tyrone quoting Baudelaire in
Long Day's Journey Into Night

Critics generally praised the opening of *"Anna Christie"* at the Vanderbilt Theatre on November 2, 1921, but they balked at what they considered a contrived marriage agreement between the heroine and her stoker
lover, Mat Burke. The drama editor of *The Evening Post*, J. Rankin Towse,
declared that "At the end of it all the impression remains that what has
been witnessed is not a near tragedy of human hearts and real circumstances but the unusual play of adroitly maneuvered stage puppets" (Jiji
74). A couple of weeks later, still referring to the improbability of the last
act, Alexander Woollcott of *The New York Times* added: "We may yet live
to see O'Neill write a play in which a crook turns out in the last act to be
a detective." O'Neill countered by arguing that audiences had misunderstood his play and that the proposed marriage at the end represented only
a pause before a new storm of problems could swell.[1] Defending his play
in a letter to George Jean Nathan, he rationalized Anna's actions at the
end by saying that "in moments of great stress life copies melodrama" (SL
148). As a fictional character, however, Anna's problems become the playwright's. O'Neill hides behind Anna's skirts instead of admitting that in
moments of great stress in which a playwright does not know how to solve
a dramatic problem he resorts to the time proven formulas that will guar-
antee a theatrical success—in this case, melodrama. Kurt Eisen calls this
play an "artistic dead end" (38), but in the words of Walt Whitman, "it

is to collect a ten-fold impetus that any halt is made." The problems that set back *"Anna Christie"* detour along the way toward artistic breakthrough. O'Neill attempts to write a play that transcends the traditional endings of comedies and tragedies but lacks the means to do it. The surprise ending in *"Anna Christie"* signifies that failure, but it also anticipates the solution to O'Neill's temporal problem that he discovered in his last great masterpieces.

O'Neill failed to present the ironic picture at the end of *"Anna Christie"* largely because he did not adequately allow for Anna's transformation to take place. He intended, of course, for the proposed marriage at the end to cast an uneasy portent for the future, but he did not establish the appropriate pattern within his play for this response to occur. His final plays, however, fulfill the intent of this early play brilliantly. It is ironic, too, that as less action occurs over a shorter period of time in the last plays, not only are these last plays superior to everything that comes before, but tragic resonance in these plays actually increases. None of the last plays, for example, ends with a death scene, the staple of the early plays in which events govern the action and a strong narrative leads to an inevitable conclusion. The final plays, too, occur in a short time span unlike the epic canvasses of earlier representations. Revelations within the plays shift from the sublime to the quotidian.

Repetition and the rhythm of everyday life surface as the dominant techniques for creating a sense of dramatic action. Of course, repetition is fundamental to Nietzsche's concept of eternal recurrence in which the same energies conserve and repeat themselves endlessly. Thematically, repetition signals human destiny which must constantly struggle and fail in the effort to survive and persevere. O'Neill's use of repetition develops the "hopeless hope" theme throughout the plays. Structurally, repetition creates the impression that O'Neill's plays resemble musical compositions.[2] Motifs and phrases repeat themselves in various combinations and resolve into a complex whole over the time of the piece. Repetition, the sense that the same things are happening again and again, creates units of action which form a pattern. This aspect of modernism is evident in Chekhov, and later Beckett, and more recently in the absurd vision of Václav Havel. In O'Neill's final dramas, the pattern serves as part for the whole. Instead of events building toward a traditional climax and conclusion, the end of an O'Neill play foretells future unrepresented events. The key to this projection into the future, beyond the represented action in the play, always involves a reading of past events, also unrepresented in the play. Retrospective action in which characters look to the past replaces a traditional progressive drive. O'Neill solves his temporal problem in drama by staging in the final plays a contest between present and past in which the future promises always to be more of the same.

Analysis of O'Neill's literary output reveals striking differences between the endings of his early plays and his later plays. Death is the final image among almost half of the twenty-seven plays prior to *"Anna Christie."* Murder (*The Web*), military firing squad (*The Sniper*), accident (*Thirst, Bound East for Cardiff*), suicide (*Recklessness, Warnings, Bread and Butter, Abortion, Before Breakfast*), tuberculosis (*Beyond the Horizon*) and old age/madness (*Where the Cross Is Made, Gold*) account for twelve of the plays. In addition, a gunshot reduces the hero of *The Personal Equation* to a vegetable state at the end of that play. Captain Keeney's wife goes mad at the end of *Ile*. The end of *The Dreamy Kid* anticipates the capture and death of the hero, and the advanced state of tuberculosis from which Eileen Carmody suffers in *The Straw* threatens to kill her at the end of that play. The bulk of the deadly endings occur in O'Neill's earliest and unproduced works.[3] Only *Bound East for Cardiff, Beyond the Horizon* and *The Straw*, from the list above, remain as enduring works in O'Neill's canon. The other sea plays from the Glencairn series, in which no deaths occur, including *In the Zone, The Long Voyage Home*, and *The Moon of the Caribbees*, comprise O'Neill's most important early dramatic contributions. The significance and value of a play inextricably ties to the nature of the ending.

Even in the experimental decade of the '20s, however, death predominates in half of the plays culminating with *Mourning Becomes Electra*, the trilogy featuring two murders and two suicides. Both Brutus Jones and Yank Smith meet death at the end of their respective expressionistic plays. The protagonists in *Diff'rent* commit suicide; Abbie and Eben prepare for judgment and likely death in *Desire Under the Elms* in recompense for an infanticide; Cybel identifies the body of William Brown as "Man" in *The Great God Brown*; an arrow mortally wounds Juan in *The Fountain*; Princess Kukachin's death frames the action of *Marco Millions*. Even Lazarus finally dies to end *Lazarus Laughed*. Perhaps the most spectacular finale occurs in *Dynamo* in which Reuben Light first kills his girlfriend and then electrocutes himself. Despite the experimental trappings of these plays, O'Neill resorts to conventional means to structure experience and end them.

Similar to Chekhov's, O'Neill's plays move from melodramatic endings, punctuated by gunshots, to truncated actions that suggest continuation and repetition rather than closure. O'Neill's final plays avoid scenes of dramatic death. In *Days Without End*, the most religious of all O'Neill plays, John Loving's idealism reveals itself in his plaintive cry for divine revelation: "A new savior must be born who will reveal to us how we can be saved from ourselves, so that we can be free of the past and inherit the future and not perish by it" (CP3 158). Although no savior does appear, John regains his faith at the foot of the Cross in a church scene to conclude the play in a fashion that doomed the play among critics who felt it was too religious and a sign that O'Neill had embraced his Catholic roots again. In fact, O'Neill, as in *"Anna Christie,"* attempted a new strategy to complement his own dramatic, not religious, compulsions. While this effort to stave off death and create a new structure did not succeed, it showed a new direction in O'Neill's work. How to conclude a play remains a daunting task. Frederic Carpenter addressed the complexity of this challenge with respect to the ending of *Days Without End*: "Ideally, however, the 'lifegiving formula' toward which O'Neill was groping would not require the final choice of one 'faith,' or ending, to the exclusion of others. It would accept uncertainty, or multiplicity of choice, as the essence of its drama; and it would not weight the scales in favor of any one character or faith" (142). The unsuccessful attempt of John Loving to write an end to his novel is analogous to the playwright struggling to conclude *Days Without End* effectively. The various alternative endings that O'Neill drafted for this play signify a search for an ending that avoids the simple or the melodramatic. That O'Neill reacted diametrically to the power of the big death scene and produced something equally melodramatic in praise of life and God ("Life laughs with God's love again! Life laughs with love!" [180]), is a first step toward a new creative pattern. A move away from the fixed ending, often ending in death, explores the unrepresented territory of the future by developing a recurring pattern in the dramatic action. The visible pattern on stage predicts the unseen future.

With the exception of Don Parritt, a supporting character in *The Iceman Cometh*, no characters die in the action of the final eight plays. Although it incites the action for the entire play, the murder of Evelyn Hickman, for example, occurs prior to the beginning. The gunshot offstage in the final act of *A Touch of the Poet* parodies a melodramatic ending by signaling an alarm of Cornelius Melody's suicide. His return to the stage dashes that expectation as he discloses that only his prize mare has died. This surprise intensifies the following scene in which Con Melody's transformation from military officer to shebeen keeper gives him death in life. The only death in *Hughie* is one that happened in the recent past prior to the action. After James Tyrone passes out at one point in *A Moon for the Misbegotten*, Josie fears that he has died. He looks like death in such repose. Despite his best efforts, though, to drink himself to death, Tyrone does not die in the action of the play. In the end, he merely walks away, albeit for the last time from the Hogan farm. The emotional power at the end stems from the simple fact that death and peace have not come yet.

Repetition motifs, rather than final tableaus of death and dying, create dramatic impact in the mature plays. The novelistic techniques that O'Neill employs to tell his stories are not nearly as significant as his discovery of a means to show dramatically that things and events repeat themselves, and that repetition is not merely a fact of life, but a cross to bear. O'Neill works neither toward the exclusion of the individual from society nor the reintegration of that individual back into society. Instead, he dramatizes a continuous struggle to stumble on without a destination in sight. He attempts to dodge the classical completeness of comedy and tragedy (ending typically in marriage or death), in favor of an "open" ending that remains unresolved, ambiguous, and ironic. Dying is easy for O'Neill, but living remains difficult. His unique conception of tragedy as endless struggle and ultimate failure has nothing to do with reaching destinations that a death provides, terminal stopping places, but in recognitions and revelations that humanity never reaches the place of desire.

Cyclical repetition serves as a major structuring device in all of O'Neill's best plays. Even plays which feature dramatic deaths strive to present a sense of ongoing struggle through repetitive motifs. As mentioned in the introductory chapter, *Bound East for Cardiff* first successfully evoked this pattern by offsetting the death of Yank with the everyday rituals of life aboard a tramp steamer. Plays of the '20s attempt these same patterns of repetition, although technical artifice often obscures repetition's importance. Most obviously, *Lazarus Laughed*, O'Neill's most Nietzschean play, with its constant refrain of "Death is Dead," consciously pronounces its theme of eternal recurrence. *The Great God Brown* and *Ah, Wilderness!* evoke seasonal recurrence at the end of each. Cybel, the earth mother prostitute in the former play, eulogizes over the body of William Brown: "Always spring comes again bearing life! Always again! Always, always forever again!—Spring again!—life again!—summer and fall and death and peace again!—[*with agonized sorrow*]—but always, always, love and conception and birth and pain again—spring bearing the intolerable chalice of life again!—[*then with agonized exultance*]—bearing the glorious, blazing crown of life again!" (CP2 532). Nat Miller, the father in *Ah, Wilderness!*, watches his son at the end of that play and quotes from the *Rubaiyat*: "Yet Ah, that Spring should vanish with the Rose!/ That Youth's sweet-scented manuscript should close!" Turning to his wife, he then adds: "Well, Spring isn't everything, is it, Essie? There's a lot to be said for Autumn. That's got beauty, too. And Winter—if you're together" (CP3 107). Emphasis upon the seasons, or, the life cycle, as opposed to individual fate celebrates or mourns ongoing life processes. Juxtaposition of youth and maturity at the end brings out a complex response. Richard's innocence is applauded but the end of innocence is near. His parents recognize that he's growing older. And with that realization comes thought of their own mortality, joy at what they've shared, but also an awareness of time passing and that their own youth is well behind them, and perhaps even a little uneasiness about what lies ahead. The final image of the play shifts focus away from Richard to his parents and how they view him: someone precious who must be protected, but also someone who will change, grow and leave. The impact of the title emerges in the final moments of the play when the focus swings to the parents' perspective of their son. Nat Miller knows what the title verse is about. "Warm stuff" he called it earlier in the play. *Ah, Wilderness!* is a nostalgic play, but it's more than a warm view of the past and the good old days. The experience of the play is also about time and the effect of looking back in time and recognizing the consequences of time. Not in a maudlin sense, but in a clear-eyed acceptance of the way things have to be. The combination of joy and sadness that marks the end of the play is life affirming and bittersweet because it attempts to embrace a wide spectrum of human responses and emotional feelings.

Generational inheritance within the family also shows cyclical repetition. The birth of Curtis Jayson's son in *The First Man* preserves the family line, represented by three generations, even in the face of Martha's death in childbirth. Curtis confronts his gathered family and swears that he will return one day to embrace his son: "When he's old enough, I'll teach him to know and love a big, free life. Martha used to say that he would take her place in time. Martha shall live again for me in him" (CP2 116). In *Desire Under the Elms*, characters describe Eben as the "spittin' image" of both his maw and Ephraim Cabot. His covetousness of the farm mirrors that of his father. The inciting moment of *Strange Interlude*, prior to the play's opening, is the death of Nina's lover, Gordon Shaw. He lives again at the end of the play in the birth of little Gordon, who, like his namesake, flies away in an airplane. His fiancée, Madeline, also functions as a replacement for an aging Nina. Both Sara Melody and her husband, Simon Harford, share characteristics of their respective parents. In *A Touch of the Poet*, Sara confides to her mother that she has seduced Simon, much the same fashion as Nora once seduced Cornelius. The greed and possessiveness that sustains the action in *More Stately Mansions*, and which is the subject of the entire cycle, seems to resolve at the end of the play with a decision to live in a little cabin in the woods. That decision marks a return to the place where the couple first fell in love. The fates of the next generation of Harford children, four boys, staked to pursue careers in trade and politics, prove that the consuming flames of desire have not burned out. *Mourning Becomes Electra*, which details three generations of the Mannon family, lays out generational repetitions most prominently. The Mannon features handed down from father to son and mother to daughter curse the offspring to become their parents.

Aside from seasonal and generational repetitions, plays depict the mere struggle to survive as a ceaseless attempt to conquer the ultimate defeat of death or failure. Juan's search for the fountain of youth or Nina Leeds' pursuit of happiness in the arms of men follows a pattern of unfulfilled struggle to achieve a desired goal. Gordon Shaw, unseen in the play, is Nina's ideal man. He is described in the play as strikingly handsome, a great athlete, and a consummate gentleman. She tries to resurrect his image by combining her "three men," Sam Evans, Ned Darrell, and Charlie Marsden, but no single man satisfies her. One of her projects in the play is to write Gordon's biography and give him the sort of immortality that literature affords. The birth of Little Gordon, Nina's son, does bring Gordon back into the action. But his physical presence only serves to remind Nina that her lover died years ago and that she, too, has aged. She sees her own life of years ago in the happy coupling of Gordon and Madeline. Nina never does recover the Gordon she seeks. Similarly, the bar exam that Jim Harris strives to pass in *All God's Chillun Got Wings* is a goal that would allow him to enter an ideal marriage with his white wife. His recurring efforts to pass the bar exam reach a crescendo in the final act. Passing is the key for Jim to enter into the white world, but he fails every time, and he speaks of his latest failure at the end of the play to his wife Ella: "Pass? Me? Jim Crow Harris? Nigger Jim Harris—become a full-fledged Member of the Bar! Why the mere notion of it is enough to kill you with laughing! It'd be against all natural laws, all human right and justice. It'd be miraculous, there'd be earthquakes and catastrophes, the seven Plagues'd come again and locusts'd devour all the money in the banks, the second Flood'd come roaring and Noah'd fall overboard, the sun'd drop out of the sky like a ripe fig, and the Devil'd perform miracles, and God'd be tipped head first right out of the Judgment seat!" (CP2 313). In each case, the hope for success but not the achievement of it defines the dramatic essence of the play. Repetition, coming up again and again to realizations of failure, ennobles human endeavor.

Repetition through yearly seasons, generations, and the struggle to survive effectively makes time the subject of O'Neill's plays. This is another consequence of his novelistic desire to tell all. Earlier, I discussed the battle between narrative and dramatic technique. Time emerges as the true subject of the novel principally because of the flexibility of the novel form and the presence of the narrator to cover vast amounts of time. John Henry Raleigh notes in *The Plays of Eugene O'Neill* that "The impulse in his earlier career to spread his dramatic action over a long period of time arose, in a general way, from O'Neill's novelistic impulse, the Proustian urge to dramatize the chemistry and the attritions of the years" (179). The action of *Beyond the Horizon* occurs over an eight year period. *Diff'rent*, a two act play, features a time elapse of thirty years between the two acts. *All God's Chillun Got Wings* covers over sixteen years in time, from the early childhood of Jim and Ella to adulthood and marriage. *Strange Interlude*, the most famous of the long plays, depicts Nina first as a young woman of twenty and ranges over twenty-five years in her struggle to attain happiness. At the age of only forty-five, O'Neill, perhaps lost in time, portrays her as a tired and post-menopausal woman!

Action in these plays tracks the ravages of time upon the characters and consequences of their choices. The second act of *Beyond the Horizon* resumes three years after the first. Stage directions describe the protagonist, Robert Mayo, as follows: "His shoulders are stooped as if under too great a burden. His eyes are dull and lifeless, his face burned by the sun and unshaven for days. Streaks of sweat have smudged the layer of dust on his cheeks. His lips drawn down at the corners, give him a hopeless, resigned expression" (CP1 608). The third and final act, another five years later, reveals Robert in the full stages of tuberculosis: "His hair is long and unkempt, his face and body emaciated. There are bright patches of crimson over his cheek bones and his eyes are burning with fever" (631–632). Ruth Mayo, his wife, undergoes a similar transformation from buoyant youth to hardened and discouraged maturity. *Bread and Butter*, O'Neill's first full-length play, shares a similar theme with *Beyond the Horizon*. John Brown, a painter, marries his small town sweetheart instead of pursuing his career as a serious artist. The action which takes place over barely four years in time greatly alters him. In the two year interval between the third and fourth acts, John, according to stage directions, has "grown stout and his face is flabby and pasty-complected, his eyes dull and lusterless" (CP1 170). Likewise, Maud, his wife, "is still pretty but has faded, grown prim and hardened, has lines of fretful irritation about her eyes and mouth, and wears the air of one who has been cheated in the game of life and knows it; but will even up the scale by making those around her as wretched as possible" (166). In both of these plays, the protagonists make a disastrous marriage choice. The consequences of those decisions wear on them physically.

The above examples show the results of time upon the characters, but the crucial aspects of the action remain absent. Time becomes the subject in the plays, but the important aspects of time passing are missing. It is as though the main action, the meaningful action, occurs in the temporal ellipses between acts. The real drama, the daily grind through the years, occurs offstage. In *Beyond the Horizon*, for example, the tragedy of the play lies in the incremental wasting away of Robert and the farm. Slowly over time all his dreams slip away. The concise and compact form of drama cannot adequately treat this subject. Instead, the playwright selects highlights to render those few times when Andrew, Robert's brother, returns home briefly. The gap of two years between the third and fourth act of *Bread and Butter* is the space in which the drama occurs in that play. Again, the dawning recognition of a bad choice of marriage for þoth John and Maud, and the effects of being stuck together with the bitterness of regret, forms the subject. Requirements to show the fateful decision and the consequences of that decision emphasize the limitations of the narrative drive in drama to deal sufficiently with the subject of time. Interest in *Diff'rent* lies in space not represented in the drama, Emma's gradual disintegration and Caleb's persistence. Every year, Caleb returns to Emma to propose marriage. Each year she rebuffs him in response to an acknowledged peccadillo from thirty years ago. Unfortunately, the play can only dramatize the last visit by Caleb. The repetition of his yearly visits is a subject which can only be stated but not shown. Instead, Benny Rogers emerges in the second act as a younger and more successful suitor. That character intercedes between the two rightful lovers and becomes the visible and melodramatic means to draw the drama to a conclusion.

Martha Jayson voices the novelized subject of time in *The First Man*: "All in the past is our work. It's my greatest pride to think so. But, Curt, I'll have to confess frankly—during the past two years I've felt myself feeling as if I wasn't complete—with that alone" (CP2 85). She speaks of her desire for a child and her pregnancy and childbirth encompasses the time period of the play. In the third act her husband, Curtis, discusses his marriage with Martha to his best friend and, again, states the temporal subject of the play: "There was something in each of us the other grew to hate. And still we loved as never before, perhaps, for we grew to pity each other's helplessness" (98). The essence of their relationship can be talked about, but it cannot be shown. When Curtis wants to confide in his wife, he calls her into his private study. No one can fully understand or even see their relationship, including the other characters in the play. What sustains the plot is not the relationship of Curtis and Martha, nor the themes articulated above, but a melodrama of small town life and family in which the Jayson clan suspects that Curtis Jayson is not even the father of Martha's child. These false suspicions spur Curtis to leave. Martha and Curt's relationship remains as opaque to the Jayson family as it does to the audience. The ostensible plot overwhelms the true subject of the play.

O'Neill solves the temporal problem in his dramas by tightening the action in the final plays and by bringing the past into the present. *A Touch of the Poet*, *The Iceman Cometh*, *Long Day's Journey Into Night*, and *A Moon for the Misbegotten* perfect what O'Neill first tried to do with *"Anna Christie."* O'Neill first narrows his scope and focuses on a single temporal event. With the exception of *More Stately Mansions*, the last plays adhere to unities of time, place and action: the anniversary of Wellington's great victory at Talavera; the annual return of salesman Hickey to Harry Hope's bar in *The Iceman Cometh*; the discovery that Mary's begun taking dope again in *Long Day's Journey Into Night*; a late night date under the stars in *A Moon for the Misbegotten*. O'Neill hinges his drama upon a single event in the future—a celebration, a date with James, Hickey's arrival—which provides an occasion (waiting) to reflect on past events. As Simon remarks in *More Stately Mansions*, "...the past is never dead as long as we live because all we are is the past" (CP3 391). O'Neill then weds the past and the present, not just thematically, but visually as well. Cornelius Melody dons his old uniform again; Mary brings down her wedding dress from the attic; Tyrone first confuses Josie with a prostitute, then uses her to act the part of his dead mother; Hickey's newfound sobriety throws a blanket on Harry's party. O'Neill effectively elides the gap between what was and what is.

Goethe's essay, "Epic and Dramatic Poetry," cites the essential difference between epic (narrative) and drama according to temporal modes. The epic poet "describes an action as being altogether past and completed, the dramatic poet represents it as actually occurring" (281). The presence of a narrator mediates the actual event of the story and the occasion of its telling. Drama, acted out by characters on stage, presents a story directly and immediately in front of an audience. Goethe describes several kinds of possible action in narrative and dramatic poetry, the first two of which are progressive and retrogressive action. Progressive action is goal oriented and is best suited for drama. *Oedipus* is an outstanding example of such action. Despite several delays in the course of the action, what Goethe terms retardative movements, and a series of recognitions and reversals, the action follows a straightforward course of relentless discovery to the end. Retrogressive action, according to Goethe, is best suited for epic or narrative poetry. This type of action draws the action away from its ultimate goal. Lukács cites Goethe in *The Historical Novel* and elaborates upon the effectiveness and dominance of retrogressive action using *The*

Odyssey as an example: "It is only because Odysseus's 'journey' is a cease-less struggle with a stronger power that every step along this path acquires an exciting significance: not a single circumstance depicted is mere circum-stance, but a real event, the result of an action, the driving cause of a fur-ther encounter between the contending forces" (146). Lukács' analysis highlights "wandering" and "journey" as essential motifs belonging to nar-rative form. The action never takes a direct path to the goal. Something always impedes progress toward a goal and prevents direct access to the end.

O'Neill's best dramas lock progressive and retrogressive modes of action in conflict. Lukács' discussion of "ceaseless struggle" in epic describes perfectly the tension in *Mourning Becomes Electra*, *The Iceman Cometh*, or *A Touch of the Poet*. Basic to all O'Neill's plays is the fact that characters do not achieve their goals, they only strive for them. "Ceaseless struggle" defines repetitive acts in the plays. Another term from Goethe, a mode of action he calls "retrospective," describes action in O'Neill. He defines retrospective action as "events that have happened previously to the epoch of the poem [which] are introduced into it" (282). This term applies to O'Neill's drama for two reasons. One reason so little happens in the late plays is that so much has already happened previous to the action. Sec-ondly, though, and more powerfully, retrospective action, with its empha-sis upon vision, suggests a mode of behavior among characters on stage. Characters in O'Neill look to the past even as time inexorably moves for-ward. The posture of retrospection and implied stasis rubs against drama's forward movement.

Repetitive acts of murder prompt Orin Mannon's downward slide and preoccupation with the past in *Mourning Becomes Electra*. Having returned from the Civil War, Orin recalls dreams of killing the same man over and over again until he discovers that man to be himself. After killing Brant, his mother's lover, Orin realizes: "This is like my dream. I've killed him before—over and over…. Do you remember me telling you how the faces of the men I killed came back and changed to Father's face and finally became my own? [*He smiles grimly.*] He looks like me, too! Maybe I've committed suicide!" (CP2 996). His mother's suicide, however, in response to this murder, damns Orin in his own eyes. He describes his spiritual descent in the third act of the final part of the trilogy, shortly before his own suicide: "The only love I can know now is the love of guilt for guilt which breeds more guilt—until you get so deep at the bottom of hell there is no lower you can sink and you rest there in peace!" (CP2 1037). At this point in the play, Orin looks like his father, the past again returns in the present. Alone in his father's dark study, he records the history of the Mannon family in a book. Lavinia's attempt to get Orin to live in the present and marry Hazel, the girl next door, fails dismally. Orin's "ceaseless struggle" with death and dying binds him fast and forever to the past.

Harry Hope's birthday party in *The Iceman Cometh* signifies an annual (repetitive) event that Hickey habitually tries unsuccessfully to avoid. Over the years he attempts to break his pattern of debauchery and become a faithful husband, but, like Jimmy Tomorrow, he prefers the drunken revels at Harry's to nights at home with his wife. This year he had promised Evelyn once again that he would not go back: "And as the time got nearer to when I was due to come here for my drunk around Harry's birthday, I got nearly crazy. I kept swearing to her every night that this time I really wouldn't, until I'd made it a real final test to myself—and to her" (CP3 699). His failure this time prompts him to destroy the illusion, held out by his wife, that he will ever reform. This particular year marks the end of Hickey's struggle with himself. Having given up his dream, he is a changed man prior to the start of the play. The bums at Harry's look forward to Hickey's arrival and the same as always good time. Hickey, on the other hand, having just walked down from Astoria, fresh from a killing, eagerly embarks to make this time different from all the rest, first of all, by justifying his actions to himself, and secondly bringing happiness to the men as further justification for murdering Evelyn. From the outset, desire for things to remain the same and competing desire for things to change structure events in the play.

An anniversary of sorts also structures *A Touch of the Poet*. Cornelius Melody celebrates Wellington's victory over Napoleon at Talavera, at which Melody played a heroic part, by dressing in his old uniform and recreating days of past triumph. He struts around reciting Byron and posing as a romantic hero, striking a discordant figure against the slovenly bar which he owns. The presence of Jamie Creegan, a man who served with Melody in former glory days, makes the retrospective action visually explicit in the play. The banquet scene in this act shows the comic contest between former days of military prowess and present ones of domestic abject poverty. Melody, with Creegan, and the rest of the no good spongers hanging about to drink Con's liquor, replay the great battle using cutlery on the dining table to stake out military positions and operations. When Melody and the men ride off at the end of the act to avenge Sara's honor by confronting the elder Harford, past and present again collide. Melody pictures himself as a fine aristocratic gentleman, but his gallop off to the Harford mansion mocks his gallant past as a military officer. Upon his return, Melody, dazed from his beating, conflates past and present, with devastating acumen: "Bravely done, Major Melody! The Commander of the Forces honors your exceptional gallantry! Like the glorious field of Talavera! Like the charge on the French square! Cursing like a drunken, foul-mouthed son of a thieving shebeen keeper who sprang from the filth of a peasant hovel, with pigs on the floor—" (CP3 267) Melody, who has held on to his pose as a Byronic hero, at last recognizes the difference between that image and who he seems to be. The repetitive act of the celebration of Talavera ultimately wakes him up to the drifting temporal gap between past and present. Melody looks at himself again in the mirror and acknowledges the difference between pose and persona: "Be Jaysus, if it ain't the mirror the alud loon was always admirin' his mug in while he spouted Byron to pretend himself was a lord wid a touch av the poet—" (277). The brogue, a sign of Melody's past, a renunciation of his musically fantastic name, repudiates his aristocratic pose. Sara, his daughter and nemesis, routinely scoffs at the hypocrisy of Con's performance. To the horror of his daughter here, Melody finally sees the laughable disparity between past and present. His humiliation at the hands of the Harfords causes him to drop his stance as something finer than he is and his surrender ends the play; Sara, his adversary throughout the play, takes up his cause and the cycle continues.

At the end of *The Iceman Cometh*, as he begins to feel the effect of liquor again, Hope recalls Hickey's unfortunate life: "Poor old Hickey! We musn't hold him responsible for anything he's done. We'll forget that and only remember him the way we've always known him before—the kindest, biggest-hearted guy ever wore shoe leather" (706). The final image in that play is devastating because it shows that nothing has changed among the men (except for Larry, of course) and that Hickey's efforts were indeed mostly in vain. At the end of a very long play, the conclusion returns to the beginning. Compared to O'Neill, modern playwrights such as Chekhov and Ibsen are masters of economy in terms of their use of repetition. What takes O'Neill an entire play to say, again and again, Chekhov condenses to the single lyrical pine for "Moscow, Moscow" in *Three Sisters*. Ibsen is the acknowledged champion of loading the past into the present. The scene in which Hedda Gabler and Eilert Lovborg look at an album and reflect upon the fact that they sat in identical positions years ago brilliantly transforms the dead past into an active and dramatic presence. By contrast, O'Neill rather crudely visualizes the past via properties (e.g., uniform, wedding dress), makeup (e.g., aging over the years in *Strange Interlude*, Mary's girlish hairstyle in the last scene), generations (e.g., *Mourning Becomes Electra*, parent/child relations), or through the effects of alcohol (Tyrone's gabbiness in *A Moon for the Misbegotten*, pipe dreams in *The Iceman Cometh*).

What really distinguishes O'Neill from Chekhov or Ibsen is sheer length. I've stressed the open ended structure and the use of repetition to give a sense of perpetual action. But, in a phenomenal sense, the duration of O'Neill's plays gives a sense also of plays without end. There is no other author like O'Neill in terms of writing such long plays.[4] To steal a phrase from John Henry Raleigh, the plays last as long as "the torments of hell" (*Plays of Eugene O'Neill* 208). *Strange Interlude* is nine acts, *Mourning Becomes Electra* is a trilogy, *The Iceman Cometh* is well over four hours in playing time, and *Long Day's Journey Into Night* is almost equally as long. *More Stately Mansions*, although only a draft, is the longest play of all, numbering 272 pages in the edition of *Complete Plays*. Among these plays, only *Long Day's Journey Into Night* is performed frequently. They all require special considerations in performance such as early curtain times and dinner breaks between acts. The length of the plays increases production costs, too, because of fewer performances in the week, added rehearsal time to get the play ready, and overtime pay for the technical crew. The obvious answer to these problems is to cut the plays to manageable length. Much theatre fare today is so short that it seems catered for the audience to enjoy dinner before or after the show and still get to bed by 11:00.[5] That's simply not possible in most O'Neill plays. *Long Day's Journey Into Night* is exactly what it says it is, a very long haul for the audience. Despite the fact that the action takes place in a single day, it seems like the action takes a full day to unfold! The length of this play and others forces an uncomfortable fit into the theatre. Either the plays must be trimmed in order to satisfy production budgets and audience expectations; or, the theatre must expand to accommodate the integrity of the plays. Certainly, the many repetitions offer an opportunity to cut material from a text without harming an understanding of the plot. The real question, then, is why are the plays so long and is such length necessary to achieve the desired emotional response?

In O'Neill's late plays, time is the subject as characters reflect upon the past and try to trace their lives back to a happier day and pinpoint the moment when life went wrong, or justify, in the case of Hickey in *The Iceman Cometh*, why they did what they did. What's unique about O'Neill, though, is that time is not only the subject of the play for the characters, but the length of time that the audience watches the play is integral to its experience of the event. A two hour production of *Long Day's Journey Into Night* is very different than a four hour production of the same play. This has less to do with the relative speeds of performances than it has to do with the aesthetic experience of time. I'm thinking now exclusively of *Iceman* and *Long Day's Journey*, O'Neill's two best plays, and two of the longest American plays. To watch an O'Neill play is to experience an exhausting event. In order to have an emotional experience at the end of the play the audience must be exhausted. Looked at from another angle, the text exhausts itself in performance. It is as though the plays want to end, but can't. There is always a search for an ending, but the final sentence cannot be said until the text exhausts completely and that moment is endlessly deferred. Watching *The Iceman Cometh*, the audience, and indeed the characters in the play, guess the end well before Hickey discloses his secret. Hickey discovers that he has not banished his last illusion or pipe dream. For the audience, this seems to be the ready answer to the play and the final piece of the puzzle, albeit an expected one. The play sets up a mechanism that seems to supply answers (humanity can't survive without pipe dreams) but ends up asking questions that fuel the desire for answers. Simply put, it says, "What are you going to do?" In time, the action exhausts various possibilities for definitive answers through contradictions and multiple points of view. In the end, only the questions remain.

Even before Hickey launches into his big speech, Rocky advises the two police officers, Lieb and Moran, about how to catch their suspect: "And if yuh want a confession all yuh got to do is listen. He'll be talkin' all about it soon. Yuh can't stop de bastard talkin'" (CP3 693). Coming at the end of a very long performance, this is a very funny line. It is also a basic principle in O'Neill's best plays. Hickey describes his wife as a saintly woman. The more he speaks of her, though, the more his description seems to satisfy only his illusions of her. The length of Hickey's monologue is dramatically viable because it seeks closure, but fails to achieve it. The more Hickey speaks, the more certain it becomes that there will be no final answer. Characters try to tell stories that will adequately explain events in the past. But the more that they talk, the less clear the explanation. Hickey's long monologue is a perspicuous example of this phenomenon.

The more he talks about what he did and why he did it, the more confusing it becomes, to him, and to the audience. The clarity of the dramatic message recedes through increased talking about it and this becomes the dramatic message. The length of the play becomes inseparable from its meaning. Likewise, each story in *Long Day's Journey Into Night* by one of the family members meant to justify or explain the way things are offers the hope of truth. Competing stories fail to locate a first cause or final cure for family ills. The layering of personal experience in both plays becomes onion-like: peeled away, there is no core. Put simply, the impulse to simplify experience results only in further complications. Small wonder that characters are all "fog people" who resort to pipe dreams, alcohol and drugs as a means to retreat from recognition of the fact that ultimate truth is illusory. The timeless and ubiquitous literary conceit of truth versus illusion gets a new dimension in O'Neill's universe.

O'Neill's great plays achieve a form unique to the twentieth century by showing that the life-force endures under the pressure of the almost unimaginable burden of time. A question that remains unanswered even at the end is simply this: How will characters bear such burdens in the future? Lukács' "ceaseless struggle" is O'Neill's pipe dream. How do characters survive once their dreams die? Cornelius Melody stands bruised and bloody in his red, torn and tattered uniform and reverts back to his thick Irish peasant brogue and says that he's awakened to his true identity. But how will he bear the loss of his prize mare? Action in the following cycle play, *More Stately Mansions*, picks up at a wake for Melody a few years later in which it is made clear that he never did recover from the previous blows to his identity. Larry Slade's last line in *The Iceman Cometh* reads, "Be God, I'm the only real convert to death Hickey made here. From the bottom of my coward's heart I mean that now!" (CP3 710). The last lines of that play, a stage direction, indicate that "In his chair by the window, Larry stares in front of him, oblivious to their [the cacophony of voices in the bar] racket" (711). Larry may be ready for death, but how will he live with himself until that day comes? Michael Manheim argues that he will continue to minister to others, living in "the unmelodramatizable mercury of the present," a spokesman for "existence in flux" ("Transcendence of Melodrama in O'Neill's *The Iceman Cometh*" 157). Unlike Melody, who cannot live without illusions, cowardly Larry Slade achieves a grandeur as he stands in for all of us, living from day to day and doing the best that he can with all that he has to offer.

It seems fitting to close a chapter on how plays end by studying the last lines of *Long Day's Journey Into Night*. To glimpse the whole in the part, O'Neill fashions an ending that reverberates tragically beyond the final lines of the play. Formal consideration reveals a pattern that echoes throughout this work and all of O'Neill in terms of love, destruction and death. Critics attack O'Neill as a poor stylist. Indeed, Edmund in this play mocks his own poetic achievements and proclaims himself a stammerer. But in this play at least, O'Neill achieves a quotidian greatness voiced in Mary Tyrone's final lines. Recalling her girlhood at the end of the play, she states simply the most significant event in her life: "Then in the spring something happened to me. Yes, I remember. I fell in love with James Tyrone and was so happy for a time" (CP3 828). The juxtaposed elegance of the passive mode in the first sentence with active mode in the

Strange Interlude, Act 6, produced in 1928 by the Theatre Guild at the Guild Theatre, directed by Philip Moeller. In the "My three men" scene, Nina Leeds (Lynn Fontanne) is surrounded by husband Sam Evans (Glenn Anders, left), lover Edmund Darrell (Earle Larimore, right), and father figure Charles Marsden (Tom Powers), and she is pregnant with Gordon, Jr. Museum of the City of New York. Theater Collection.

last points up the sharp distinction and tension in the play between concepts of ordained fate and human will. The passive mode indicates an abdication of will, the presence of forces beyond human control which claims victims. "Something happened to me." As if there were no possibility for things turning out otherwise, as if there were no volition to determine the outcome of events. Something happened, a surprise turn of events. Everything led in one direction until a major peripety, the stuff of drama, reversed the currents of history. On the other hand, the final lines with the "I" at the head of the sentence indicate a particular choice. Indeed, Mary names the object of her affection. And the sentence continues to deliver a direct cause and effect: "I fell in love with James Tyrone and was so happy for a time." The switch between passive and active modes vacillates between

Strange Interlude, Act 8. Over twenty years pass between acts 6 and 8 and the movement in time displays the "attritions of the years." Nina, an "old woman," regrets that her son is about to marry and fly away and she seeks the comfort of "Dear Old Charlie." Pictured above are Tom Powers and Lynn Fontanne. Museum of the City of New York. Theater Collection.

victimization at the hands of fate or circumstance and the powers of individual choice. These two approaches, viewpoints of the world, cross dramatically throughout the play. The inseparable struggle between two modes of being, victim and author, impacts the action and shapes the determination of ultimate responsibility.

Choice of the word "happy" sends a red flag up for interpretive inquiry in one of O'Neill's saddest and most tragic plays. Repetition of the word, in this play as well as throughout O'Neill's work, signals revaluation of its meaning. Recall that the first three acts of O'Neill's previous play, *The Iceman Cometh*, end with Hickey telling his trapped audience at Hope's saloon that he wants them to be happy. I began this chapter with a consideration of the happy ending of *"Anna Christie"* and O'Neill's intent to

Act 1 of *Long Day's Journey Into Night*, 1956, directed by José Quintero at the Helen Hayes Theatre, with (left to right) Bradford Dillman as Edmund Tyrone, Jason Robards, Jr., as James Tyrone, Jr., Florence Eldridge as Mary Cavan Tyrone, and Fredric March as James Tyrone. This early scene, bright and promising, in which Edmund (Dillman) tells the story of Shaughnessy's pigs, is the only shared one between all of the family members. Museum of the City of New York. Theater Collection.

produce quite the opposite effect. In that play, the end represented only a pause before life continued. In a world of exaltation, happiness remains a petty emotion and a temporal state destined to pass into something else, tragedy perhaps, when the individual transgresses all human limitation and runs into an inevitable defeat, death or failure. In *Long Day's Journey Into Night*, the end looks not forward to the future so much as back to the past. Mary uses the word "happy" in conjunction with her guilt concerning the death of her second son: "Eugene was the same, too, happy and healthy, during the two years he lived before I let him die through my neglect (781)." Prior to this, Mary makes a more telling statement: "Only the past when you were happy is real" (777). Only the past exists;

The final scene in *Long Day's Journey Into Night* shows the splintering of the family, the ravages of time (in only one day) and the effects of alcohol and drugs late at night. Mary's girlish hairstyle, along with her rheumatic fingers which can no longer play the piano, and the wedding dress held by Tyrone are grotesque images of spent youth. O'Neill, in this play, no longer needs an epic narrative to dramatize time. Billy Rose Theatre Collection. The New York Public Library for the Performing Arts. Astor, Lenox and Tilden Foundations.

present events are merely dancing chimeras. Indeed, throughout the action, all the characters construct the past through either an alcoholic or drug induced haze. Quoting Kipling near the end of the play, after a long and drunken monologue about his night's adventure in the local whorehouse, Jamie yarns:

> Speakin' in general, I 'ave tried 'em all,
> The 'appy roads that take you o'er the world [817].

He goes on to say: "Happy roads is bunk. Weary roads is right. Get you nowhere fast. That's where I've got—nowhere. Where everyone lands in the end, even if most of the suckers won't admit it" (817). All the characters stand at the end of a weary road in *Long Day's Journey Into Night*.

Jamie's drunken cynicism, fueled by self-contempt, does not carry the spirit of the play. It is only one note in the musical score composed of all four Tyrone voices. The action of the play looks back at happiness and struggles through human suffering toward tragic epiphany forged not by understanding but simply through surviving the pain of existence. Repetition impacts the action. On the brink of perhaps kicking her drug dependency, Mary reverts to her former habit. Once again, the family suffers through all the familiar signs and repercussions of Mary's illness. From the beginning, repetition simultaneously heightens dramatic impact and places the represented action within the context of larger lives. Implications of the final phrase "for a time" strike to the core of the play's action. How long did Mary's happiness last? Where did it go? Action searches the past as the key to identity and happiness. It is evident that none is happy now, only perhaps "for a time." O'Neill dramatizes the tortured space of now in the present and the fervent desire to recapture a lost happy time. Time once again becomes the subject of the play, but in contrast to earlier plays, when O'Neill announced his desire to write a play with a theme for a novel, this great play represents action dramatically in the present.

The end juxtaposes past and present in one of O'Neill's most spectacular scenes. The entire final act anticipates Mary's entrance. From the beginning of the fourth act, Mary paces the floor upstairs in her most drug induced state. She has been taking more and more injections of morphine throughout the day. In Act 2, Tyrone warns: "For god's sake, don't dig up what's long forgotten. If you're that far gone in the past already, when it's only the beginning of the afternoon, what will you be tonight?" (765). In Act 3, Tyrone further proclaims: "You'll be like a mad ghost before the night's over!" (790). Act 4 begins with Tyrone playing solitaire, waiting to go to upstairs until his wife goes to bed in order not to face her. Both Edmund and Jamie return, also hoping to avoid Mary, and all three gather in the main room when Mary makes her surprise and climactic entrance. She remains out of sight for an extended period of time. First, light bulbs go on in the hall, and then Mary begins playing a Chopin waltz badly with her crippled hands, a recollection of her youthful desire to become a concert pianist. Jamie anticipates her appearance with his typically cynical introduction: "The Mad Scene. Enter Ophelia!" (824). The grotesque entrance of Mary, however, warrants such a prolonged preparation. Mary, a woman in her mid-fifties, joins the men as if she were the schoolgirl of her convent days. She wears her hair, the hair that she's been self-conscious about throughout the play, in braids as if she were a girl. Her beautiful wedding dress, which she described earlier, trails behind her. But she is no blushing bride in this scene. Carrying the dress, off-handedly letting Tyrone take it from her, captures a further grotesque image as she remembers her lost chaste adolescence. The image visualizes Mary's assertion from the second act: "The past is the present, isn't it? It's the future, too. We all try to lie out of that but life won't let us" (765). Whatever happened in the past cannot be forgotten. What's more, past actions inform the present and dictate the future. Within the intimacy of the family, a shared past affects all the characters. One of the dominant images and topics for conversation throughout the play is the omnipresent bottle of whiskey on the table. Each act features drinking in it. Edmund, in conversation with his father, points out that they drink in order to forget about what's happening to Mary. Alcohol serves as refuge from the weight of time. Edmund quotes from Baudelaire in the fourth act: "If you would not feel the horrible burden of Time weighing on your shoulders and crushing you to the earth, be drunken continually" (797). There is no escape from the reality of Mary's desperation and that of the men who love her.

Total lack of irony amplifies the pathos of the final tableau. In Chekhov, perhaps, a male chorus upstage might comment upon the lone woman's monologue downstage. The point might be that things change with the passing of time. Mary once loved her husband but realizes that she does not love him any longer. There is no such experience in O'Neill. The simple enduring truth of Mary's last line registers tragic impact: "I fell in love with James Tyrone and was so happy for a time." Pathos comes from the fact that Mary remains in love with her husband now and forever and he loves her passionately as well. Events changed the course of their lives, they all blame each other for a variety of sins, but nothing changes the fact of their love for each other. The absolute commitment of that relationship bonds the family together even as they tear each other apart for reasons that they seem unable to control. Earlier in the play, in Act 3, Mary recalls her romance with Tyrone: "Thirty-six years ago, but I can see it as clearly as if it were tonight!" (778). Action uncovers the secrets of the family as the play moves back to the beginning of that relationship. The beginning of the play welcomes back Mary to the family after a long stay at a sanitarium with high hopes of a cure and a new beginning for the family. James announces early: "This home has been a home again" (734). But the end of the play forces a realization that Mary's addiction starts a new beginning with a familiar pattern: "Every day from now on, there'll be the same drifting away from us until by the end of each night—" (760). This is where the play ends, opening up old wounds and forcing the family to endure them, to face the new day, which is really a return of an old pattern.

Retrospective action in the play reveals the entire history of the Tyrone family. Strategically, however, overt plotting gives the appearance of moving action forward. These two movements, forward and backward in time, grind against each other and provide dramatic resonance for the action. At the gross level, the title dictates progression from morning to night. The play captures a sense of the whole in the part through its rhythmic intervals of each act: morning, noon, evening, and midnight. Thus the movement from daylight to pitch darkness signifies the inevitable and symbolic movement toward death. More important to this inquiry, the movement from light to darkness retreats from knowledge and truth, from sight to blindness. The most optimistic moments of the play occur in the opening moments. The rest of the action gets increasingly dark or bitter, culminating in the final scene described above. The movement according to the clock in the play is not linear, however, but circular. The resonance at the end of the play comes with the recognition that the same things will happen again tomorrow. The most stunning image of the fog makes this most clear. Early in the play, Mary warns the men to "take advantage of the sunshine before the fog comes back" (736). By late night, the fog returns to envelope the little summer house. The established pattern, then, is one of obscured vision, followed by clarity, followed by obscured vision. Alternation and repetition of these two modes of vision amplify the psychological and physiological states of the embattled Tyrone family.

The plot, itself, on one level, veers toward melodrama with the discovery and subsequent discussion of two family secrets.[6] The first, of course, is that Mary is not cured from her addiction to morphine but has just begun during the previous evening to take the drugs again.[7] At the beginning,

Mary has been home for two months from a sanitarium and has been doing very well. Jamie reports later that he had just begun to hope again that this time she could beat the game. But on the morning in which the play opens, there is palpable tension in the air. All the men watch Mary very closely, so much so that she exhibits extremely nervous behavior, worrying over her hair and allowing her hands and fingers nervously to flutter over the tabletop. She addresses her husband within the first few pages of the play: "You really must not watch me all the time, James" (721). Later, after Mary has exited for a few moments, Jamie observes: "Outside of nerves, she seems perfectly all right this morning" (734). But it is clear that something bothers the men and soon it is disclosed that Mary was up in the night and that Jamie heard her in the spare room upstairs, always a sign in the past that she was taking drugs again. The men do not want to give in to their suspicions but neither can they ignore what all the visual signs tell them. Significantly, they do not discuss Mary's disease directly.

The other major plot development is the discovery and naming of Edmund's disease. Prior to the first scene, he has been to see the doctor, who is supposed to call during the morning to give his report (after having called in a specialist). O'Neill's initial description of Edmund pointedly marks his lapsed physical condition: "He is plainly in bad health. Much thinner than he should be, his eyes appear feverish and his cheeks are sunken. His skin, in spite of being sunburned a deep brown, has a parched sallowness" (723). From early hints in the play, it's evident that both Tyrone and Jamie know what's up with Edmund, that he has contracted consumption and will have to go to a sanitarium, but they play an elaborate game in order to conceal the truth from Mary. Since her father died of consumption, they fear that news of Edmund's illness would throw her into a nervous panic from which she could not recover. So, in spite of all the physical evidence to the contrary, Mary clings to a story that Edmund has just a cold and will be well as soon as he gets some rest.

As Mary injects more morphine in each successive act, the discourse surrounding her addiction becomes more frank. The men do not concede that Mary has been taking drugs again until they return from yard work at noon for lunch (Act 2, scene 1). Jamie, naturally, is the first to admit the truth verbally: "The truth is there is no cure and we've been saps to hope—" (758). Tyrone always speaks of the drug as the "poison." Upon his last entrance in the play, Jamie inquires: "Where's the hophead?" (818). None of the men's judgments can compare with Mary's own self-condemnation in the third act. Alone onstage after talking to Cathleen about her romance with Tyrone, Mary reflects upon her early days at the convent and begins to recite the Hail Mary before stopping abruptly: "You expect the Blessed Virgin to be fooled by a lying dope fiend reciting words! You can't hide from her! I must go upstairs. I haven't taken enough. When you start again you never know exactly how much you need" (779). This act of harsh naming receives amplification through repetition in the next scene in which Edmund attempts to confront his mother by telling her that he is very sick. He earlier called his sickness a touch of malaria, and Mary later refers to it as a slight case of grippe, but in this scene Edmund attempts to break through the haze surrounding his mother, address the truth, and receive the nurturing that he desires and needs from his mother. Ironically, this confrontation occurs immediately after Mary rebukes Edmund for failing to understand and forgive his father's failings. Ignoring her, Edmund launches his attack, excerpted in detail below:

> EDMUND: All this talk about loving me—and you won't even listen
>   when I try to tell you how sick—
>
> MARY: [*with an abrupt transformation into a detached bullying moth-*
>   *erliness*] Now, now. That's enough! I don't care to hear
>   because I know it's nothing but Hardy's [the doctor's] igno-
>   rant lies. [*He shrinks back into himself. She keeps on in a forced,*
>   *teasing tone but with an increasing undercurrent of resentment.*]
>   You're so like your father, dear. You love to make a scene
>   out of nothing so you can be dramatic and tragic. [*with a*
>   *belittling laugh*] If I gave you the slightest encouragement,
>   you'd tell me next you were going to die—
>
> EDMUND: People do die of it. Your own father—
>
> MARY: [*sharply*] Why do you mention him? There's no compari-
>   son at all with you. He had consumption. [*angrily*] I hate
>   you when you become gloomy and morbid! I forbid you to
>   remind me of my father's death, do you hear me?
>
> EDMUND: [*his face hard—grimly*] Yes, I hear you, Mama. I wish to God
>   I didn't! [*He gets up from his chair and stands staring con-*
>   *demningly at her—bitterly.*] It's pretty hard to take at times,
>   having a dope fiend for a mother! [788]

The anguish and brutality of this scene stem from mutual acknowledgment of each's condition laid out in the most direct terms. While Mary condemns herself in her monologue before this scene, she cannot face her son's accusations. Neither can she accept what he tries to tell her, although it is clear that she knows that he is very sick. Despite many assertions on her part that Edmund has just a cold, the more she repeats that line, the more apparent it is that she resists a growing awareness that he has contracted the very disease that killed her father. Edmund's illness demonstrates Mary's inability and refusal to deal effectively or even acknowledge what's happening in the present. Edmund will, it turns out, go to a sanitarium, but Mary never accepts the truth of the situation. Instead, she wards off her son's advances and as Edmund's situation develops into diagnosis and a posed solution, Mary shrinks from the family. After this climactic scene in Act 3, Mary goes upstairs and does not return again until her final entrance at the end of the play. Just before that, however, she meets her husband for a brief exchange. After first insisting again that Edmund just has a summer cold, she collapses against James and sobs: "I know he's going to die!" (789). For a moment she unpacks all the guilt she's been carrying for years: "I should never have borne him. It would have been better for his sake. I could never hurt him then. He wouldn't have had to know his mother was a dope fiend—and hate her!" (790). Mary composes herself quickly and momentarily excuses herself from dining in order to go up to take more drugs. Her own father's death from tuberculosis, in addition to the loss of her baby Eugene, fuels Mary's morbid fears that Edmund will die as well. The past is the present which continually haunts Mary for things she's done and not done. Morphine provides the only escape possible for her.

Drug addiction moves Mary into the past as an escape from an unbearable present. During the journey in time back to when she was a girl, Mary recounts her experiences of her doting father, life at the convent in the Middle West, dreams of becoming a concert pianist and meeting James Tyrone for the first time. Ultimately, she pines most for her lost religious convictions. Her physical description changes back in time as well. The stage directions for her final appearance note a remarkable makeover: "The uncanny thing is that her face now appears so youthful. Experience seems ironed out of it. It is a marble mask of girlish innocence, the mouth caught in a shy smile" (823). Mary's drift from the present into the past draws the rest of the family into the central action of retrospection as well. Certainly, revelations of Mary's condition and knowledge of her returning to addiction devastates them all. Drinking rituals help them cope with the truth that they do not want to face. Speaking of her husband in Act 3, Mary tells Cathleen: "He has such a good excuse, he believes, to drown his sorrows" (774). As the action progresses, however, the men explore the past without referring to Mary's addiction. Act 4, in addition to Mary's climactic story, features dialogues between Tyrone and Edmund and Edmund and Jamie. All three of the men offer narrative explanations of the past meant to help the listener understand them. Tyrone tells a story about his youth and his desire to go on the stage inspired by his love of Shakespeare. Edmund trades on alcoholic reverie with his father: "You've just told me some high spots in your memories. Want to hear mine? They're all connected with the sea" (811). Jamie, the most drunk of all, staggers back to the house and indulges in a series of monologues capped by a warning of his rotten influence upon his brother: "Listen, Kid, you'll be going away. May not get another chance to talk. Or might not be drunk enough to tell you truth. So got to tell you now. Something I ought to have told you long ago—for your own good" (820). He goes on to explain how he deliberately led his kid brother down the road to ruin as revenge against him for stealing his mother's love. Mary's return to the spare room, then, provides only the inciting incident that inspires the entire family to look back and examine the past. By speaking of it, they all hope to exonerate themselves from the guilt that haunts them.

Earlier plays such as *Beyond the Horizon* and *Strange Interlude* show the effects of past choices upon the present. Too much so, in fact, to the point that every action tethers to an appropriate reaction. These plays move forward in time and allow for a retrospective glance only after the action's done. In each of these plays it is possible to trace how the characters arrived at certain decisions and places as a result of those decisions. By contrast, *Long Day's Journey Into Night* takes place in only one locale and in only one day, but looks back on an entire lifetime in order to recall the history of the Tyrone family. Drugs and alcohol, omnipresent in this play, naturalize the narrative techniques that allow characters to speak their minds without the requirement for dialogue. The beginning of Act 3 provides an excellent example of this technique in which Mary talks to the second girl, Cathleen. Ostensibly, they have a conversation, but Mary, under the effects of morphine, and Cathleen, a bit tipsy from the whiskey offered to her by Mary, don't listen to each other. Mary speaks of her love of the fog, her desire to hide in it and be hidden by it. Cathleen, on the other hand, talks about the impudence of the family driver, Smythe, and his wandering hands that she vows to smash some day. Two seemingly unconnected monologues exist side by side, with neither character listening to the other. Jamie's drunken confession to Edmund in the final act claims to be "in vino veritas" (820). But the speech may not have complete truth value. His confession absolves him, as though speaking of such things relieves him of the responsibility of his actions toward his brother. One of the triumphs of this play is that narratives always reflect desires to both explain past events concerning the family interactions but also to absolve guilt, either through denial or confession. Every story in the play can only be understood in terms of the context in which it arises and to whom it is addressed. Almost always a story is told between husband and wife, father and son, and mother and son. There are no prolonged discussions among the entire family sitting around the dinner table. Despite the fact that family meals organize the first three acts, the dining room remains offstage and out of sight. This marks a significant difference between this play and *Ah, Wilderness!*, in which the second act centers around the dinner table and the family meal. Almost all of the important revelations in *Long Day's Journey Into Night* occur in a confrontation between one family member and another and often the subject of discussion is another family member who is not present. Discussions range from Mama's drug addiction, Edmund's tuberculosis, Eugene's death, to Tyrone's stinginess. But these are only the most glaring problems. In addition to Mary's problem, the telltale signs of familial disarray are the children. Jamie is thirty-four years old and an alcoholic who spends all his money on Broadway whores. He still takes money from his father and his only available job is as an actor, playing roles given him by his father, and as a gardener for his father. Edmund, on the other hand, has run away from home and traveled around the world as a seaman, and only lately returned in ill health. Although still young at 24, he's been thrown out of college, made a failed suicide attempt, and his only future apparent at this moment is as a reporter at the local provincial newspaper.[8] The question among the characters as they argue, fight, and make up with each other is who is to blame for the way things are.

Unlike the early plays, action in *Long Day's Journey Into Night* overdetermines responsibility for past actions. It's easy to discover the culprit and tidy up the action in most plays, but the genius of this one is that guilt circulates among all the Tyrones and none is either fully guilty or innocent. There are several causes for Mary's addiction, which began after she gave birth to Edmund. The doctor Tyrone got for her was not first rate and he prescribed morphine for her in order to cope with the pain. All the family members accuse Tyrone of being a miser, and indeed he acts the part with his attempts to turn the light bulbs out to avoid paying the Electric Light Company in the final act. Tyrone saved money by getting his wife a quack doctor. In the action of the play, too, Tyrone pleads poorhouse for Edmund's treatment and initially elects to send him to a state institution. Only after Edmund appeals to his pride does he suggest a costlier and better place to go for Edmund to recover. All this, of course, backs a claim that sees Tyrone as the man most blameworthy. But if this were truly so, there could be no accounting for the weight of guilt borne by his two sons in the play. Edmund would never have been born if Eugene, the second son, had not died of measles contracted from exposure to Jamie, then seven years old. Mary blames Jamie for deliberately exposing the baby to the disease out of jealousy. He hated the baby because Eugene got more attention than him. And that situation, of course, reflects upon the parents who never seem to extend themselves to their first-born. In the last act, Jamie sneers at Edmund as "Mama's baby and Papa's pet! The family White Hope!" (819). Jamie hates Edmund for precisely the same reasons that led him to murder Eugene. Yet how conscious could he have been of those motives when he was seven years old? Even if what Mary says is true, can Jamie be responsible for that act? Jamie accessed Eugene's room only because Mary left him in the care of her mother to be with James Tyrone on the road. Mary, too, blames herself at one point: "It was my fault. I should have insisted on staying with Eugene and not have let you persuade me to join you, just because I loved you. Above all, I shouldn't have let you insist I have another baby to take Eugene's place, because you thought that would make me forget his death" (766). Mary accuses Tyrone of jealousy of her babies and she blames herself for not being able to resist his invitations to join him on tour. Edmund, finally, wears the curse of just being born. The fact of him reminds his mother of her dead baby and she feels that she does not deserve him. Temperamentally, too, he has her same nervousness, and the guilt she feels about having him in the world is compounded by her guilt that something will happen to him to further punish her: "He was born nervous and too sensitive, and that's my fault. And now, ever since he's been so sick I've kept remembering Eugene and my father and I've been so frightened and guilty—" (766). The family tries to shield Mary from the knowledge of Edmund's disease for fear of driving her back into drug use as an escape. That fear began, however, with his birth, and Edmund carries knowledge of that with him throughout the play.

Action similarly overdetermines the cause of Edmund's disease. Certainly, he carries a genetic predisposition to it, which, for Mary, represents a curse to punish her for sins of neglect. Mary blames James, too, for never providing a proper home for the family. Much is made of the fact that the house in which the action takes place is only a summer house. Edmund's hard living, bumming around seaports and sleeping on park benches also accounts for his physical deterioration. Tyrone blames Jamie for being a bad influence upon his brother. And, Jamie admits culpability for leading his brother down the wrong path. Edmund, too, faults his mother for lack of nurturing. Indeed, Tyrone and Jamie shielded him from knowledge of her drug habit for many years. Once he did find out, one way Edmund dealt with that discovery was to stay away from the house so he didn't have to face reminders of his mother's addiction and the guilt that his birth created it.

While the above examples suggest the ease with which ample blame falls on any of the characters, another strong strain in the play suggests that no one is responsible for what happens to the family members. After upbraiding her older son for sneering at his father, Mary changes tack abruptly: "None of us can help the things life has done to us. They're done before you realize it, and once they're done they make you do other things until at last everything comes between you and what you'd like to be, and you've lost your true self forever" (749). Repetition of "done" and the passive construction underscores the twisting responsibility for actions. In the absence of apparent choice, events victimize characters. Speaking to Edmund about Jamie, Mary adds: "It's wrong to blame your brother. He can't help being what the past has made him. Any more than your father can. Or you. Or I" (751). The passive voice abdicates choice and responsibility but, in light of the comparison between this late play and the early ones, another reading emerges. Early plays isolate ramifications of particular choices, in which characters inevitably make the wrong choices and pay for their decisions. There is no longer a clear distinction between a good and bad choice in *Long Day's Journey Into Night*. Any action has the possibility of turning out badly because characters can only see limited options and cannot foresee the consequences of certain actions. In the early plays, the dilemma is often whether or not the principal character should marry. Later actions verify that they should not. In the second act of *Long Day's Journey*, Mary, too, attacks her husband: "You should have remained a bachelor and lived in second-rate hotels and entertained your friends in barrooms! [*She adds strangely, as if she were now talking aloud to herself rather than to Tyrone*] Then nothing would ever have happened" (753). And yet, if this were true, she would be negating an essential part of herself that she did will. The early plays show the characters fall out of love with each other. Time changes them. But, in this play, things that happen do not diminish the bond between characters, but instead make events more painful. What this play opens up is the possibility that there may be choices, but no matter which choice is made things may yet turn out badly. The struggle of every character to reconcile all the choices that have been made defines the tragic perspective embraced in all of O'Neill. Fending off Edmund's accusations against her drug use, Mary explains: "I never lied about anything once upon a time. Now I have to lie, especially to myself. But how can you understand, when I don't myself. I've never understood anything about it, except that one day long ago I found I could no longer call my soul my own" (769–770). Characters long to claim all their choices, in all their disparity and particularity, and to integrate them into an understandable whole. That search constitutes the retrospective action in the play. What happened?

Marriage remains first cause for the family's dysfunction. A split in Mary's identity drives a wedge between her and the family that began with marriage to Tyrone. At the beginning of the third act, after she has returned from the drug store and taken more "medicine," she explicitly talks about her dreams of the past. Her two desires, she tells Cathleen, were to become a nun or a concert pianist. But she segues immediately from those thoughts to a detailed description of her first meeting with the actor James Tyrone. The amount of detail signifies the importance of the memory to her. He was playing a Romantic hero from the French Revolution and his performance completely swept her off her feet. But when Cathleen leaves, Mary returns from her reverie to remark bitterly about herself: "You're a sentimental fool. What is so wonderful about that first meeting between a silly romantic schoolgirl and a matinee idol? You were much happier before you knew he existed, in the Convent when you used to pray to the Blessed Virgin" (779).

Tyrone embodies a similar dividedness within his character. On the one hand, his family regards him as a tightwad in fear of poverty and the poorhouse. On the other hand, among his barroom cronies he's a spendthrift always happy to buy the next round. His family makes fun of his many real estate deals that almost always turn out poorly and unprofitable. But this in turn leads to further speculation. He attempts to explain the cause of this aberration or idiosyncrasy to Edmund late in the play. Mary took up his part early by trying again to tell her sons of the dire poverty in which Tyrone grew up. In his long monologue to Edmund in the fourth act, Tyrone speaks of his transformation from sweatshop worker to actor. He discovered Shakespeare and educated himself with the Bard's great poetry. He would have acted in his plays for free, he claims, just to say those words. He got rid of his Irish brogue through practice and self-mastery so that he could act in Shakespeare plays. He developed into a fine actor with the potential to be the greatest Shakespearean actor of his day. He takes particular pleasure reveling in playing *Othello* with Edwin Booth, exchanging lead roles nightly, and earning Booth's praise. Tyrone laments that he could have been a great artist, but he traded that opportunity away to play in a great moneymaker. Years of easy success in one part ruined his talent and made him unfit for any other role: "…and then life had me where it wanted me—at from thirty-five to forty thousand net profit a season!" (810). Moments after this speech, he refutes Edmund's challenge that life is "so damned crazy" by quoting from *Julius Caesar*: "The fault, dear Brutus, is not in our stars, but in ourselves that we are underlings" (810–811). Tyrone blames himself for his decisions, but also accuses fate, or life, for destroying his happiness.

Repeated invocation of "home" throughout the play hallmarks family dysfunction. At the beginning Tyrone remarks happily that "This home has been a home again" (734). The reference is to Mary's return from the sanitarium and the perception of her cure. The implication, of course, is that it was not a home previously due to Mary's condition. Mary invokes the word repeatedly throughout the play. For her, it is just a cheap summer house that employs poor help (Cathleen and the cook, Bridget) and a second hand car and driver: "I've never felt it was my home. It was wrong from the start. Everything was done in the cheapest way. Your father would never spend the money to make it right" (738–739). The men are all comfortable in the house, Edmund even says he likes it, but that is partly because he can and does leave the house. While Mary drifts away from the family back into the past, the men literally leave her for long periods of time by herself, completely trapping and isolating her. The men go to town, to bars, to the Club or the Inn to drink and cavort with each other, leaving Mary alone. The isolation of Mary is one of the haunting images throughout the action. Tyrone keeps buying property outside, but never gives Mary a sense of home. Speaking to him in the second act, she insists that there was never a home, even before her addiction began: "And for me it's always been as lonely as a dirty room in a one-night stand hotel. In a real home one is never lonely. You forget I know from experience what a home is like. I gave up one to marry you—my father's home" (756).

Tyrone's profession as an actor keeps them from having anything but a summer house. For nine months of the year he tours the country and so they stay in a series of hotels often playing for only one night at a time. But the one-night stand hotel produces sexual images of prostitution and carnality. A home, on the other hand, is clean and orderly. Theatrical life is opposed to home life. Speaking to Cathleen, Mary makes the distinction clear: "I've never felt at home in the theater. ... They have always been kind to me, and I to them. But I've never felt at home with them. Their life is not my life. It has always stood between me and—But let's not talk of old things that couldn't be helped" (775). It's possible to infer that the word Mary leaves out is "home" and that home represents a clean and respectable life, one that she's used to, a part of herself that she has had to let go. She's unable to hold on to any part of her old self with her marriage to Tyrone. She laments the fact that she has no friends and that she has no one to visit and that no one visits her. She has to turn to the stupid second girl, Cathleen, for any female companionship. All her old friends cut her or felt sorry for her when she married an actor. She cannot hold on to her image of herself. The reality of past dreams slips away:

"For a time after my marriage I tried to keep up my music. But it was hopeless. One-night stands, cheap hotels, dirty trains, leaving children, never having a home—" (777). Years of traveling on the road with Tyrone have worn Mary's sense of herself away, but that has taken years, not a matter of one or two seasons. She has fought against the ceaseless repetition of the actor's life: "Even traveling with you season after season, with week after week of one-night stands, in trains without Pullmans, in dirty rooms of filthy hotels, eating bad food, bearing children in hotel rooms, I still kept healthy" (765). Her husband, James, was unavailable, first at a performance and later at the bar. Mary recounts how even on her honeymoon her husband was absent and drunk and was brought up to her hotel room and left outside the door. She comments simply: "I didn't know how often that was to happen in the years to come, how many times I was to wait in ugly hotel rooms. I became quite used to it" (783).

No decent girls will have anything to do with the Tyrone sons. This, too, is attributable to a lack of home. Jamie spends all his time in hotel rooms with Broadway whores and bonded liquor. The connection with one-night stands gets its carnal incarnation with images of Jamie coupling with whores. Mary defends him against her husband: "He's not to blame. If he'd been brought up in a real home, I'm sure he would have been different" (762). Instead, he enjoyed a life on the road in the same hotels. Tyrone spoon fed both children whiskey to cure any ailments they may have had: "Always a bottle on the bureau in the cheap hotel rooms!" (782). Mary addresses her own sense of guilt when she laments the fact that her babies did not have a proper home in which to grow up: "I knew from experience by then that children should have homes to be born in, if they are to be good children, and women need homes, if they are to be good mothers" (766). For Mary, home is a clean and non-sexualized space. One-night stands, whiskey bottles, dirty hotel rooms, are part of the sexualized world of the theater from which Mary recoils and reacts with middle class contempt: "I was brought up in a respectable home and educated in the best convent in the Middle West. Before I met Mr. Tyrone I hardly knew there was such a thing as a theater. I was a very pious girl. I even dreamed of becoming a nun. I've never had the slightest desire to be an actress" (775). She did want to become, however, a matinee idol's wife, the essence of which was sexual attraction.

In light of the sexual connotations involved in repeating the word "home," Tyrone's reference to the fact that "This home has been a home again" deserves a closer look. He recognizes Mary's sexuality as a huge part of their attraction and relationship and thirty-six years of marriage. There are several clues that Mary is not nearly as pious as she says she is.

Cathleen, for example, says: "Well, I can't imagine you a holy nun, Ma'am" (775). About his wife, Tyrone corrects some of Edmund's misconceptions: "She was never made to renounce the world. She was bursting with health and high spirits and the love of loving" (801). Mary fusses constantly over her physical appearance throughout much of the play and worries that her looks are leaving her. Tyrone is always happy to compliment her appearance as well. When Mary describes her meeting with Tyrone, she speaks of how attractive she was as a young girl. In the action of the play, she worries about her crippled hands and talks about how beautiful they once were. One of the great causes of guilt for Mary is the fact that she left her baby in order to be with Tyrone on the road. Presumably, she could have had a permanent home if she were content to stay at home. But her longing to be with him and he to have her with him primarily fulfills a sexual need for both of them. Mary is completely incapable of integrating her own sexuality into her sense of self-conception and role within the family.

The very first line of the play hints at Mary's sexuality and her subsequent shrinking from it. Coming from breakfast, Tyrone's arm is around Mary's waist and he says: "You're a fine armful now, Mary, with those twenty pounds you've gained" (719). Added weight and vitality is a sign of healthy sexuality, but throughout the rest of the play Mary refuses meals in order to rest up in her bedroom. The first suspicious sign of Mary's renewed drug use is the fact that Tyrone notices that she doesn't eat much breakfast. The full implications of weight and sexuality repeat in a funny and macabre story of Jamie's visit to the local whorehouse and his selection of Fat Violet for the night. "I like them fat," he claims, "but not that fat" (816). The grotesque image at the moment in the play when Jamie has given up all hope for his mother is at once comical and tragic. He tells a funny story about it, but his account of crying in the hallway with the fat whore connects with his mother. Later in the same scene with Edmund he recalls when he first found out that she was a drug addict: "Christ, I'd never dreamed before that any women but whores took dope!" (818). He associates his mother as a kind of whore. Sleeping with whores is a kind of punishment against her, a desire to be close to her, and an act of self-defilement. This debasement reaches its apex in the story of Fat Violet, who "weighs a ton," according to Edmund. Jamie concludes his account of the night's escapade with a comic epiphany: "By applying my natural God-given talents in their proper sphere, I shall attain the pinnacle of success! I'll be the lover of the fat woman in Barnum and Bailey's circus!" (817). The grotesque humor of the image and the joke masks the pain which drove Jamie to Mamie Burns' house in the first place.

Like Mary's sexuality, Tyrone's miserliness also remains divided within his character. "It was at home I first learned the value of a dollar and the fear of the poorhouse," (806) he claims. Just as Mary learned about "respectability" from her family home, Tyrone, learned a lesson too well from his own life experiences. The very first story in the play, an anecdote about the tenant farmer Shaughnessy and the millionaire Harker, reveals Tyrone's split character through eliciting his reactions to the story that Edmund tells.[9] Certainly, the story does much to start the play in a light tone and to establish family atmosphere (it's one of the only exchanges in which all four characters are present). Indeed, this scene bookends one end of the play against Mary's entrance at the other end. The story tells how the underdog poor man, the Irishman Shaughnessy, gets the best of his millionaire neighbor through the use of his wits. It is a very funny story and while Tyrone holds initial hostility against his tenant, he begrudges him respect as the story unfolds and even has to suppress a laugh at the thought of the poor man defeating the rich man. Ultimately, though, he stops laughing and becomes angry when he thinks that he himself might land in a lawsuit as a result of the squabble. The described scene lays out who Tyrone was (a poor Irishman) and who he would like to become (a rich American). His sentiments lie with the Irishman, but he can't ultimately defend him. Tyrone cannot reconcile and integrate the two sides of himself and even thinks that his two sons are laughing and plotting against him by telling the story. What begins as a tale about pride bonding all of the Tyrones ends up in another argument with belligerent feelings and divided self-consciousness.

As a result of Mary's inability to reconcile all aspects of her identity, she pulls away from the family and retreats into the spare bedroom. Repeated use of the word "spare" connotes several meanings. Is it spare in the sense that it is an arid room, or an extra room, or spare in the sense that there is nothing extraneous in it? Similar, perhaps, to a room Mary stayed in at the convent as a girl. It is clearly spare as a non-sexualized space. She moves into the spare room when she starts up with morphine again. In the preceding night to the play's actions, she moves from her husband's bed to the one in the spare room. She complains of the foghorn, but jokes about her husband's snoring as a foghorn—the presence of him next to her makes her nervous. In the second act, Cathleen tells Edmund that Mary was "lying down in the spare room with her eyes wide open" (744). She has begun to move away from the family, away from her responsibilities as wife to James and mother to Edmund and Jamie. She moves back in time in search of innocence, which again has a physical as well as spiritual sense. Speaking of the fog in Act 3, Mary remarks: "It hides you from the world and the world from you. You feel that everything has changed, and nothing is what it seemed to be. No one can find or touch you any more" (773). She's talking about the effect of the drugs as well; she has cut herself loose from the family and drifts away from physical touch, away from the three men in her life.

The fog returns at the end of the play to shroud characters from themselves and each other. At the start of Act 3, evening, the fog "is like a white curtain drawn down outside the windows" (772). The characters cannot see what they're looking for. Mary asks about her glasses throughout the action. In Act 3, after recollecting the prettiness of her wedding dress, she says: "Where is it now, I wonder? I used to take it out from time to time when I was lonely, but it always made me cry, so finally a long while ago—I wonder where I hid it?" (785). She enters the final scene with this same wedding dress, but she passes beyond the dress to her other preoccupation—her girlhood innocence. "I'm going to be a nun—that is, if I can only find—What is it I'm looking for? I know it's something I lost" (825). Her religious faith is lost, and she won't be able to find it in the Tyrone living room. She, like the rest of the family, is lost in the fog, stumbling into the furniture and family members, unable to find her way. As always, Tyrone mirrors his wife's condition with almost identical words. After telling his life story to Edmund and talking about how much money he made while he wasted his talent on a crowd-pleaser, he ends bitterly: "What the hell was it I wanted to buy, I wonder, that was worth—Well, no matter. It's a late day for regrets" (810). He cannot remember or even make sense of his actions even in the past tense. His actions remain a mystery to him. He goes on, though, to talk of Edwin Booth's praise for him and the fact that he kept a written copy of it: "I kept it in my wallet for years. I used to read it every once in a while until finally it made me feel so bad I didn't want to face it any more. Where is it now, I wonder? Somewhere in this house. I remember I put it away carefully—" (811). Edmund makes the parallel construction of this story with Mary's explicit: [*with a wry ironical sadness*] "It might be in an old trunk in the attic, along with Mama's wedding dress" (811). Things long ago, memories, packed up in old trunks, tucked away in attics, cannot easily be remembered and reconstituted.

Edmund returns in the fourth act after walking home in the fog and the images of that experience echo Mary's earlier desire to find a place beyond human touch, of peace and solitude: "The fog was where I wanted to be. Halfway down the path you can't see this house. You'd never know it was here. Or any of the other places down the avenue. I couldn't see but a few feet ahead. I didn't meet a soul. Everything looked and sounded unreal. Nothing was what it is. That's what I wanted—to be alone with myself in another world where truth is untrue and life can hide from itself" (795–796).

Edmund seeks transcendence in the fog. Later in the act, he speaks of other such moments that have happened to him, all connected to his journeys at sea: "The peace, the end of the quest, the last harbor, the joy of belonging to a fulfillment beyond men's lousy, pitiful, greedy fears and hopes and dreams! … Like a saint's vision of beatitude. Like the veil of things as they seem drawn back by an unseen hand. For a second you see—and seeing the secret, are the secret. For a second there is meaning! Then the hand lets the veil fall and you are alone, lost in the fog again, and you stumble on toward nowhere, for no good reason!" (812).

Jamie, at once the most cynical and necessarily the most hopeful for Mary's recovery, finally gives up hope for the family's salvation. He offers a fitting benediction on the play's action, after Mary has entered and launched into her search for faith and the Blessed Virgin. O'Neill sets up the scene so that Mary barely notices the presence of the men in the scene, who are left to their drinks and to comment upon the action. Jamie fittingly quotes from Swinburne's *A Leave-taking*. Significantly, he cannot look at Mary. Stage directions indicate that he *"drops his hand from his face, his eyes on the table top"* (825). He recites:

> Let us go hence, go hence; she will not see.
> Sing all once more together; surely she,
> She too, remembering days and words that were,
> Will turn a little toward us, sighing; but we,
> We are hence, we are gone, as though we had not been there.
> Nay, and though all men seeing had pity on me,
> She would not see [826–827].

She would not, could not see. The past cannot be remembered, the future cannot be seen. Competing narratives in the action do not answer the mystery of the play. Mary admonishes Edmund early in the play for scoffing at his father and she explains that he grew up poor and that that accounts for his stinginess with a dollar. Edmund complains that he's heard the story of his father's poverty in Ireland and America a thousand times before. Mary tells him that he's listened but he hasn't understood. At the end of James telling Edmund essentially the same story at the end of the play, Edmund says, "I'm glad you've told me this Papa. I know you a lot better now" (810). What is it he knows remains a mystery. It is not so much that he knows his father better, but in the quiet of the early morning scene he's able to see his father in a different light than he's been able to in the past. He views him sympathetically and fondly. All the stories, the blame, the excuses, the guilt, don't add up to a total narrative that can be easily explained. What makes the play tragic is the fact that the pain cannot be dismissed nor can the characters move totally away from each other. The cyclical action returns again, and the men can only hope that Mary will come back to them again at some later time. Mary cries out to James in the second act in an attempt to ward off any future incriminations: "We've loved each other! We always will! Let's remember only that, and not try to understand what we cannot understand, or help things that cannot be helped—the things life has done to us we cannot excuse or explain" (764). The play dramatizes the inability of individuals to see themselves or others in complete totality and the failure to accept the partial vision that is the only one available as sufficient. Love endures, but it doesn't make the pain of existence any easier. In fact, love makes life more painful. Othello's final lines, from the play in which Tyrone achieved fame, makes a perfect closure. Tyrone instructs his sons that anything worth saying can be found in Shakespeare and perhaps he's right. Othello instructs his captors at the end that he "loved not wisely but too well." No better statement could adequately describe the Tyrones. The play ends with fog rolling in upon the harbor town once again, enveloping the little house, metaphoric, of course, for the state of Mary's mental condition, but also for every member of the house, in which the love they share for each other fights with hate, admiration with disgust, affection with disdain. Indeed, they are all messed up, it's nobody's fault, and they keep going in a direction that they cannot determine, always banging into each other, always hurting each other, mostly unintentionally, but unavoidably. Night brings a new day and the torments begin again as the fog rolls in once more.

Chapter 5

Tragic Vision

"Fog, fog, fog, all bloody time. You can't see vhere you vas
going, no. Only dat ole davil, sea—she knows!"
—*Chris Christopherson in* "Anna Christie"

One of the things O'Neill did when he didn't do assigned readings
his freshman year at Princeton was to read Nietzsche.[1] He discovered *Thus
Spake Zarathustra* in Benjamin Tucker's bookshop in Greenwich Village
in 1907. As late as 1927 he claimed to have reread it every year or so since
first purchasing it. Although as a mature man he did not accept all of Zarathustra's teachings, he felt that it was the most important book that he
had ever read (SL 245–246). Similarly, he also read and admired very
much Nietzsche's first book, *The Birth of Tragedy*. In 1936, O'Neill confirmed Nietzsche's influence upon him publicly through his short acceptance address for the Nobel Prize. In it, he accorded debt to Strindberg
and Nietzsche. Speaking of the former, O'Neill wrote: "For me, he remains,
as Nietzsche remains, in his sphere, the master, still to this day more modern than any of us, still our leader" (Gelb 814). The basis for O'Neill's
tragic vision is profoundly Nietzschean.

For Nietzsche, life remains unfathomable and his dominant image
to portray the world is an abyss into which one cannot see due to its immense
size and depth. Reason and intellect fail to shine light into the abyss. *The
Birth of Tragedy* vilifies Socrates as a logical thinker who cannot adequately
explain existence through reason: "...there is, to be sure, a profound *illusion* that first saw the light of the world in the person of Socrates: the
unshakable faith that thought, using the thread of causality, can penetrate
the deepest abysses of being, and that thought is capable not only of knowing being but even of *correcting* it. This sublime metaphysical illusion

accompanies science as an instinct and leads science again and again to its limits at which it must turn into *art—which is really the aim of this mechanism*" (95–96). Aesthetic Socratism is the desire to make everything clear and understandable. In Nietzsche's scheme, rational thought represents an unreachable ideal. Art is the means by which humanity copes with the harshness and hardness and essential unreasonableness of existence. Nietzsche's analysis of Greek civilization refuted the idea of the Happy Greeks basking in a superior cultural life. His re-evaluation figured Greek tragedy as the means to make sense and give form to a world that remained essentially out of view and beyond interpretation. Myth attempts to make sense of the world. Tragic insight, according to Nietzsche, occurs at precisely the moment of recognition that science or knowledge fails to explain the mysteries of existence and that the horrors of the unexplained abyss still loom in view. Art protects against the fall into that imposing abyss of ignorance (*Birth* 97–98). Socrates' reliance upon knowledge as virtue murdered the grandeur of Aeschylean tragedy. Nietzsche insists that reason fails to explain existence: the more you know about reality, the more you realize how frightful it really is. Leonard Chabrowe observes in *Ritual and Pathos* that "The tragic myth on the stage revealed suffering as the underlying reality of existence, enabling the audience to experience and accept it as such. In a metaphysical sense suffering was justified as an aesthetic phenomenon" (7). Suffering results from both the inability to see and as a reaction from seeing too well. Dionysus, in whose praise Nietzsche writes *The Birth of Tragedy* is also the god of wine. Not only is tragedy a means to cope with an unexplainable universe, but wine is drink to make suffering more palatable as well.

Suffering as the context from which tragedy emerges leads to the individual's ultimate failure or death. Nietzsche views this struggle as spiritually uplifting. Speaking of the Overman in the fourth part of *Zarathustra*, Nietzsche explains: "The higher its type, the more rarely a thing succeeds. You higher men here, have you not all failed?" (*Portable Nietzsche* 404). The higher type aspires to achieve more than the lower type, and aspiration dooms the higher type to ultimate failure. Death, of course, is the universal fate that separates humanity from the immortal gods. Aspiration and ambition and drive for distinction separate and individuate human endeavor such that it isolates the one from the many and assures an often violent, premature failure. Zarathustra admonishes his followers not to despair about failure, but to rejoice in its liberating possibilities: "You higher men, the worst about you is that all of you have not learned to dance as one must dance—dancing away over yourselves! What does it matter that you are failures? How much is still possible! So *learn* to laugh away over yourselves! Lift up your hearts, you good dancers, high, higher! And do not forget good laughter. This crown of him who laughs, this rose-wreath crown: to you, my brothers, I throw this crown. Laughter I have pronounced holy; you higher men, *learn* to laugh!" (*Portable Nietzsche* 407–408).

Only through the will of higher types pushing the boundaries of what is humanly possible is any notion of progress possible. Laughter disregards death as the ultimate failure and celebrates the life force running through all humanity. Denial of human limitation (death) creates possibilities for future accomplishments. Nietzsche denies humanity a fixed nature; it is always in the state of becoming. If existence is unknowable through science, if empirical clarity remains out of sight, then the desire to impose a world view upon things is entirely creative. Nietzsche's will to power is such a creative power, a power that creates illusion and creates meaning (Habermas 95). The Overman refers to a strong individual unwilling to follow the common herd, who impresses an individual mark upon the world. The parables of Zarathustra define humanity in a struggle to merge with the life force in a continual process of becoming that has no final destination: "Man is something that shall be overcome" (*Portable Nietzsche* 124) serves as mantra to introduce the concept of the Overman who must struggle to transcend human limitations: "Man is a rope, tied between beast and overman—a rope over an abyss. A dangerous across, a dangerous on-the-way, a dangerous looking-back, a dangerous shuddering and stopping. What is great in man is that he is a bridge and not an end" (*Portable Nietzsche* 126–127). Outlines of Nietzschean Overmen may be seen in the title characters of *The Emperor Jones* and *The Hairy Ape* as well as Con Melody in *A Touch of the Poet* and even Edmund in *Long Day's Journey Into Night*. In each of these plays, characters experience frustration with their inability to impose their visions of the world upon surrounding events in the plays.

Tension between individuation, epitomized by the excellence of the higher types or the Overman, and the life force, eternal recurrence, in which current all living things run confluently, stages the dramatic contest according to Nietzsche. Death of the individual leads to the end of individuation that motivates the celebration of Dionysus. Nietzsche articulates the mystery doctrine of tragedy in *The Birth of Tragedy* as "the fundamental knowledge of the oneness of everything existent, the conception of individuation as the primal cause of evil, and of art as the joyous hope that the spell of individuation may be broken in augury of a restored oneness" (74). The fate of the tragic hero inspires communal suffering which gives shape to dramatic structure. Individuality must suffer and die in order for the community to survive and prosper and achieve an identification of oneness. If individuation rests on one side of the continuum of dramatic struggle, eternal recurrence is, on the other, an assertion that maintains: "Must not whatever *can* happen have happened, have been done, have passed by before?" (*Portable Nietzsche* 270). To merge with the life force requires abdication of the individuating qualities that led to pursuit of the life force in the first place.

This continual battle between the one and the many inextricably links Nietzsche and O'Neill, according to Gerhard Hoffman: "The notion of eternal recurrence serves as a bridge between individuation and oneness, the oppositional basis of Nietzsche's and O'Neill's concepts of tragedy" (199). Nietzsche's philosophy inspires O'Neill's recurring theme of belonging. In *The Hairy Ape*, O'Neill's final stage direction, after Yank's death, reads that the protagonist "at last belongs" (CP2 163). This belonging figures visually as a return to an already established pattern. In the first scene of that play, on board ship in the stoker's furnace, O'Neill describes the environment as a kind of steel cage in which the stokers hunker like filthy apes shoveling coal into the mighty furnaces. In the last scene, Yank takes the place of the gorilla at the zoo, who slams the door on the cage leaving Yank alone to die. The final direction, then, is not without irony. The way in which the ends of plays repeat the beginnings and form a pattern that implies repetition is the visual representation of eternal recurrence.[2] In *Mourning Becomes Electra*, O'Neill describes the physical similarities of parents and children to the extent that Lavinia becomes her mother and Orin becomes his father. Directors can emphasize this transformation further by repeating gestural patterns and blocking later scenes in ways which recall the same images from earlier in the play. Likewise, in *Strange Interlude*, a director might stress the similarity of Nina's father, who only appears in the first act, to Charles Marsden, her surrogate father, in whose arms Nina rests at the final curtain. O'Neill points out the physical similarities of Sara Melody to her father in *A Touch of the Poet*. This is a sign for the director to stage the end of the play in such a way that Sara will continue her father's fight against the Harfords well past his death. In *The Iceman Cometh*, the director must balance Larry Slade, the one character profoundly changed by the action, with the rest of the gang at Harry's saloon, who joyfully return to happy drunkenness as they did at the beginning, on the other side of the stage. A final interpretation of this play hangs in the relationship between the one and the many. The director must ask: How much has changed? How much remains the same?

Visibility, itself, is the source of conflict in O'Neill's plays. Nietzsche's abyss becomes O'Neill's fog. While fog actually appears in only seven O'Neill plays, it remains the most visible expression of O'Neill's tragic vision and seems to appear in all of the plays.[3] Stumbling in the fog receives its most eloquent description in *Long Day's Journey Into Night*. At the beginning of the third act, Mary praises the fog's cloaking genius: "It hides you from the world and the world from you. You feel that everything has changed, and nothing is what it seemed to be. No one can find or touch you any more" (CP3 773). Later, in the final act, Edmund returns home late at night and affirms his need for the fog: "The fog was where I wanted to be. Halfway down the path you can't see this house. You'd never know it was here. Or any of the other places down the avenue. I couldn't see but a few feet ahead. I didn't meet a soul. Everything looked and sounded unreal. Nothing was what it is. That's what I wanted—to be alone with myself in another world where truth is untrue and life can hide from itself" (795–796). Despite the final reconciliation of the two lovers in *"Anna Christie,"* the end creates an unsettling effect at the end of the play when Anna's father looks out over the water into the night: "Fog, fog, fog, all bloody time. You can't see vhere you vas going, no. Only dat ole davil, sea—she knows!" (CP1 1027). These curtain lines echo Mat's resolution to leave things up to the will of God. The sea functions as fate, buoying its passengers along, but the thick fog prevents them from seeing where they're going. Anxiety and foreboding for what may come in the future fuels doubt and creates the sense of impending tragedy.

Even in the plays in which fog does not appear, however, the retreat from reality to illusion persists as a dominant theme, and the visual image of fog receives metaphorical treatment. Alcohol, for example, produces a haze through which characters act in many of the plays. In all of O'Neill's late plays, including *A Touch of the Poet*, especially *The Iceman Cometh*, *Long Day's Journey Into Night*, and *A Moon for the Misbegotten*, drinking plays a formidable role. The presence of a bottle on stage and the effects of alcohol form significant motifs in each play and relate in a direct sense to the need to forget as well as the inability to do so. The bums who inhabit Harry Hope's saloon drink in order to keep their pipe dreams alive. Conversely, James Tyrone, Jr., drinks in order to numb the guilt for which he can't forgive himself or forget in *A Moon for the Misbegotten*. Similarly, all the male characters in *Long Day's Journey Into Night* imbibe in order to get drunk and block the pain of present circumstances with Mary. In all cases, they drink in order to survive. Characters don't drink socially in O'Neill's plays. They drink prodigious amounts of liquor in order to get drunk and distort their perceptions of the way things are. In *"Anna Christie,"* Mat Burke embarks on a three day's drunk to drown the memory of Anna's confessed life as a prostitute. Melody drinks throughout *A Touch of the Poet*, a visible sign of his pain and discomfort about playing an ill-fitting role. An alcoholic fog within the head of any of these characters is as dense as any fog that surrounds them.

Tragic vision is the Dionysian nightmare of night and fog, confusion and doubt. O'Neill's characters grope and flail and stumble in the dark, afraid to turn on the light, or having done so, they fear to confront what appears before them. The inability to see, or to gain visual proof of what one sees, creates a context for tragic events. In *Desire Under the Elms*, for example, tragedy arises at the moment when Eben cannot see Abbie's love for him and demands proof of it. Orin's guilt and fears of abandonment fan his incestuous desire for Lavinia in *Mourning Becomes Electra*: "How else can I be sure you won't leave me? ... Damn you, don't you see I must find some certainty some way or go mad?" (CP2 1041). The desire to see clearly, to obtain visual proof, requires strong actions in both plays (e.g., infanticide; incest) which lend themselves directly to melodramatic expression. Extended treatments of both of the above plays conclude this essay in an attempt to show how each drama embodies melodramatic aspects but how the action ultimately subverts them.

At the opposite end of tragic experience, far apart from Nietzschean concepts of the dark abyss, boundless aspiration, and eternal recurrence, melodramatic expression relies upon extreme gestures, high contrast and fixed endings to reinforce its reassuring message of visual clarity. It represents an idealized world, a wished-for fantasy of easy distinctions between right and wrong, good and evil, high and low. This is the dream world of Nietzsche's Apollonian vision. By way of example, Augustin Daly's *Under the Gaslight* (1867) offers a study in melodramatic visual expression which, above all else, attempts to be easily read.

The tableau in the production poster (see illustration, page 170) catches the action at its most intense and most gruesome and balances three elements. Although Daly did not invent the train scene, he perfected it by tying a helpless victim to the tracks in front of an onrushing locomotive. The locomotive, with an inhuman headlight shining down upon the writhing one-armed Civil War veteran Snorkey, bears down relentlessly along the tracks. On the left, Laura, the heroine, bursts from the shed, arms akimbo, as if to extend protective wings over the innocent prey tied to the tracks. The onrushing locomotive and plucky heroine buttress the image of the innocent and helpless victim. The tracks, destiny, cut diagonally from bottom left to top right. Snorkey's figure forms a diagonal in the opposite direction, and the female figure above him extends the diagonal. The intersection of two lines, then, almost the center of the

Part of David Belasco's turn-of-the-century production poster for Augustin Daly's *Under the Gaslight*. Emphasis upon action, suspense, grand gestures, and the polarities of good and evil certify this image as melodramatic. Billy Rose Theatre Collection. The New York Public Library for the Performing Arts. Astor, Lenox and Tilden Foundations.

image, forms a point of maximum contrast. Light projecting from the train contrasts with the trailing veil of black smoke emanating from the stack. Bright moon and cloud banks mix the nighttime sky of light and dark across the horizon. The heroine represents angelic purity in contrast to the personified villainy of the black and menacing train. The sensation scene, as such moments were called, packages a highly theatrical scene into a suspenseful, action-packed moment. Speaking of the play in general, Daniel Gerould notes its appeal to the spectator: "The world of melodrama—with its radical polarities and colorful simplifications—is in many respects akin to the fairy tale" (19). Fairy tale is analogous in this context to the idealized world of melodrama that I described earlier. The riches to rags to riches plot of Daly's play reveals a kind of wish fulfillment on the part of the audience. Laura, poor girl, turns out, in the end, to be the aristocrat she assumed herself to be at the beginning. After sympathizing with her plight and recognizing her character as humble, hardworking and charitable, ultimately the audience discovers that she possesses those qualities because of her aristocratic birth after all, and the action of the play reinforces class distinction and values based upon birth. The drama plays out a fantasy that the audience, too, will discover someday that it descends from royal blood.

In *The Melodramatic Imagination*, Peter Brooks terms the genre a "drama of morality" and goes on to articulate the importance of visual display by calling melodrama a "dramaturgy of virtue misprized and eventually recognized. It is about virtue made visible and acknowledged, the drama of a recognition" (27). Virtue, morality, reducing the plane of action to worldly human actions, supplants the gods. Nietzsche's most famous dictum, "God is Dead," heralds a significant change in the drama. Previously, the idea and presence of god(s) gave not only meaning to the drama, but provided a structure for histrionic display. The tripartite stage of Shakespeare with heaven above and hell below expanded the drama beyond the plane of the stage to assume cosmic proportions. To compensate for the absence of the gods, melodrama shows the reign of virtue on earth.[4] Melodrama attempts to invest the mundane world of quotidian events, the world of the novel (which also rises during this period), with theatrical, that is, visual, interest. The preoccupation of melodrama to make everything visible led to innovation in terms of the means of production. Throughout the 19th century, the scenic means of expression achieved technological brilliance and playwrights employed devices to promote visual recognition of the message of virtue. The tableau, the first or final moment of scenes and acts, when all action remained frozen, highlighted and magnified the visual code of the stage picture. Brooks again comments: "In the tableau more than in any other sign device of dramaturgy, we grasp melodrama's primordial concern to make signs clear, unambiguous, and impressive" (48).

Emphasis upon clarity and size suggests the externalization of drama. Formerly, there were the gods. Without them, only human virtue upholds a moral universe. Goodness, in melodramatic terms, requires that the interior self match the exterior presentation, requires persons not to be hypocritical but to be whom they seem to be. The dramatic possibilities of playing goodness are quite limited. Vice, not surprisingly, is fun to play. Richard III, Shakespeare's most melodramatic villain, delights an audience with duplicity and the mask of respectability and nobility which he wears over a scheming villainy. With showmanship bravura, speaking directly to the audience of evil intent, then turning a smiling face to the scene at hand to court favor, Richard woos Lady Anne in the first of many examples of brilliant acting. Villains in standard melodramas get similar rewards to that of playing Richard. If all acting is duplicitous, such roles double that dimension. It plays better to be bad than good. In *Under the Gaslight*, Laura's essential character never changes, only the conditions forced upon her change from immense wealth to dire poverty and back again. The scene around her changes but it is essential to the values and meanings of the play that her character remains the same. Such immutability creates the dramatic message and allows her virtue to be recognized in the bold relief of contrasting economic and social positions. Changes within Byke, the villain of the play, motivated not, in the end, by evil per se, but by economic necessity, ultimately portray his actions sympathetically. The course of events reveal a past for him that does not reconcile itself to his overt actions in the play. The "inside" does not match exactly with the "outside."

Melodrama, insistent upon virtue and sympathy for a solid hero or heroine, depends almost wholly upon events rather than character development in order to sustain action. Matching inner reality with exterior presentation in melodrama accords with Robert Heilman's concept of wholeness introduced first in *Tragedy and Melodrama: Versions of Experience*, in which the conflict occurs between the subject and other outside things or characters. Focus upon events thus externalizes the drama. Since all elements are visible on the surface, the need to explore "depth" does not arise. "...In this structure," Heilman maintains, "man is pitted against a force outside of himself—a specific enemy, a hostile group, a social force, a natural event, an accident or coincidence" (79). Dividedness within the individual, on the other hand, typifies tragedy. Aspects within the individual which do not fit or match battle each other. External appearance no longer accurately measures the reality of inner feeling and belief. Such dividedness extends beyond hypocritical playing in *Richard III* between the self and others. In Heilman's sense of the tragic situation, the individual suffers from lack of self-knowledge. Fooling others, including the audience, results from primary ignorance of the self. *The Iceman, the Arsonist and the Troubled Agent: Tragedy and Melodrama on the Modern Stage* (1973) reveals Heilman's further elaborations on his concepts of melodramatic wholeness and tragic dividedness. Tragedy concerns, according to him, ordering of the self. Ambiguity hallmarks the genre. Melodrama, concerned with external events, orders the world as a result of single-mindedness (wholeness) on the part of the characters.

Emphasis upon events or plot in melodrama at the expense of character makes choice largely irrelevant (choice is a traditional dramatic means of revealing character). The size of imposing outside events (e.g., a chugging locomotive) turns virtuous characters into victims of circumstance, in which they must react to that which befalls them. Laura reveals her virtue by chopping her way through the shed in order to rescue Snorkey at the last possible moment. Snorkey exclaims in excited relief as the curtain comes down: "And these are the women who ain't to have a vote!" (Daly 177). Daly's political message reveals Laura as exactly the character whom the audience knows her to be. Such an ending satisfies morally and appeals visually precisely because of the character's integrity. The entire stage picture reads clearly and therefore reassuringly. As Heilman says, "Melodrama is alluring; as tonic or tranquilizer, it unifies. It may be that our tendency to use the generic term disparagingly reflects an unarticulated resistance against an unacknowledged seductiveness" (*Iceman* 57). Concepts of unification and wholeness reassure hopes that all things can be made clear and understandable. Melodrama is the drama of light. The "unacknowledged seductiveness" of melodrama refers to the appeal of a world in which things are what they seem to be and require no further interpretation. Not only does melodrama represent, in Eric Bentley's terms, "the quintessence of drama" (216), with its strong visual appeal and high contrasts between opposites, but it represents an aspirational goal for living as well. Wholeness, as an image, represents a kind of ideal.

Tragedy begins with recognition of the impossibility or falseness of achieving complete wholeness. The "unarticulated resistance" about which Heilman speaks is the gnawing doubt that things are ever all that they appear to be, fueled by the awareness of an individual's innate dividedness. Ambiguity in tragic dividedness results from doubt and inability to see the self clearly and measure how all things fit: "that we are not all of a piece, that we can make wrong choices, that we are vulnerable to the consequences of any choice" (Heilman, *Iceman* 34). The subject of dividedness becomes the essence of O'Neill's dramatic exploration. Summarizing O'Neill's dramatic achievements in 1964, John Gassner addressed his principal preoccupation: "Like his exemplary modern playwright, Strindberg, O'Neill made division itself the subject of his plays and expressed it formally in his work with expressionistic devices, masks, and interior monologues" (168). The problem for O'Neill becomes using the devices above as an external means to show the tensions of dividedness within the individual. He tries to make the invisible visible and give dramatic expression and theatrical (visual) impressiveness to that which cannot be seen.

Dividedness may be the subject of O'Neill's drama, but his father, actor James O'Neill (1846–1920), embodied melodramatic wholeness in the role of Edmund Dantés in *Monte Cristo.* The action presents Edmund as the victim of an evil plot and traces his plight from haggard prisoner at the Château d'If to aristocratic swordsman, the Count of Monte Cristo. As with Laura in *Under the Gaslight,* Dantés changes costume but never wavers in character. He is a victim of outside forces. Ultimately, his triumph, monetary rewards, an aristocratic title, and reunion with his family, owes to his fixed and virtuous character. Upon his imminent escape from prison, he states the course of future narrative action in succinct fashion: "I must live. I have the wicked to punish and the good to reward. Your will be done!" (Fechter 237). Moments later, rising up from the sea, he proclaims his new wealth and promise in life: "The world is mine!" Thereafter, he dispatches his enemies, Villefort, Fernand, and Danglars, and records the notches: "One"; "Two"; "Three." The action ends with reconciliation and recognition between Edmund and his lover, Mercédès, and his son Albert. The riches to rags to even greater riches tale spans over 18 years and ultimately rewards good and punishes evil. Each scene ends with a powerful moment designed to carry the action along into the next scene (e.g., arrest of Edmund in act one; his decision to escape in act two; his rise from the sea in the following scene; the death of Villefort (One!) at end of act three; the revelation that Albert is his son in act four; the deaths of Fernand and Danglars (Two! Three!) followed by Mercédès' revelation to Albert that Edmund is his father, the curtain line of the play. Virtue recognized and rewarded, evil vanquished, emphasis upon action, impressive gestures, maximum contrast (rich/poor, good/evil) constitute elements which make this romantic tale a model of melodramatic action.

Certainly, James O'Neill's many performances in *Monte Cristo* influenced his son's playwriting career. The exact nature of that influence is difficult to pinpoint, however. On the one hand, it's easy to see the son's career as a revolt against the father and all of his experimentation as a dramatist as an attempt to vanquish the father. On the other hand, growing up in the theatre as he did, O'Neill knew first-hand how to grab hold of an audience and manipulate its feelings. The Gelb biographers note O'Neill's theatrical heritage as an important part of his talent as a playwright: "The intimate knowledge of stagecraft and actorcraft he had acquired from association with his father's companies made him acutely conscious of everything from the proper placing of doors to the timing of costume changes" (568). They quote O'Neill as telling a friend: "I know more about a trap door than any son of a bitch in the theatre" (568). John Henry Raleigh argues that the popular stage tradition in the 19th century influenced O'Neill's career just as much as his allegiance to Strindberg and Nietzsche. In "Eugene O'Neill and the Escape from the Château d'If," he theorizes that O'Neill's bad plays owe allegiance to *Monte Cristo*, whereas the late masterpieces represent an escape, analogous to Edmund Dantés' escape from prison after eighteen years. He cites the revenge plots in O'Neill, emphasis upon history, and "hammer-strokes" that end scenes as evidence of a melodramatic inheritance by the son from the father.

Identifying melodramatic elements in O'Neill's early plays is akin to shooting ducks in a barrel. You can't miss. Collectively, these plays sympathetically portray struggles of the underclass, the battles of youth against age, and the artist against the bourgeois world. Beyond subject matter, however, mechanical plotting and obvious staging mark them as inferior plays. Robert Brustein maintains in *The Theatre of Revolt* that in his early plays O'Neill "is incapable of *thinking like a dramatist*, communicating his ideas through significant action" (333). In other words, he can only present his ideas by overtly expressing them in terms of stage directions, character expression, and plotting of the play. At the end of *The Web* (1913), to cite a crass example, at the moment Rose realizes that all is hopeless, the stage directions read: "She seems to be aware of something in the room which none of the others can see—perhaps the personification of the ironic life force that has crushed her" (CP1 27–28). As the policemen lead her away out of her squalid hotel room, she stops to perform a big gesture and says: "Gawd! Gawd! Why d'yuh hate me so?" (28). At this point in his career, O'Neill's "ironic life force" exists only in the heavy handed pen of the playwright. Full of ideas, O'Neill remains unable to express them in such a way that shows a scene without commenting upon it. In *Recklessness* (1913), imitative of Strindberg's *Miss Julie*, a jealous maid spies on the two lovers with "vindictive hatred shining in her black eyes" (CP1 56). In *Thirst* (1913) stage directions state that "The sun glares down from straight overhead like a great angry eye of God" (CP1 31). Similarly, in *Fog* (1914), "A menacing silence, like the genius of the fog, broods over everything" (97). The primary action in these early efforts reduces to a neat fable. John Brown chooses between an artistic career or a hardware store with his hometown wife in *Bread and Butter* (1914). He makes the wrong choice and ends up killing himself. Emphasis upon action in all of these plays, exterior action between people and events, defines the experience as melodramatic. Equally defining, too, is the degree to which the plot neatly resolves the action. Endings in each play drive home a thematic point.

O'Neill registered his first production with *Bound East for Cardiff* in 1916, and a comparison of later companion pieces, *In the Zone* (1917) and *The Moon of the Caribbees* (1917), best shows the difference between the old and new drama. These plays of the sea, along with *The Long Voyage Home* (1917), represent the finest work of O'Neill's early career, and embody the full range of melodramatic plotting and tragic experience. O'Neill much preferred *The Moon of the Caribbees* to *In the Zone*, and felt that the commercial success of the latter play proved that "something is rotten in Denmark." In his letter to critic Barrett Clark, O'Neill considers

"*In the Zone* a conventional construction of the theatre as it is, and *The Moon* an attempt to achieve a higher plane of bigger, finer values" (SL 87). The weaker play is all plot and suspense as the ship's crew suspects that their mate is a spy carrying a bomb. The suspense breaks with a reversal in the plot which brings sympathy for the outcast and an end to the action. There is a single focus in this play, whereas in *The Moon of the Caribbees* the action highlights the entire ship's crew set against the distant background of a tropical island. This play is rich in atmosphere of a crew at liberty: drinking and dancing, and the scenic split between land and sea, bridged by the arrival of native women with rum and promises of more intimate gifts. Instead of a strong narrative, the action depicts the sailors' environment and shows the economy of the ship without judgment. For example, ship commanders condone drinking and fraternization with native women as a necessary reward for the crew. The exchange of money shows how sailors never actually retain money once they get to shore. Brutal and appalling behavior ends in a knife fight. One sailor, Smitty, isolated on another part of the stage, stands in contrast to the loud debauchery of his comrades. His moral judgment of others, and his self-pitying lament of his own relations with women, spins a melodrama of its own, but this isolated story complements and contradicts the rest of the play and the simplicity and beauty of the scenic landscape which hovers over everything adds silence to the overall sound of the play. Smitty's whining, habitual behavior, repeats a maudlin exercise of self-pity dwarfed by the mute beauty of the poetic landscape.

While the two plays above provide good examples of what may be called old and new drama, they represent tendencies which are rarely mutually exclusive. O'Neill does not dispense with one form and move to another. Even in *The Moon of the Caribbees*, its greater value as a play over *In the Zone* lies in the way that melodramatic presence, the character of Smitty, wars with competing elements, the other members of the crew, women, the landscape. O'Neill's later (and better) plays do not simply eliminate melodrama. Instead, as in the above example, melodrama meets its match in charged theatrical images which blunt, if not contradict, melodrama's persuasive visual power. Theatre historian Thomas Postlewait revises the notion of a smooth transition from 19th century melodrama to 20th century realism in a recent anthologized article: "Melodrama may be defined as a theatrical form of polarized excesses, articulating and resolving primary conflicts, but this does not mean that its relation to realism is equally polarized. Most of the time we can find melodramatic elements in realistic drama and realistic elements in melodramatic plays" (54–55). Historically, O'Neill figures as the leader who closes the breach

The Provincetown Players produced *The Moon of the Caribbees* at the Province-town Playhouse, New York City, in 1918. The "finer values" to which O'Neill ascribes this play include the triumph of atmosphere over plot, ensemble over star acting, and multiple points of view and playing areas as opposed to a single focus. The play of light and shadow in this photograph connotes a brooding uncertainty very different from the black and white polarities of *Under the Gaslight*. Museum of the City of New York. Gift of Mr. Louis Shaeffer.

between melodrama and realism, the old and the new. Postlewait's insistence upon melodramatic and realistic (or tragic) commingling demonstrates how the relationship between the two creates dramatic tension. Kurt Eisen's thesis in *The Inner Strength of Opposites* contends that O'Neill does not transcend melodrama so much as revel in and reveal melodrama's "inescapable power" (29). The dramatic power of melodrama proves to be half of O'Neill's dramatic formula for success, complemented by devices from the novel which add sophistication to dramatic form. Novelistic desire to complicate competes with the melodramatic urge to simplify (11). Revision of Eisen's argument for my present purposes simply formulates this conflict in visual terms. The desire for clarity (melodrama) fights with the simultaneous desire for ambiguity (tragedy). In keeping with Nietzschean perspectivism, it's not a question of either melodramatic or tragic aspects in O'Neill. Limiting an argument between tragedy and melodrama to visual terms avoids a hierarchical value statement about the two genres. Instead, tragedy and melodrama exist as radical tendencies on a dramatic continuum. Clarity and striking contrast and conflict represent the essence of the melodramatic impulse. Attraction to this side of the continuum causes a reaction and retreat toward mysterious, dark, unseen forces which characterize tragedy. The paradox of seeing in O'Neill's vision is that clarity brings recognition that all certainties are false and thus stirs new impulses to retreat further into fog. In *Struggle, Defeat or Rebirth: Eugene O'Neill's Vision of Humanity*, Thierry Dubost asserts that "...all genuine self-knowledge brings with it an overturning of certitudes and, when this process begins, the seeds of turmoil are sown in the minds of those who can no longer ignore the nightmarish vision before their eyes" (155). The urge for clarity, toward melodrama, halts with the realization that clarified vision, all things visible in bright particularity, represents an ideal that cannot sustain life.

Over the past twelve years, Michael Manheim has written a series of articles detailing the transcendence of melodrama in O'Neill's best plays: *A Touch of the Poet*, *A Moon for the Misbegotten*, *The Iceman Cometh*, *Long Day's Journey Into Night*.[5] Even these plays partake heavily in melodramatic elements. The first two adhere to a melodramatic structure in plot. Melody's revenge against the Harfords for his daughter's honor (and his own) is an old melodramatic plot. Similarly, Hogan, another father, plots to catch Jim Tyrone in bed with his daughter in *A Moon for the Misbegotten*, a contrivance which reeks of melodrama. Manheim convincingly argues that the latter play "goes beyond the gentle mocking of melodrama in *A Touch of the Poet* to an actual displacement of it as the play's basis of construction" ("O'Neill's Transcendence of Melodrama in *A Touch of the Poet* and *A Moon for the Misbegotten*" 153). The beautiful dawn at the end of the play, a sign of Josie's abiding love, transcends Tyrone's reference to the theatrical David Belasco dawn, associated with melodrama, which is representative of Tyrone's cynicism and self-loathing (157). *Long Day's Journey Into Night* and *The Iceman Cometh* borrow less from the intrigues of melodrama than they do from the melodramatic urge to simplify versions of experience into "good" and "evil" designations. Yet the competing melodramatic stories which the bums and the Tyrones trade in their respective plays often contradict each other and never reconcile into one verifiable narrative. In *The Iceman Cometh*, O'Neill weaves disparate melodramatic pipe dreams and sad histories into a fabric that appears much more complex than any one individual story. Melodramatic versions of the past never explain the complexity of the present. Manheim designates *Long Day's Journey Into Night* as a tragedy precisely because "it does not reduce existence to 'good' and 'evil' alternatives" ("The Transcendence of Melodrama in *Long Day's Journey Into Night*" 33). All the Tyrones are at once culpable and innocent of what befalls them. There are no heroes and no villains. Both of these dramas exploit contradiction as opposed to certainty. As Manheim states provocatively and elegantly: "What appears to exist may indeed exist, yet something quite the opposite may also exist" (36). Arriving at his estimation of these plays as tragedies, Manheim elevates contradiction as a defining element: "...it is not suffering and stamina alone, important as these qualities are in tragedy, which contribute to the greatness of a work but also the range of often contradictory feelings underlying the characters' statements and actions" ("The Stature of *Long Day's Journey Into Night* 206). The contradictions that Manheim sees in dramatic structure are analogous to the dividedness that Heilman sees in the tragic character.

It is not so much that characters cannot face the truth and require illusions to live. The more difficult question is which truth to face? Or, whose truth? The pipe dream is a method to simplify experience and block out recognition of the vagaries of existence. The binary opposition of truth/illusion is analogous to the polarization of good and evil in melodrama. They both represent extreme and simplified versions of experience, and because of that, they are much desired. Just so, *The Iceman Cometh* and *Long Day's Journey Into Night* strive and fail to achieve the comfort that melodramatic experience affords. In O'Neill's best plays the illusion of this *or* that masks a more complex choice of this *and* that ... and that ... and that! Robert and Andrew Mayo make poor choices in *Beyond the Horizon* and suffer the consequences of their single decisions. Similarly, O'Neill splits his protagonists in *The Great God Brown*. *Strange Interlude*, while in itself not a strong play, shows more clearly the vision of "this *and* that. Nina Leeds ages and burns out over the course of the action in pursuit of her lost Gordon. Each encounter with a man is only a piece of her ideal man and she continually tries to add them up and make a whole. *A Touch of the Poet* reveals two aspects of Con Melody's identity, both of which are authentic, if opposite, and this revelation hints at the possibility that much more remains hidden. The action of *Hughie* portrays "Erie" Smith as a loser masquerading as a winner, but also shows him as generous, lonely, desperate, mournful, sentimental, callous, humorous, and crass. In short, the complexity of Smith makes facile designations such as "winner" and "loser" irrelevant and meaningless. The contradictions in these plays, to go along with Manheim's contentions, create a tragic context as a result of lack of certitude. The melodramatic urge toward simplification, toward clarity, toward a unified and uniform vision opposes the tragic fog of uncertainty and doubt. Such oppositions create resonance in the plays. To the extent that these oppositions fully develop, the better plays achieve better balance as they complicate and enrich vision.

   Desire Under the Elms (1924) and *Mourning Becomes Electra* (1931) are the two best plays from O'Neill's "middle period" because they both exemplify the melodramatic urge toward simplicity yet gain strength from an inability to fulfill such a vision. Travis Bogard hails *Desire Under the Elms* (1924) as the first important American tragedy (200), and it marks O'Neill's first attempt to borrow audaciously from the Greeks. According to the Gelbs, "The opportunity for such artistic plagiarism was so obvious that no other American dramatist had dared to try it" (540). The plot owes debt to Euripides' *The Hippolytus* and *Medea* as well as Sophocles' *Oedipus*. The sexual attraction between step-mother and step-son drives the play, an infanticide clinches a tragic ending, and the Oedipal love of a son for his dead mother creates the setting for the action. Twentieth century psychology and Freud in particular influence an understanding, if not the actual writing, of the play. O'Neill made the statement to a friend, perhaps consciously, that the entire play came to him in a dream. Indeed, critics analyze *Desire Under the Elms* as his unconscious autobiographical drama (as opposed to the conscious one, *Long Day's Journey Into Night*). In such studies, O'Neill's mourning over the recent deaths of his mother and brother and all the dead O'Neills inspires the artistic work.

   On the surface of the text, though, much melodramatic evidence defies an estimation of the play as inherently great. The action appears simple, even simple-minded at times. The first confrontation between the step-mother, Abbie, and her step-son, Eben (Part II, scene 1), offers a glimpse of the whole in the part. Stage directions read as follows: "They stare into each other's eyes, his held by hers in spite of himself, hers glowingly possessive. Their physical attraction becomes a palpable force quivering in the hot air" (CP2 341). Abbie addresses Eben: "Ye been fightin' yer nature ever since the day I come—tryin' t' tell yerself I hain't purty t'ye. [*She laughs a low humid laugh without taking her eyes from his. A pause— her body squirms desirously—she murmurs languorously.*] Hain't the sun strong an' hot? Ye kin feel it burnin' into the earth—Nature—makin' thin's grow— bigger 'n' bigger—burnin' inside ye—makin' ye want t' grow—into somethin' else—till ye're jined with it—an' it's your'n—but it owns ye, too—an' makes ye grow bigger—like a tree—like them elums—[*She laughs again*

softly, holding his eyes. He takes a step toward her, compelled against his will.]
Nature'll beat ye, Eben. Ye might's well own up t' it fust 's last" (CP2
341–342).

Abbie's speech encapsulates (or, is a synopsis of) the action of the
entire play. Desire for ownership by possessors who will be dispossessed
by passion and sensuality and the power and fecundity of nature over-
powers the senses. I frequently ask students in class to discuss what this
play is about and watch them avert their eyes and squirm (certainly not
desirously) in their seats. They would be much more willing and comfortable to talk about meaning in *Hamlet* than to embrace the primitive
sexuality and covetousness in this play. Joel Pfister claims that the reliance
upon psychosexual dynamics masks the significance of history, class and
economic divisions. According to him, "Members of the Greenwich Village Theatre audience who felt owned by corporations or more generally
dominated by the production of life under capitalism now see that they
are possessed by something more elemental, a force originating in their
very own depths—desire" (91). This argument suggests that the strength
of desire blinds an audience (and the characters within the play) to other
possible interpretations. Desire, then, signifies a potent melodramatic
device that simplifies a vision of the way things are.

Frank and open desire for love and for land creates melodramatic
space which drives the action. Prior to possession, the viewer must behold
the object of desire. Indeed, the first line of the play finds Eben staring
at the new dawn and proclaiming it "Purty," echoed immediately thereafter by his brother Simeon. Abbie exclaims her first lines as she walks
into her new house: "It's purty—purty! I can't b'lieve it's r'ally mine" (335).
In Part II, the following dialogue reveals Cabot's boundless desire as well
as Abbie's contempt for him:

> CABOT: Purty, hain't it?
>
> ABBIE: [*crossly*] I don't see nothin' purty.
>
> CABOT: The sky. Feels like a wa'm field up thar.
>
> ABBIE: [*sarcastically*] Air yew aimin' to' buy up over the farm too? [*she snickers contemptuously.*]
>
> CABOT: [*strangely*] I'd like t' own my place up thar [344].

Anything the eye can see falls prey to desire. Cabot associates the sky with
the fields that he plows and cultivates. "Purty" also refers to sexual as
opposed to acquisitive desire. Abbie's speech above begins by invoking
"purty" in terms of Eben's attraction to her. The tie between sexual desire

and desire for the land is made fast in the figure of Minnie, a woman from a nearby town, who, over the years, has slept with all the Cabots: Ephraim, Peter and Simeon, and finally, Eben. Just as Cabot refers to the "purty" sky as a warm field, Eben projects Min as a nurturing, earth figure offering warmth and protection: "she's like t'night, she's soft 'n' warm, her eyes kin wink like a star, her mouth's wa'm, her arms're wa'm, she smells like a wa'm plowed field, she's purty ... Ay-eh! By God A'mighty she's purty, an' I don't give a damn how many sins she's sinned afore mine or who she's sinned 'em with, my sin's as purty as any one on 'em!" (326). Visual appeal sparks all subsequent and consuming desire in the play.

The excessiveness and ubiquity of desire creates a melodramatic experience in the sense that this elemental force lacks any nuance or subtlety. Since desire requires a direction away from the self, since it is directed at other things (avarice) or characters (sexual desire), that sort of action lends itself to melodramatic experience because conflict remains external and can be shown easily. Part of the discomfort that students have talking about this play has to do with the frankness of the emotions and the histrionic display of the characters. After seeing the scene between Abbie and Eben above, there may very well be little left to say. The high visibility of melodramatic expression, equated here with verbal expression as well as physical gesture, renders commentary redundant and useless. Unlike psychological realism, with its explosive subtext but often mumbled text, this scene hides nothing. Everything, every emotion is exposed and made vulnerable (subject to view). The plot of *Desire Under the Elms*, centering upon the desire for a farm but also a romantic triangle between an older man, his young wife, and his son, sets up a scenario for a rich melodrama of great dramatic tumult. The seduction of Eben by Abbie and their passionate relationship is exciting because their desire for one another is completely visible to the audience.

Despite over-the-top clarity in the above speech by Abbie and throughout the dominant love plot, three subsequent scenes feature the presence of something unseen that counters melodramatic visibility and hints at something more complex in the making. In Part II, scene 2, set in the interior of the two upstairs bedrooms of the Cabot New England farmhouse, Cabot unburdens his soul to Abbie in one bedroom, while Eben sits on his bed in the opposite room, seemingly aware of Abbie's presence on the other side of the intervening wall. Instead of listening to Cabot, Abbie focuses entirely upon Eben, though, of course, she cannot see him, but only "feels" his presence. The richness of the scene derives from the frustrated desire of the two future lovers to see each other and the audience's frustrated desire at seeing them apart. Simultaneously, Cabot's monologue reveals his loneliness and pathos, made more painful by virtue of the fact that Abbie does not listen to him. At the end of his speech, Cabot realizes that he's wasted his words and threatens Abbie that she must produce a male heir for him and the farm, a message upon which the action turns. Ironically, Abbie assures him that he'll have a son "out o' me" and promises that she has "second sight." Cabot immediately leaves the house, clearing the room for the two young lovers, and heads down to his barn to sleep with the animals. An unseen presence spooks him in his own house: "It's cold in this house. It's oneasy. They's thin's pokin' about in the dark—in the corners" (350). What he senses but cannot see is his rival, his own son, in the other room. Cabot's inability to see and subsequent departure from the scene paves the way for a dramatic and fateful collision between Eben and Abbie. On the one hand, this scene features the palpable intensity of feeling, desire, between Abbie and Eben. The wall that separates them adds tension in the scene but gives the scene a marvelously melodramatic texture. Another component, Cabot, layers another dimension to the scene, and one that belongs to a tragic sensibility.

The presence of something unseen acknowledges this counter force within the scene. Tragic vision is that which remains inscrutable. In Part I, scene 2, Eben rages to his two half-brothers, Simeon and Peter, about how his maw worked tirelessly for Cabot's behalf. He concludes: "[*fiercely*] An' fur thanks he killed her!" Simeon responds: "[*after a pause*] No one never kills nobody. It's allus somethin'. That's the murderer" (322). Simeon's thoughtful statement anticipates the rest of the action in the play. While Eben insists that Cabot is to blame for his maw's death, Simeon provides a more enlightened and detached view. Eben sees the family history as a kind of melodrama and a simple vision of those events comforts him. Ironically, Simeon, described as a kind of herd animal slumping to its evening meal, offers the first insight toward a more complicated version of the past. It's a more complicated vision simply because it refuses to assign blame. Something is the murderer, not even a someone. Who is really to blame remains a mystery. A few lines later, Simeon confronts his younger sibling: "What've ye got held agin us, Eben? Year arter year it's skulked in yer eye—somethin'" (323). Later, Cabot refers to his uneasiness in his own bedroom as "something" poking around in the dark. Unseen things play as pivotal a role in the play as the "purty" things. If desire spawns a melodrama of high visibility, "something" hallmarks the tragic vision of ambiguity and darkness. The strength of the play attests to the coexistence of dual visions. Without desire, the play would have no drive to see more, to possess all. But without "something" to elude the

Desire Under the Elms (1924), designed by Robert Edmond Jones. The division of the house into cubicles and the presence of both interior and exterior space allows the audience to see several "scenes" simultaneously, but it also constrains the characters' ability to see their surroundings. In the above photograph, the three main characters all seem to search for "something" that they cannot see. Photograph by Vandamm Studio. Billy Rose Theatre Collection. The New York Public Library for the Performing Arts. Astor, Lenox and Tilden Foundations.

eye, to remain in shadow, the action could not sustain itself as a full-length drama. The combination of clarity and doubt offers a provocative collision of perspectives.

A second scene which pits dark over light takes place in the parlor room downstairs: "A grim, repressed room like a tomb in which the family has been interred alive" (352). Not coincidentally, Abbie and Eben attempt to consummate their sexual union in a space formerly inhabited by Eben's maw. This time, Abbie feels the presence of something unseen: "When I fust come in—in the dark—they seemed somethin' here" (353). The parlor was Eben's mother's room, and the scene plays out as an exorcism for the dead. Abbie claims to hear Maw's voice and tells Eben what he must do: "She's tellin' ye t' love me. She knows I love ye an' I'll be good t' ye. Can't ye feel it? Don't ye know? She's tellin' ye t' love me, Eben!" (354). Finally, Eben justifies embracing Abbie, his father's new wife, by concocting a simplified version of experience. He tells Abbie that "I see it! I sees why. It's her vengeance on him [Cabot]—so's she kin rest quiet in her grave!" (355). This is one of the most bizarre scenes in all of dramatic literature. It begins in the dark parlor room with Eben calling upon her, hat in hand, and Abbie sitting properly on the sofa. It ends with a "bruising kiss" during which it is clear that Abbie functions as mother, lover, and friend. The room itself is where Maw was laid out after she died, and no one has used the room since her death. Her voice in the room, heard only by Abbie and Eben, but not the audience, directs him to sleep with Abbie as part of a revenge plot, the essence of melodrama, a wholly external action. Possessive desire focuses the action between characters (e.g., Eben and Abbie; Eben and Cabot) and between characters and things (e.g., the farm). Accordingly, this scene colonizes another space. Formerly dark and foreboding and off limits, Eben and Abbie possess the parlor as well as each other. At dawn, as Eben leaves the house, Abbie flings the window open and the shutters back to let dawn's light into this reclaimed territory, a gesture designed to register the triumph of desire, of melodrama, over something unseen and unexplainable.

Part III resumes a year later, after the birth of Abbie's son, and reveals the fact that "something" has not yet disappeared. In the kitchen, a chorus of townspeople gather to drink and dance in celebration of the new Cabot. Ephraim rules the party and proves himself a better and stronger dancer than anyone else there. He alone does not realize that all of the gathered guests can see what he cannot: that Eben is the father of Abbie's son. Eben sits in one of the bedrooms upstairs. In the other bedroom, a candle lights a cradle. The raucous party and fiddle music in the downstairs kitchen contrast with the dark solitude of the upstairs scene. Abbie leaves the party to join Eben and together they peer into the cradle. "Ain't he purty?" Abbie remarks, but Eben cannot shake his dark mood and resentment about having to call what's his, Cabot's. The end of the scene reverses the visual image with which the scene began. Abbie, Eben and the baby form a community upstairs, while Cabot leaves the house and stands outside alone by the gate to the farmhouse. He laments: "Even the music can't drive it out—somethin'. Ye kin feel it droppin' off the elums, climbin' up the roof, sneakin' down the chimney, pokin' in the corners! They's no peace in houses, they's no rest livin' with folks. Somethin's always livin' with ye" (363). Simultaneous staging in the scene visualizes the perspectives with which characters interpret events. The stage picture juxtaposes the blindness and anxiety of Ephraim with the insight and calm of Eben and Abbie, but the provisional peace that the two lovers enjoy only lasts momentarily in the bedroom before the major problem arises.

Desire dispossesses the lovers in the play as it transforms into doubt. The problem confronting Eben and Abbie is not different than the one of change and visual proof facing Anna and Mat Burke in *"Anna Christie."* Like Anna, Abbie claims to have changed in the course of the drama. Originally, she arrived at the Cabot household in search of a home of her own and she initially bragged to Eben that the farm would be all hers someday. Her past, too, like Anna's, has been hardship at the hands of men. These reported yet unseen factors make her motives behind the initial seduction of Eben difficult to determine accurately. In addition, Cabot's demand that she bear him a son overdetermines the plot. Eben accuses her of using him to get what she wants: secure ownership of the farm by virtue of an heir who will eventually disinherit Eben completely. The argument in Part III arises because Eben refuses to believe that Abbie loves him. He can only accept a single and simplified motive on Abbie's part. His melodramatic vision cannot see the contradictions in the situation and in his relationship with Abbie. With Eben, it's all or nothing. Like Anna, Abbie must somehow demonstrate her change in feelings and motivations from those of lust and desire and manipulation to love. Looking at his son, Eben says: "I wish he never was born! I wish he'd die this minit! I wish I'd never sot eyes on him! It's him—yew havin' him—a-purpose t' steal—that's changed everythin'!" (367). Just as Mat Burke demanded that Anna swear her love on his mother's rosary, Eben Cabot looks for a sign of love from Abbie. From this encounter, Abbie discovers the one action that will prove her love to Eben. She commits infanticide and removes the barrier between them. This murderous act of high visibility signifies a move beyond desire to prove allegiance and love to Eben.

Eben, in turn, makes a dramatic gesture to trump Abbie's infanticide. Initially, he recoils and runs to town to summon the sheriff, a move that beckons to complete the melodramatic action. After doing so, however, he regrets this decision and returns to take responsibility for the crime along with Abbie. The final recognition and reversal occurs offstage when Eben realizes his love for Abbie. Such admission finally brings tenderness and vulnerability into the play. He realizes that he motivated her actions and that she performed the deed on account of her love for him. Eben acknowledges his role as an accomplice in the murder: "An' it is true—way down. I did help ye—somehow" (375). He recognizes that although he didn't tell Abbie to kill the baby, he created the situation which made the murder possible and encouraged her to do it without ever saying so or even realizing the stakes of the matter. If Abbie's love could be shown only through the murder of the child, Eben's love can match Abbie's only by his accepting partnership and responsibility for the crime. This bonding which acknowledges their love publicly, and even wins the grudging admiration of Cabot ("Purty good—fur yew!" [377]), comes at the expense of their freedom and perhaps even their lives.

The main plot of *Desire Under the Elms*, the adulterous, near incestuous romance between Abbie and Eben ends with irony disguised as tragedy. The couple accepts love (and death) only when they give up desire. This paradigm is consistent with *Marco Millions* and *Mourning Becomes Electra* and especially with the theme of the elaborate cycle plays. In O'Neill's universe, however, the most tragic characters are those who remain unyielding. Ephraim Cabot, not Eben, the third member of the triangle, emerges as the central character of a tragedy about perseverance in the face of not being able to see. Cabot's outstanding physical characteristic, in addition to his strength, is the fact that he is nearly blind. Despite nearsightedness, however, he stands resolute in his convictions, including steadfast belief in an Old Testament God of retribution. Oppositions of hard and soft dominate the play. Stage directions show the tension in Cabot's face: "as hard as if it were hewn out of a boulder, yet there is a weakness in it, a petty pride in its own narrow strength" (334). Rocks on the farm form images of hardness on the New England landscape. Not by accident, the play is set in 1850, the year following the start of the California gold rush. In response to the life of hard stones on the farm, Simeon and Peter, Cabot's two sons by his first wife, rush off in Part I to prospect and pan for soft money in the Far West. They describe Eben both like his Maw, who was soft, and as the "spittin' image of the old man." Ultimately, Eben chooses to follow the "soft" path of his maw and make himself vulnerable to love. Only Cabot remains unbowed at play's end.

Cabot, however, does undergo shifts throughout the action of the play. Prior to his first entrance in Part I, his sons describe him as hard and unflinching. Indeed, that is the picture of him when he first appears with his young bride at the end of the first part. In the middle section of the play, though, his demeanor changes from hard to soft. This is due to the influence of Abbie upon him. Stage directions record: "The hard, grim expression of his face has changed. He seems in some queer way softened, mellowed. His eyes have taken on a strange, incongruous dreamy quality" (343). Like Ezra Mannon, the general in *Mourning Becomes Electra*, Cabot attempts to unburden his lonesome thoughts to his wife. He reveals his softer side as he talks about the past to Abbie in their bedroom. His fate is not Mannon's, though, but Lavinia's. Both of them share similar physical characteristics and undergo similar transformations throughout the action in their respective plays. Both of them vacillate between "hard" and "soft" over the course of the play. In his long monologue to an uncomprehending Abbie in Part II, Cabot admits that he once forsook his farm to pursue easy planting in the West where "Ye'd on'y to plow an' sow an' then set an' smoke yer pipe an' watch thin's grow" (349). He returned to New England quickly thereafter with the realization that "God's hard, not easy!" (349). Near the end of the play, Cabot decides to give up the farm once again and go after the easy money in California looking for gold, following the same path as his two sons, Simeon and Peter. He reverses himself quickly thereafter and elects to stick it out on the farm: "It's a-goin' t' be lonesomer now than ever it war afore—an' I'm gittin' old, Lord—ripe on the bough…. [*then stiffening*] Waal—what d'ye want? God's lonesome, hain't He? God's hard an' lonesome!" (377).

As much as Abbie or Eben, Cabot experiences heartfelt pain with the loss of the baby boy. Stage directions again reveal cracks in his stony exterior: "[*He lapses into crushed silence—then with a strange emotion.*] He's dead, sart'n. I felt his heart. Pore little critter! [*He blinks back one tear, wiping his sleeve across his nose.*]" (373). Yet, no sign remains of this tender "softness" by the end of the play. He exits, "his shoulders squared, his face stony, and stalks grimly toward the barn" (377). His demeanor at the end mirrors that of the beginning. Both Cabot and Lavinia refuse to submit to their soft and vulnerable sides. Rigidity gives these two unique characters the status of tragic heroes in O'Neill's plays. The focus turns to Cabot at the end as he leaves to round up his stock again. Only Cabot returns to his workaday world. The action ends at sunrise, just as it began. Again, Eben invokes the sky as "Purty," but the sheriff adds the last ironic line surveying the surroundings: "It's a jim-dandy farm, no denyin'. Wished I owned it!" (378). Cabot does own it and continues to work on it. Desire transforms into love among the young couple, but desire to possess perseveres in the aging and unyielding Cabot who endures to toil alone. His two former wives both died, and Abbie, his third, cuckolds him. He tried to be tender with Abbie, but she did not hear him or love him. Despite his 76 years, he can physically dominate younger men, his own sons, in the fields. He sleeps with his animals in the barn for company. His desire endures and even achieves new resolve at the end. He owns the property and devotes his life to plowing the fields, building fences, and making things grow out of rocks. The action of the play demonstrates the price of ownership and the futility of desire. For all his work, for his endurance, for his strength, Cabot remains alone at the end of the play. He has no wife, no sons, and no heir to the farm. When he decided to leave the farm, he determined to burn it to the ground so that no one could have any part of it in the future. Cabot figures to end his legacy in almost as dramatic a fashion as Lavinia snuffs out the Mannons in that play. Cabot's contempt for Eben's softness is similar, too, to Lavinia's relationship to her guilt-ridden brother. Both Cabot and Lavinia place themselves beyond the judgment of any other character. Both of them are completely alone and answer individually to their god. The defiance of their actions, the one against the many, inspires awesome respect. Cabot continues to plow stony fields and endure the hardships of New England farming. Lavinia lives completely alone. Their isolation is a kind of willful blindness. At the end no one can get to them. They are completely invulnerable and appease their gods through suffering and perseverance.

Mourning Becomes Electra borrows its plot from Greek tragedy far more extensively than *Desire Under the Elms*, yet old fashioned melodrama prevails in much of the play. Based on *The Oresteia*, though without resorting to gods, this psychological drama details the Mannon family and portrays most strongly their sexual appetites. A study of the repressed puritan New England spirit, Oedipal/Electra complexes orchestrate the pattern of events that play out in the trilogy: *The Homecoming*; *The Hunted*; *The Haunted*. However much O'Neill thought that he was exploring the interior and hidden psyches of his characters, external events, the stuff of melodrama, offer even more compelling viewing. Orin, the Orestes figure, chronicles a family history in the last play to absolve his guilt but also to secure his fate with his sister. He records a three generational Mannon melodrama that begins with grandfather Abe, descends to father Ezra, and ends with the children, Lavinia and Orin. It tells the story of two brothers, Abe and David, in love with the family nurse, Maria Brantôme. When David married her, Abe cast him from the family home. Unable to support a family, including a son, Adam, David committed suicide.

Years later, Adam returned from the sea to find his mother on her deathbed and vowed vengeance against the Mannons. Ezra, Abe's son, married a woman who looked very much like Marie, Christine. But on his wedding night, his sexual advances repulsed Christine and strained the marriage ever after. They had two children, Lavinia and Orin. The girl looked like her mother but loved only the father. The boy took after the father but doted on his mother. After years of frustration, Christine took a lover, who turned out to be the same Adam Brantôme, now Adam Brant, who was the son of David Mannon. Together they murdered Ezra. Lavinia suspected her of the crime, however, and she and Orin watched the two lovers meet secretly aboard Adam's ship in Boston only a couple of days after Ezra's murder. After Christine departed, they murdered Brant and returned home to confront Christine with the news. Devastated, Christine committed suicide. After the deaths of both parents, Lavinia and Orin traveled to the South Sea Islands where Lavinia transformed sexually and physically into the image of her mother. Orin, conversely suffered horribly from guilt as he began to resemble his father and all the male Mannons. The full story of the House of Mannon thus reveals a narrative chock full of betrayal, sex and murder.

A veil of secrecy and scent of scandal surrounds the estate and entices onlookers from the periphery to speculate about the nature of events and things that take place indoors and out of sight. Watching becomes the real subject of the play as the watched participate in a melodrama that thrills observers. O'Neill employs a chorus of townspeople who appear at the start of each play to comment on the action and to recapitulate events. Stage directions describe the townspeople as "a chorus representing the town come to look and listen and spy on the rich and exclusive Mannons" (CP2 894). They assemble to watch the Mannons and they direct the audience's focus to see the play through their eyes. The citizen chorus in Greek drama often tempers the hubris of the tragic hero and serves in a moderating and advisory capacity. Certainly, it fulfilled a narrative function as well. O'Neill's modern chorus executes this latter purpose and ably supplies expository material and fills in gaps of knowledge and events between each play of the trilogy. Unlike the Greek chorus, though, they remain completely detached from the main action, quite afraid of the proud and domineering Mannons. They function best as observers of the action and as a kind of audience, they visually reinforce the subject of spectatorship in the play. In *The Homecoming*, the visitors are eager to get a look at Christine Mannon, about whom one describes as "handsome," then adds: "There's somethin' queer lookin' about her face" (896). Once again, as in *Desire Under the Elms*, "something" appears to block a melodramatic interpretation of experience. The secret mask that Christine seems to wear, along with all the Mannons, prevents anyone from knowing them and solving the mystery of their lives. The inscrutable look of the Mannons fuels further desire to see on the part of the townspeople, and by extension, the audience as well. They continue a few lines later to dig at the melodramatic roots of the story: "Tell Minnie about old Abe Mannon's brother David marryin' that French Canuck nurse girl he'd got into trouble" (897). *The Hunted*, the second play in the trilogy, takes up with the townspeople's speculation about the nature and timing of Ezra's death. The preceding play ended with Christine poisoning her husband. Here, on the outside of events, a group gathers to discuss possible interpretations. They misread Christine's agitated emotional state for grief and Lavinia's calm for coldness. Taking the daughter's defense, a woman declares: "She feels it as much as her mother. Only she's too Mannon to let anyone see what she feels" (952). The Mannons frustrate the desire to see clearly into their affairs. The chorus only appears in exterior scenes in front of the house, but they desire to see what transpires inside the house. The action alternates between public and private spaces. Ironically, General Mannon, who has survived the bloodiest war in American history, returns home to die ignominiously in his own bedroom. In the absence of a clear interpretation of what happened, the chorus offers various readings to explain Ezra's death: the hand of fate; angina; love. About the last, the doctor pulls one friend aside to explain hastily: "I haven't asked Christine Mannon any embarrassing questions, but I have a strong suspicion it was love killed Ezra! ... Leastways, love made angina kill him, if you take my meaning" (954). Given what has transpired, these interpretations border on the comic as they illustrate the difference between the inside and the outside.

Comic aspects of frustrated desire to see inside the Mannon house reach their zenith in the final play, *The Haunted*. After Adam Brant's murder and Christine's suicide, Lavinia and Orin lock up the house and leave for a long voyage. The empty house beckons the nosy townspeople to go inside and to see if the place is truly haunted as it is reported. Seth Beckwith, the Mannon's gardener, and essentially the chorus leader, has, in fact, planted the story that there are ghosts in the house in order to frighten onlookers away and stop the rumors surfacing about the Mannons. Indeed, his plan works well as one of the drunken townsfolk emerges from the house screaming that he "seed Ezra's ghost dressed like a judge comin' through the wall" (1011). Seth's own misgivings about the place, however, undercut the comic response to a bunch of drunks acting on a dare. Publicly, he gets a laugh from the foolish spectacle: "That was Ezra's picture hangin' on the wall, not a ghost, ye durned idjut!" (1012). Privately, though, entering the dark house frightens him as well: "But there is such a thing as evil spirit. An' I've felt it, goin' in there daytimes to see to things—like somethin' rottin' in the walls!" (1013). Hazel Niles, Orin's friend and neighbor, backs up Seth's claim: "There is something queer about this house" (1013). That "something" remains a mystery in the play. It suggests a force that cannot be seen or defined, one that always escapes ocular perception. That which cannot receive direct representation, a presence yet not a thing, represents the arena in which tragic experience blossoms, characterized by darkness and ambiguity. For all the explanations of events in the play, for all the family history, events do not add up to form a coherent reason for things in the play. More importantly, the presence of "something" always prevents a ready and simplified vision of events to define experience completely. The undefined presence of something counters the heavy handed melodrama of the story in which so much is clearly stated and easily visible to the eye.

While the townspeople observe the Mannons from the outside, the nuclear family spies upon each other as well. Lavinia discovered her mother's affair with Adam Brant by following her to his apartment in New York. In the confrontation that follows, Christine attacks her daughter as a rival in love: "I know you, Vinnie! I've watched you ever since you were little, trying to do exactly what you're doing now! You've tried to become the wife of your father and the mother of Orin! You've always schemed to steal my place!" (919). Christine glimpses desire and covetousness in her daughter, signs that remain only prescient for the moment. Lavinia retaliates by warning her mother that she will be watching her and that she must give up her lover or face punishment. After Ezra's death, Lavinia hounds her mother even more closely than before. Christine tries to put an end to it but to no avail: "Why do you keep following me everywhere—and stare at me like that?" (960). Lavinia searches for the sure signs of guilt upon her mother. She found the pill box which contained the poison but she looks to gather direct proof. In order to prove her mother a murderer she plants the pill box on her father's corpse and gathers her brother to watch her mother's reaction when she sees it. Later, she and Orin follow her mother to Boston to spy on her with her lover in the scene that precipitates murder and alters the direction of all future events.

As one who is watched, Christine functions in the play as a melodramatic heroine. O'Neill's initial stage directions give her distinctive and vibrant physical characteristics: "Christine Mannon is a tall striking-looking woman of forty but she appears younger. She has a fine, voluptuous figure and she moves with a flowing animal grace. She wears a green satin dress, smartly cut and expensive, which brings out the peculiar color of her thick curly hair, partly a copper brown, partly a bronze gold, each shade distinct and yet blending with the other. Her face is unusual, handsome rather than beautiful" (896). Color for Christine contrasts her with all the other members of the Mannon family. In the first half of the play, Christine maintains all of the focus in the play. Not only is she the observed character, but she responds by performing in a series of highly melodramatic scenes. She persuades her lover, Brant, to aid her in the murder of her husband by taunting his manhood and arousing his jealousy and physical desire for her. Later, after having poisoned her husband, Ezra, she faints and sprawls across the floor. When she sees the box of poison placed upon Ezra's laid out corpse awaiting burial, "she starts back with a stifled scream and stares at it with guilty fear" (982). Melodramatic foreboding fills her parting words to her lover aboard his clipper ship: "Good-bye my lover! I must go! I must! Oh! I feel so strange—so sad—as if I'd never see you again! Oh, Adam, tell me you don't regret! Tell me we're going to be happy! I can't bear this horrible feeling of despair!" (993). When her children thrust the newspaper account of Adam's death in her face, Christine "looks at the paper with fascinated horror. Then she lets it slip through her fingers, sinks down on the lowest step and begins to moan to herself, wringing her hands together in stricken anguish" (1000). In all of the above examples, Christine plays visually expansive, excessively theatrical scenes which satisfy an audience's desire to see events clearly and without contradiction.

Lavinia, on the other hand, balances the melodramatic picture with her reserve and deliberate non-theatricality. She does have moments of emotional explosiveness, when she confronts Brant and especially when she loses her father at the end of the first play: "Father! Don't leave me alone! Come back to me! Tell me what to do!" (947). On the whole, though, Lavinia suppresses emotional display. She is "twenty-three but looks considerably older. Tall like her mother, her body is thin, flat-breasted and angular, and its unattractiveness is accentuated by her plain black dress. Her movements are stiff and she carries herself with a wooden, square-shouldered, military bearing" (897). After being the observer in the first two parts of the play, Lavinia takes her mother's place as the observed in the last play of the trilogy. Lavinia transforms into Christine and even wears the color green. In action, too, Lavinia pursues her sexual desires for the first time. The action picks up a year later and commences with the return of Lavinia and Orin to New England after having sailed abroad, including a stop at one of the South Sea Islands. Orin hints at the possibility that Lavinia engaged in a sexual affair with an islander there. In any event, once she's back, Lavinia overtly pursues her old suitor and neighbor, Peter Niles. Just as Lavinia turns into Christine, Orin turns into Ezra and he regards Vinnie's sexual awakening with jealousy. Orin's transformation offsets the robust change evident in his sister. He now plays the role which she played formerly. Upon his entrance, stage directions read: "He carries himself woodenly erect now like a soldier. His movements and attitude have the statue-like quality that was so marked in his father. ... He has grown dreadfully thin and his black suit hangs loosely on his body. His haggard swarthy face is set in a blank lifeless expression" (1014–1015). Lavinia takes her turn as the vibrant melodramatic heroine, and Orin plays the part of her dark nemesis. While Lavinia looks forward to the future and prospects of happiness, Orin drags his memory through the past. He locks himself within his father's dark study day after day to record the litany of Mannon crimes. Gazing at a portrait of his father, Orin's first speech in Act 2 of the last play begins: "The truth, the whole truth and nothing but the truth! Is that what you're demanding, Father? Are you sure you want the whole truth? What will the neighbors say if the whole truth is ever known?" (1026). Written in secret, Orin's history threatens to expose the Mannon family to public shame. The prospect of townspeople finally satisfying their curiosity contrasts starkly with the image of Orin slaving over his manuscript in the dark. Lavinia encourages him to seek fresh air, but he responds, harshly: "I hate the daylight. It's like an accusing eye! No, we've renounced the day, in which normal people live—or rather it has renounced us. Perpetual night—darkness of death in life—that's the fitting habitat for guilt!" (1027). Orin attempts, within this dark tomb, to discover the cause of blood guilt in the Mannon family and to gain insight concerning the future. He confesses the extent of his narrative project: "I've tried to trace to its secret hiding place in the Mannon past the evil destiny behind our lives! I thought if I could see it clearly in the past I might be able to foretell what fate is in store for us...." (1029). Orin's history details a family melodrama which brings the past to light and seeks to explain everything. He promises to publish the manuscript if his sister ever attempts to leave him and marry Peter. "I'll be watching you!" (1032), he reminds her, in a threatening voice that recalls the same tone Lavinia formerly leveled against her mother. Orin's emotional instability increases as the fear of abandonment and isolation escalates. After seeing Hazel with an envelope containing the manuscript, Lavinia promises Orin that she will do anything if he will only retrieve it. Striking that bargain, Orin takes the final step to signal a transformation in his relationship with Lavinia from brother to lover. Incest recreates the parental past of Ezra and Christine. At this point in the play, too, it provides melodramatic spectacle and indicates Orin's descent into madness due to overwhelming guilt: "How else can I be sure you won't leave me? You would never dare leave me—then! You would feel as guilty then as I do! You would be as damned as I am!" (1041). Lavinia rebukes him; Orin, horrified with what he has become, dreadful to himself in his own eyes, commits suicide. Like Eben, Orin's guilt leads him to seek punishment, leaving Lavinia as the only survivor.

Orin's prurient story threatens to disgrace the Mannon name, but Lavinia's family pride motivates her to secure Orin's manuscript and never allow anyone outside to read it. She suppresses publication of this melodrama in which she plays a starring role. Immediately after the report of Orin's death, Lavinia spies one of the Mannon portraits staring accusingly at her and she attacks the image: "Why do you look at me like that? Wasn't it the only way to keep your secret, too? But I'm through with you forever now, do you hear? I'm Mother's daughter—not one of you! I'll live in spite of you!" (1043–1044). Stage directions indicate that she squares her shoulders, military fashion, before marching from the room to end the act. The return to military posture, father-style, marks another transformation in the play and a return to how things were in the beginning. Striving to follow in her mother's path, the persona of father begins to win her back. The gesture of squaring her shoulders also echoes the bearing of Cabot in *Desire Under the Elms* and suggests that bucking up under adversity will define Lavinia as a tragic character. Just as Cabot emerges as the most tragic character in the earlier play, Lavinia's will to survive and struggle warrants admiration in this play. An alliance between Cabot and Vinnie highlights values of resistance, determination, and will. Mocking the family portraits prior to his final exit, Orin exclaims: "You'll find Lavinia Mannon harder to break than me! You'll have to haunt and hound her for a lifetime!" (1041). Indeed, Lavinia's hardness suggests that she deserves a far more creative and enduring punishment than death affords.

Lavinia completes her regressive transformation in the last act of the final play. "Her body, dressed in deep mourning, again appears flat-chested and thin. The Mannon mask-semblance of her face appears intensified now. It is deeply lined, haggard with sleeplessness and strain, congealed into a stony emotionless expression. Her lips are bloodless, drawn taut in a grim line" (1046). Watching her brace up after yet another funeral (Orin's), Seth, the leader of the watch, admires Vinnie's return to old form: "They'll never git her to show nothin'" (1045). Lavinia shows no traces of Christine's theatricality, and hides all expression. She refuses to play a melodrama from which signs could easily be read by an audience. She reverts to the colorless performer of the opening act. Her refusal to engage in melodramatic theatrics reaches a crisis point when Hazel, the personification of neighborly virtue, confronts her regarding her intentions of marriage to her brother Peter. Not known for a crackling wit, O'Neill provides a moment of comic insight once Hazel leaves with Lavinia's bitter comment: "I hope there is a hell for the good somewhere!" (1049). Lavinia condemns the genre in which she refuses to play a part any longer. It's a very funny line which acknowledges the clashing strain of genres at the end of a long trilogy dominated by melodrama.

Melodrama's last gasp rises with Lavinia's final clutch at happiness. She embraces Peter and asks him to marry her immediately, but in her desperate attempt to save herself and grab onto Peter, she calls him "Adam" and the motivating secret of the play is out. Like Hickey in *The Iceman Cometh*, whose own words take him by surprise and reveal more about his motives than he knows, so, too, Lavinia reveals that her revenge against her mother was not so much out of love, honor and devotion to father, but because she loved Adam, too, and jealously resented his love for her mother. Having given voice to this in the final scene, Lavinia realizes that she can never escape punishment for being a Mannon and she drives Peter away, under the false pretext that she had been the fancy woman of a native islander while she was away. She does this in order to silence the rumors concerning her family. The punishment that she designs for herself, self-interment, is a final act of concealment: "I'll never go out or see anyone! I'll have the shutters nailed closed so no sunlight can ever get in. I'll live alone with the dead, and keep their secrets, and let them hound me, until the curse is paid out and the last Mannon is let die!" (1053). A play that is about seeing and watching, ends with the negation of spectacle. Closing the household from view, at last, resists the visual demand of melodrama to see everything.

A theatrical event is obviously staged for people to see, but Lavinia and Cabot reveal O'Neill's ambivalence about histrionic display. Their revolt against the medium in which they play a part inspires respect. Despite O'Neill's copious stage directions and his desire to make every aspect of his plays visible and apparent, Cabot and Lavinia, two of his favorite characters, prove mysterious and elusive. Their staunch silence and military bearing possess theatricality, but in the end, they remain inscrutable. Their defiance resists the desire for closure, easy answers, and happy endings. They fend off the audience's quest to invade their privacy. Tragic vision in these plays suggests that there is always more to see, that "something" always remains unseen, and that the tragic heroes will never bow to a spectator's desire to expose them. O'Neill's plays displace the covetous desire of lust, greed, and power within the action of the plays and transfer it to the watching and waiting audience. In so doing, the action implicates the audience in a consideration of boundaries between public and private space.

Conclusion:
Resonant Emotion

"Our emotions are instinctive. They are the result not only of our individual experiences but of the experiences of the whole human race, back through all the ages. They are the deep undercurrent, whereas our thoughts are often only the small individual surface reactions. Truth usually goes deep. So it reaches you through your emotions."

—Eugene O'Neill

Matthew H. Wikander's essay, "Eugene O'Neill and the Cult of Sincerity," included in *The Cambridge Companion to Eugene O'Neill*, edited by Michael Manheim, is the most recent example (1998) of a phenomenon in O'Neill criticism which has no precedent among studies of modern European dramatists such as Ibsen, Chekhov, and Strindberg. It is inconceivable that a volume on one of those three would include an article that attacked the integrity or legacy of the artist. O'Neill, however, seems to inspire dissenting opinion. Virgil Geddes wrote one of the first assaults against O'Neill, although *The Melodramadness of Eugene O'Neill* (1934) preceded O'Neill's best works. Two anthologies, *O'Neill and His Plays: Four Decades of Criticism* (Cargill et al., 1961) and *Eugene O'Neill and the American Critic* (Jordan Y. Miller, 1973) attest to the presence and persistence of negative views on America's foremost playwright. In his book, *The Making of Modern Drama*, Richard Gilman admits in the preface that he doesn't like O'Neill and proceeds to dismiss him entirely from any discussion thereafter.[1] What accounts for such hostility against O'Neill?

One only has to survey O'Neill's plays to spot vast targets for rebuke. His plays are melodramatic and overreaching; dialogue often seems inadequate and unpoetic; there are few ideas and those few are obvious; beyond the persistent themes of the desire to belong, the need for the "hopeless hope" and the pipe dream, there is little else; psychological depth revealed in plays such as *Strange Interlude* appears laughable. Even mature plays such as *Dynamo* and *Days Without End* seem adolescent matched against O'Neill's grandiose rhetoric about them.[2] O'Neill's apologists admit his many flaws but argue that his dedication and discipline as an artist overcomes them through time to write his final masterpieces "of love and forgiveness." Wikander argues that the last plays are better simply because they are better written, and that plays such as *The Iceman Cometh* and *Long Day's Journey Into Night* testify to rage rather than forgiveness (228–233). With this conclusion, Wikander puts O'Neill on the opposite end of the emotional continuum from his accustomed position. This dramatic revision, with emotion as a common denominator, exposes this conflict of interpretation as a site for further investigation.

O'Neill, himself, championed the importance of emotion, and, like Nietzsche, found it superior to rational thinking. In an early interview in *American Magazine*, he stressed the value of emotion in the theatre: "Our emotions are instinctive. They are the result not only of our individual experiences but of the experiences of the whole human race, back through all the ages. They are the deep undercurrent, whereas our thoughts are often only the small individual surface reactions. Truth usually goes deep. So it reaches you through your emotions" (Mullett 27). There are so many things "wrong" with this statement that I scarcely know where to begin a response. O'Neill seems to suggest that he is the purveyor of Truth, but more insidiously, he assumes that there is such a thing as common experience among all people, regardless of race, class, and gender. Invoking emotions at all seems suspect and a decidedly nonacademic enterprise. As a scholarly pursuit, it is difficult to substantiate and justify emotional display. I mentioned earlier an anecdote about the discomfort my students (and I) felt when talking about *Desire Under the Elms*. I don't think that such self-consciousness was a product so much of their immaturity (or mine) as it was created by the classroom environment itself. School is a place where cognitive learning occurs. O'Neill, as I've said, doesn't have much to teach on that level.

It would be difficult to like O'Neill and, say, Brecht, equally well. Not surprisingly, Eric Bentley, one of O'Neill's harshest critics, introduced Brecht to an American audience. O'Neill appeals to the sentimental emotions of an audience directly, while Brecht remains wary of them. Yet,

Brecht's drama is tailor-made for the classroom. An abundance of his theory, especially concerning the mysterious alienation effect, puts his drama in straight order. Brecht's Marxist politics, too, are at once both explicitly coherent and widely applicable to current critical theories. His insistence upon a scientific method for the theater makes him a model playwright within the university curriculum. When I teach Brecht, all the smart students raise their hands and refer to dog-eared copies of *Brecht on Theatre*. There is no such bible when we turn to O'Neill. There are no groovy politics and neat theories to hide behind. Reliance upon biography has been one convenient strategy to transfer emotion from the work to the playwright. Documenting O'Neill's life in his works roots the plays in the emotional experience of the creative artist. I've tried to shift that emotional experience back to the plays, themselves, apart from the author. Formal struggle in the work creates emotional space in the gap between desire and attainment. O'Neill asks you to "make yourself vulnerable to the material" (Quintero). The times when I've been successful leading a discussion of O'Neill have been when we, as a group, lost sight of the fact that we were in a classroom and allowed the work to penetrate our intellectual defenses. On those rare but glorious occasions we delved into, not Truth, but the truths of our emotionally shaken collective.

O'Neill's modernism attempts to dramatize inscrutable forces at work within the drama. He claimed that he was not interested in depicting interpersonal relationships but only the relationship between Man and God. O'Neill, however, was a non-believer. In a world in which God is dead, the question remains: how to present the invisible and how to name it? How to see that which cannot be seen? How to suggest the presence of something that may not even be there? As a dramatist, O'Neill bears the burden of materially showing everything. The demand to show events leads to melodrama (the desire to show and tell all) and simultaneously reacts against it. The written text circumvents the actor in an effort to resist visual spectacle; characters project masks, real and figurative, in order both reveal and conceal identity; what happens offstage, out of view, influences what happens onstage in front of an audience; what happens after the play ends, the implied action beyond the representation, establishes recurring patterns which extend meanings. In a profound sense, much more than a judgment of O'Neill's inadequacies, failure constitutes the organizing principle of his drama; it is the prevailing "structure of feeling," in the words of Raymond Williams. Success, visual clarity, brings down the barrier between the visible and invisible but ends the drama.

Recently, several excellent books on O'Neill attest to a variety of critical experience that can be gleaned from the works. Nineteen hundred eighty-eight marked the centenary of O'Neill's birth and coincided with the publication of important critical works in addition to the first complete edition of all O'Neill's plays in three volumes by the Library of America. Travis Bogard published a revised edition of *Contour in Time*, which details each play chronologically in terms of the writer's life. Bogard's analysis remains the standard to measure O'Neill criticism. He, along with Jackson R. Bryer, also published the most complete edition of O'Neill's letters, *Selected Letters of Eugene O'Neill* (Yale 1988), an indispensable volume for the O'Neill scholar and anyone interested in the American Theatre. The portrait of O'Neill that emerges catches O'Neill in all his domestic and professional contradictions which make him such a fascinating figure. Ronald Wainscott's *Staging O'Neill: The Experimental Years 1920–1934* (Yale 1988) is the first volume to study the original staging practices of all the major O'Neill productions during his lifetime with the exception of *The Iceman Cometh*. Kurt Eisen's *The Inner Strength of Opposites: O'Neill's Novelistic Drama and the Melodramatic Imagination* (Georgia 1994), anticipates my work by examining the relationship between twin impulses in O'Neill's plays. *Staging Depth: Eugene O'Neill and the Politics of Psychological Discourse* (North Carolina 1995), by Joel Pfister, critiques the social and historical roots of O'Neill's drama and ends with a brilliant re-reading of *Long Day's Journey Into Night*. Thierry Dubost adds a European perspective on O'Neill with his *Struggle, Defeat or Rebirth: Eugene O'Neill's Vision of Humanity* (McFarland 1997), which adopts a thematic approach and argues against the received opinion of O'Neill as a depressing playwright. *The Cambridge Companion to Eugene O'Neill* gathered new essays from a wide variety of current O'Neill scholars. Stephen A. Black's new psychoanalytic biography, *Eugene O'Neill: Beyond Mourning and Tragedy* (Yale 1999) promises to complement the Sheaffer and Gelb volumes. The Gelbs are completely rewriting in three volumes their landmark biography, *O'Neill*; Applause Books published the first volume, *O'Neill: Life with Monte Cristo*, in early 2000.

The same diversity found in recent academic publications is present in notable theatrical productions as well. On a weekend in New York in spring 1998, it was possible to see an uptown production of *Ah, Wilderness!* at Lincoln Center, a downtown version of *The Emperor Jones* by the Wooster Group at the Performing Garage, an Off-Broadway production of *Long Day's Journey Into Night* by the Irish Repertory Company in Chelsea, and a studio production of *Beyond the Horizon* in Mid-town. A revival of *"Anna Christie"* (1993) by the Roundabout Theatre, starring Natasha Richardson and Liam Neeson, directed by David Leveaux, helped to restore the ambiguous ending of that play. Al Pacino directed and starred in *Hughie* to tremendous accolades a couple of years later (1996) at Circle in the Square. The Wooster Group's acclaimed production of *The Hairy Ape* (1997), featuring Willem Dafoe, moved from their tiny space in SoHo to the Selwyn Theatre in midtown. Along with *The Emperor Jones*, this work explored issues of race and identity along with the group's trademark interest in technologies. Outside New York, Michael Kahn directed a brilliant production of *Mourning Becomes Electra* at the Shakespeare Theatre in Washington, D.C., in 1997. A televised version of the excellent Stratford Shakespeare Festival (Ontario) production of *Long Day's Journey Into Night* appeared on public television in 1999. The Playwrights Theatre, operating in the refurbished Provincetown Playhouse in Greenwich Village, is dedicated to producing all of O'Neill's plays during the next several years. They began in 1998 by staging, in a modest fashion, the earliest and until now unproduced works. Spring 1999 featured the return of O'Neill to Broadway with the first revival of *The Iceman Cometh* since Quintero and Robards collaborated in 1985. This production, a limited run at the Brooks Atkinson Theatre, was first produced in London where the American actor Kevin Spacey won critical acclaim as the protagonist Hickey. In early 2000, Daniel Sullivan directed Cherry Jones in *A Moon for the Misbegotten* at the Walter Kerr Theatre.

The range of emotional experiences possible within the works keeps readers and audiences coming back to O'Neill. It is not a question of rage or forgiveness in *Long Day's Journey Into Night*, but a question of rage *and* forgiveness. Engagement with form will continue to spawn new and exciting critical and theatrical interpretations of O'Neill's work. Passionate struggle with the form produces emotional experience. Despite all the difficulties in casting O'Neill's plays due to exacting physical standards set forth by the playwright, Colleen Dewhurst, one of the greatest interpreters of O'Neill's work, star of the 1973 revival of *A Moon for the Misbegotten*, said this about the real hardships and beauties in O'Neill's plays:

> I've seen O'Neill productions that were wonderful where I have sat and felt that that night, that moment in space and time in my life I was forced to assess something. He will not permit you to sit complacently and observe. He reaches out and he asks you to understand the state that we are in as human beings, always a wonderful storyteller but underneath always is a request, I always feel, a question, his need, tremendous need, tremendous crying out.... Somehow in the theatre he is able to give that cry to each one in the audience [*Eugene O'Neill: A Glory of Ghosts*].

In a good performance of an O'Neill play, characters stand stripped and naked at the end. The extreme visibility of human vulnerability always precipitates the final curtain. Emotional rawness onstage reflects what may play in the reader's or viewer's head. That confrontation produces a cathartic theatrical event of clarifying, purifying, or purging emotional experience.

Appendix I: Chronology

1888   Eugene Gladstone O'Neill born October 16 at Barrett House Hotel, N. E. corner of 43rd St. and Broadway in New York City, formerly Longacre Square, now known as Times Square. Eugene is the third son and last child born to Mary Ellen (Ella) Quinlan O'Neill (b. 1857) and actor James O'Neill (b. 1846). Older brother is James, Jr. (Jamie) (b. 1878); Edmund (1883–1885) died of measles. Eugene spends early years traveling with family on James' theatrical road tours and summering in New London, CT, at Monte Cristo Cottage, named for James' most profitable and prolific role.

1895   Enters Mount St. Vincent Academy boarding school (NYC).

1902   Enters Betts Academy (Stamford, CT).

1906   Enters Princeton University, but is dismissed after one year for poor academic standing. Reads *Thus Spoke Zarathustra*.

1907   Sees Ibsen's *Hedda Gabler* ten times with Alla Nazimova in title role.

1909   Secretly marries Kathleen Jenkins; James O'Neill disapproves and arranges for Eugene to leave from San Francisco on gold prospecting trip to Honduras.

1910   Returns to New York and takes job as assistant stage manager on James' touring production of *The White Sister*. Son Eugene, Jr., is born. Sails to Buenos Aires on *Charles Racine* and works a variety of ill-paying jobs, lives in cheap hotels, and patronizes waterfront dives.

1911   Returns to New York and lives at Jimmy-the-Priest's, a water-front flophouse on the Lower East Side. Makes transatlantic crossing and returns as able-bodied seaman. Divorces Kathleen Jenkins. Sees entire touring repertory of Abbey Players on six-week engagement in New York.

1912   Makes failed suicide attempt with overdose of Veronal (sleeping drug) at Jimmy-the-Priest's. Joins family on western vaudeville circuit and plays minor roles in abridged version of *Monte Cristo*. Returns to New London and takes job on local newspaper staff. Diagnosed with tuberculosis and enters Gaylord Farm, private sanitarium in Wallingford, CT.

1913   Released from Gaylord Farm, determines to become a playwright. Reads Strindberg and other plays, returns to New London, and begins to write one-act plays.

1914   Enrolls as special student in George Pierce Baker's English 47 playwrighting class at Harvard University.

1916   Sees production of Hauptmann's *The Weavers* six times. Visits artist community in Provincetown, Massachusetts. Amateur group produces *Bound East for Cardiff* at the Wharf Theatre. O'Neill helps to organize the group's move to New York and recommends name for space on MacDougal Street in Greenwich Village: the Playwrights' Theatre.

1918   Marries writer Agnes Boulton.

1919   Moves to Peaked Hill bar on eastern side of Cape Cod, a former Coast guard station given to the O'Neills as wedding present from his father. Boni & Liveright publishes *The Moon of the Caribbees and Six Other Plays of the Sea*. Second son, Shane Rudraighe O'Neill, is born.

1920   *Beyond the Horizon* wins Pulitzer Prize. James O'Neill dies.

1922   Ella Quinlan O'Neill dies in Los Angeles. *"Anna Christie"* wins O'Neill's second Pulitzer Prize. Buys thirty acre estate, Brook Farm, in Ridgefield, CT.

1923   Brother Jamie dies in a sanitarium as a result of alcoholism. O'Neill assumes control of Provincetown Players with critic Kenneth Macgowan and designer Robert Edmond Jones in an organization known as the Experimental Theatre, Inc.

1924   Strindberg's *The Spook Sonata* (*The Ghost Sonata*) is the premiere production of the Experimental Theatre; O'Neill writes program notes exalting the Swedish playwright.

1925 Daughter Oona is born.

1926 Buys house in Bermuda: Spithead. Spends summer in Maine and is visited by Eugene, Jr., and Carlotta Monterey, who played Mildred in the Broadway production of *The Hairy Ape*.

1928 *Marco Millions* begins association with the Theatre Guild. O'Neill awarded third Pulitzer Prize for production of *Strange Interlude*. Leaves the United States for France with Carlotta Monterey.

1929 Marries Carlotta Monterey after divorce from Agnes Boulton becomes official.

1931 Returns to United States to prepare rehearsals for *Mourning Becomes Electra*.

1932 Moves into new house at Sea Island, Georgia, named Casa Genotta (derived from "Eugene" and "Carlotta").

1934 Theatre Guild production of *Days Without End* is O'Neill's last Broadway play for 12 years.

1935 Begins work on a cycle of American history plays.

1936 Moves to Seattle, Washington. Awarded Nobel Prize for Literature. Moves to San Francisco.

1937 Moves to new home near Danville, CA: Tao House.

1939 Tremor in hands worsens. Suffers from exhaustion and neuritis.

1941 Tremor diagnosed as Parkinson's disease.

1943 Destroys notes for seven plays he does not expect to finish. No longer capable of controlling pencil and incapable of composing on typewriter.

1944 Sells Tao House and moves to hotel in San Francisco. Burns manuscripts of two unfinished plays.

1945 Moves to Hotel Barclay in New York in preparation for rehearsals of *The Iceman Cometh*.

1946 Moves with Carlotta to Boston and buys house overlooking Atlantic Ocean in Marblehead Neck, MA.

1949 Tremor in hands worsens.

1950 Eugene, Jr., commits suicide.

1951   Moves to Shelton Hotel and does not leave his suite, except for medical reasons, for the remainder of his life. Donates large archive of literary material to Yale University.

1952   Destroys drafts and scenarios of unfinished cycle plays.

1953   Dies of pneumonia at Shelton Hotel on November 27. Near the end, utters his last words: "Born in a hotel room—and God damn it—died in a hotel room!" (Gelb 939). Autopsy reveals rare degenerative disease of cerebellum, superficially resembling Parkinson's, as primary cause of tremor. Buried without ceremony at Forest Hills Cemetery in Boston.

1956   José Quintero directs celebrated revival of *The Iceman Cometh* at the Circle in the Square Theatre. *Long Day's Journey Into Night* is published and produced in Stockholm, Sweden, and then New York. Wins fourth Pulitzer Prize. O'Neill's plays have been regularly produced on Broadway, Off-Broadway, and in regional theatres ever since.

Appendix II:
Play Abstracts

The plays are listed in order of their composition as documented by Travis Bogard in O'Neill's *Complete Plays*. The production history, list of principal characters, essential action, and commentary condense O'Neill's output into a brief context. The end of nearly every entry has a "DISCUSSION" section that refers to topical analyses in the text of this book. The production history is limited to American productions with the exception of the Swedish premieres of O'Neill's posthumous productions, and furthermore, mainly to New York productions. My sources for all production information are from Miller's *Eugene O'Neill and the American Critic*, 2nd ed. (New York: Archon, 1973), Bogard's *Contour in Time*, rev. ed. (New York: Oxford, 1988), and John Willis' *Theatre World* (New York: Crown).

A Wife for a Life (1913)

MAJOR PRODUCTIONS: None.

PRINCIPAL CHARACTERS: The Older Man, Jack.

DRAMATIC ACTION: The Older Man discovers that his wife never betrayed him and that her chaste lover is his best friend and partner who once saved his life.

COMMENT: Not really a play but a vaudeville skit, O'Neill's first effort at playwriting reveals characteristic novelized stage directions and reliance upon narrative monologue in place of dialogue. Use of "ironic fate" is obvious and heavy handed. Melodramatic asides allow the Older Man to confess interior experiences to the audience yet mask them from Jack. Concluding Biblical lines, "Greater love hath no man than this that he giveth his wife for his friend," receive similar expression later in *Long Day's Journey Into Night* when Jamie concludes his narrative with a final warning about his negative influence upon his brother: "Greater love hath no man than this, that he saveth his brother from himself." The Older Man's inability to love and accept the love of his wife, largely unexplored in this play, is similar to the principal male characters in *The Iceman Cometh*.

The Web (1913)

MAJOR PRODUCTIONS: None.

PRINCIPAL CHARACTERS: Rose Thomas, Steve, Tim Moran.

DRAMATIC ACTION: A consumptive prostitute tries to save her baby and escape to happiness in the arms of a bank robber, but her jealous pimp returns to kill her protector and frame her for his murder.

COMMENT: Stage directions mention presence of "ironic life force." Action of this melodrama attempts to make this force visible by showing the bleak conditions under which the lovers live, their attempt to break free from constraints, and a sudden and final reversal which creates an even worse situation than the former one. Sympathetic treatment of prostitute trapped within a squalid environment depicts her and her would-be lover, a bank robber on the lam, as victims of "what life does to people." Quite melodramatically, they share experiences that project them as innocent and incapable of directing their fate. The pimp is a cartoonish villain who fulfills necessary plot function. Action of play depicts "hopeless hope" for happiness. Just as skies brighten for the couple, the play turns.

DISCUSSION: early plays ending in death, 128; melodramatic expression, 175.

Thirst (1913)

MAJOR PRODUCTIONS: The Wharf Theatre, Provincetown, MA, August 1916 (The Provincetown Players, prod.; George Cram Cook, dir.; with Cook, Louise Bryant, and O'Neill as the Mulatto Sailor). A "rehearsal" scene from this play is depicted in Warren Beatty's film *Reds* (1981), about John Reed and Bryant, in which Jack Nicholson plays a very romantic Eugene O'Neill.

PRINCIPAL CHARACTERS: A Gentleman, A Dancer, A West Indian Mulatto Sailor.

DRAMATIC ACTION: Three shipwreck survivors float on a raft and slowly go mad from the heat and lack of water.

COMMENT: Highly melodramatic plot climaxes with the Dancer's erotic descent into madness. First hint of simultaneous action with long dialogue between Gentleman and Dancer while the Negro Sailor watches and sings. Exotic setting on endless sea, surrounded by sharks, defies theatrical practice. Irony in the play is obvious (surrounded by water, the survivors are dying of thirst). Attempt to go beyond the capabilities of the theatre evident in the theatrical setting.

DISCUSSION: early plays ending in death, 128; melodramatic expression, 175.

Recklessness (1913)

MAJOR PRODUCTIONS: None.

PRINCIPAL CHARACTERS: Arthur Baldwin, Mildred Baldwin (his wife), Fred Burgess (their chauffeur), Gene (their maid).

DRAMATIC ACTION: A jealous husband learns of his wife's infidelity, kills her lover, and sadistically tortures his wife and drives her to suicide.

COMMENT: O'Neill borrows from *Miss Julie* to create a love match between Mildred and her chauffeur. Most of the melodramatic play is a set-up for the scene between the husband and wife, the first time O'Neill is able to write effective dialogue in which subtext and situation is more important than what is said. Unfortunately, a jealous maid is the plot device to turn the drama, and the end comes almost as an afterthought. None of the characters is believable. Fred aspires to greater things ("As soon as I've passed those engineering examinations—and I will pass them—we'll go away together" CP1 57). Arthur Baldwin is inexplicably evil. It's unclear what motivates his wife, Mildred, other than a desire to get away from her husband.

DISCUSSION: early plays ending in death, 128; melodramatic expression, 175.

Warnings (1913)

MAJOR PRODUCTIONS: None.

PRINCIPAL CHARACTERS: James Knapp (wireless operator of the "Empress"), Mary Knapp (his wife), Charles and Dolly (two of their children), Captain Hardwick of the "Empress," Mason (First Officer), Dick Whitney (wireless operator of the S.S. *Duchess*).

DRAMATIC ACTION: A wireless operator, on the verge of going deaf, goes on a last voyage in order to support his family. The inevitable happens at sea and Knapp is directly responsible for the sinking of the ship; as a result, he kills himself.

COMMENT: A one-act play split into two scenes juxtaposing personal and professional responsibilities. O'Neill presents a sympathetic portrait of a large family in dire economic need, yet the wife is characterized as nagging and shrewish, the first in a line of female characters that extends all the way to *The Iceman Cometh*. O'Neill loads the deck in the first scene by showing that Knapp receives too little pay, is too old to get another job, and has too many mouths to feed (five children). The second half switches to the ship and depicts the consequences of Knapp's decision to make one last trip in terms of loss of life and destruction of property. The dilemma of the play is simply this: given the situation, what should Knapp do? Unfortunately, the action of the play presents Knapp as a victim of circumstance without indicting the society in which he lives or showing another possible outcome. The turn of events is formulaic and expected. Given the way that the action sets up, the outcome is predetermined by the opening scene.

DISCUSSION: early plays ending in death, 128.

Fog (1914)

MAJOR PRODUCTIONS: January, 1917, The Playwrights' Theatre (The Provincetown Players, prod.).

PRINCIPAL CHARACTERS: A Poet, A Man of Business.

DRAMATIC ACTION: Two shipwreck victims, a businessman and poet, adrift in a lifeboat in the cold sea, are rescued by the mysterious cries from a dead child.

COMMENT: First use of fog in plays, which gives the play a surreal quality. Rescue of the men cannot be rationally explained. O'Neill aligns himself with the poet, a self-portrait of himself ("big dark eyes and a black mustache and black hair pushed back from his high forehead"), against the privilege and money of the businessman. Sympathetic treatment of underclass runs through all of O'Neill's work. Question between the two men is the merits of saving oneself or saving others. That question is so loaded in favor of the poet's humanism that the debate doesn't get a fair shake in the action.

DISCUSSION: melodramatic expression, 175.

Bread and Butter (1914)

MAJOR PRODUCTIONS: None

PRINCIPAL CHARACTERS: John Brown, Maud Steele (his wife), Edward Brown (his father), Edward, Jr. (his brother), Richard Steele (Maud's father), Bessie Brown (John's sister), "Babe" Carter (art student), Eugene Grammont (Master of an Art School).

DRAMATIC ACTION: A man must choose between his artistic career or domestic bliss with his hometown wife. He makes the wrong choice and commits suicide.

COMMENT: O'Neill's first full-length play is a prelude to *Beyond the Horizon*. John Brown is a painter, another autobiographical "artist" in the canon. The prosaic name shows what he's up against (Brown is the surname of the non-artist in *The Great God Brown*) in the Connecticut town of Bridgetown, which is probably a picture of New London. This dreary play advances all the romantic and tired notions of the artist as a superior creature who is misunderstood by the unwashed masses. Bessie predicts that John and Maud will "grind together until both are worn out," but the action does not show this event. Instead, O'Neill presents a before and after sequence. The real drama of the play occurs in the elliptical space between acts three and four. O'Neill did not have the technique yet to show the regrets of past acts as he displays in *Long Day's Journey Into Night*. And, the characters, too, in the early effort are almost wholly good or wholly unpleasant. John's brother, Edward, for example, is a stereo-typical politician and a mouthpiece for middle-class values. That Maud could be attracted to him and his brother is not credible. Her transformation from a sweet, relative innocent to a hardened cynic is yet another melodramatic effect.

DISCUSSION: self-portrait of the author, 7–8; early plays ending in death, 128; shows effects of time over years, 133–134; melodramatic expression, 175.

Bound East for Cardiff (1914)

MAJOR PRODUCTIONS: July 28, 1916, The Wharf Theatre, Provincetown, MA (The Provincetown Players, prod.); *S.S. Glencairn* [*Bound East for Cardiff*, *The Moon of the Caribbees*, *In the Zone*, and *The Long Voyage Home* together on a single bill], 1924, Provincetown Playhouse (James Light, dir.); *S.S. Glencairn*, 1937, Lafayette Theatre (WPA Federal Theatre Project, prod.; William Challee, dir.; Canada Lee as Yank in an all–Black cast); *S.S. Glencairn*, 1948, New York City Center (New York City Theatre Company, José Ferrer, prod.); *S.S. Glencairn*, 1978, Long Wharf Theatre.

PRINCIPAL CHARACTERS: Yank, Driscoll, Cocky, Davis, Scotty, Olson, Paul, Smitty, Ivan, The Captain, The Second Mate.

DRAMATIC ACTION: Driscoll provides comfort and companionship for a dying seaman, Yank, aboard the S.S. *Glencairn*.

COMMENT: First O'Neill play to be produced, and one of his very best early plays. Unlike previous plays, does not impose a melodramatic narrative upon a dramatic situation. Repetitve life at sea balances the finality of death and height-ens the emotional effect of the play. Various dialects of the characters used effec-tively. Class issues of crew vs. officers handled in a complex way for the first time. Fog used again effectively as symbol and image of fate or destiny. After Yank dies, a crewman reports that the fog has lifted. Dialogue between Yank and Driscoll is O'Neill's best thus far because the talk disguises what the men most fear (death). Timidity and tenderness of the characters, revealed in their comradeship, belie their gruff personas. O'Neill played small part of the Second Mate in an early production.

DISCUSSION: poetic title/prosaic contents, 10–11; composite example of methods, 23–25; mask of bravado, 72; early plays ending in death, 128; an important early dramatic contribution, 128; repetition of ship's routine, 130; later companion pieces, 175.

Abortion (1914)

MAJOR PRODUCTIONS: None.

PRINCIPAL CHARACTERS: Jack Townsend, John Townsend (his father), Evelyn Sands (his fiancee), Joe Murray (a machinist).

DRAMATIC ACTION: A college athlete, fresh off the playing field in a championship game, kills himself when faced with the scandal that the illicit abortion that he paid for caused the death of an innocent girl.

COMMENT: O'Neill's contempt for university life is apparent in this one-act play as he portrays the hypocrisy of a college boy who tries to reason his way out of responsibility for a cowardly act. Joe Murray, the dead girl's brother, confronts Jack with a pistol, but runs away. Once again, O'Neill sympathetically portrays the underclass and the plight of the dead girl. The sexual politics of good girls/bad girls are interesting from an historical perspective, one in which O'Neill seems particularly enlightened. Still, this remains a very conventional melodrama in which all questions are duly answered and the intrusion of Murray is the plot twist to force the reversal of fortune and final recognition. The final moments of the play in which an approaching crowd sings "For he's a jolly good fellow" as Jack shoots himself are very effective theatrically.

DISCUSSION: early plays ending in death, 128.

The Movie Man (1914)

MAJOR PRODUCTIONS: None.

PRINCIPAL CHARACTERS: Henry Rogers (Earth Motion Picture Company), Al Devlin (photographer), Pancho Gomez (Commander-in-Chief of the Constitutionalist Army), Anita Fernandez.

DRAMATIC ACTION: A movie producer barters for a political prisoner's life in order to impress the condemned man's daughter.

COMMENT: The premise of O'Neill's first comedy is the most interesting thing about this slight piece: an American movie company finances the Mexican Civil War in order to take pictures of the battle scenes. Gomez is modeled after the legendary Pancho Villa.

Servitude (1914)

MAJOR PRODUCTIONS: None.

PRINCIPAL CHARACTERS: David Royleston (author), Alice Royleston (his wife), Ethel Frazer, George Frazer (her husband).

DRAMATIC ACTION: An Ibsenite woman discovers the meaning of love when she encounters an egotistical writer.

COMMENT: A bald thesis play ("Servitude in love, love in servitude") which ends in double reconciliations between two sets of spouses. This is O'Neill's thoroughly uninteresting answer to Ibsen's Nora. Mrs. Frazer leaves her husband to learn from her literary mentor. Mrs. Royleston teaches her and her husband a lesson about love; Royleston learns the lesson and recognizes that a "good woman" has been behind him all through the years. That Mrs. Royleston could endure her pompous husband and enjoy it defies credibility. Pride in such love surfaces again in Nora Melody and finally, in a quite interesting way, in Josie Hogan. Here, Mrs. Frazer, although an imitation of the Ibsen woman, is the most interesting character in the play and the most interesting female character that O'Neill had written up to this point.

DISCUSSION: self-portrait of the author, 7–8; pride as mask, 64; theme of sacrifice compared to *A Moon for the Misbegotten* 80, 90.

The Sniper (1915)

MAJOR PRODUCTIONS: February 16, 1917, The Playwrights' Theatre (The Provincetown Players, prod.; with George Cram Cook as Rougon).

PRINCIPAL CHARACTERS: Rougon (a Belgian peasant), Village Priest, German Captain.

DRAMATIC ACTION: An old man, having lost all his family in the War, takes up a rifle and begins to shoot, even though he knows such an act is suicidal.

COMMENT: Set in Belgium during World War I, this anti-war one-acter models after *Antigone*. Mourning the death of his son, Rougon subsequently learns that his wife and daughter have also been killed by the Germans. He knows the edict that all civilians who take up arms will be shot. Nevertheless, he picks up a rifle and begins shooting anyway to avenge his family's losses. At the end, he faces a firing squad and a priest remarks in the curtain line: "Alas, the laws of men!" Rougon's decision to take up arms is an early vestige of the "hopeless hope" that will emerge as a dominant theme in later plays. Here, the plot, as in all melodramas, drives the action.

DISCUSSION: early plays ending in death, 128.

The Personal Equation (1915)

MAJOR PRODUCTIONS: None.

PRINCIPAL CHARACTERS: Thomas Perkins (2nd engineer), Tom (his son), Olga Tarnoff.

DRAMATIC ACTION: A young man proves his mettle to his anarchist lover by blowing up a ship guarded by his father, who accidentally shoots him in defense.

COMMENT: O'Neill's third full-length play once again looks for balance between the personal and professional (political). Olga Tarnoff was apparently modeled after Emma Goldman. O'Neill portrays the anarchist movement much more interestingly in *The Iceman Cometh*. Here, the issues are all stock, idealistic ones. Olga, a zealot, becomes much less interested in Tom's involvement in the Movement once she becomes pregnant. For his part, Tom is only involved with it to get the girl. Tom's father, the one who ultimately stops Tom, is the most interesting character and O'Neill originally called the play *The Second Engineer*. His devotion to the engines of the ship foreshadows Reuben Light's love for the dynamo in that later play. The final image of *The Personal Equation* is the most interesting in which Olga and the elder Perkins join together at Tom's bedside and Olga speaks of a better future, while Tom, clearly brain-damaged, echoes: "Long live the Revolution!" As evident in many of the early plays, O'Neill is capable of putting a good ending on his plays. But the irony of this final stage picture is not preceded by any in the previous action. As a result, the end is theatrically effective, but not genuinely moving emotionally.

DISCUSSION: theme of servitude compared to *A Moon for the Misbegotten* 90; early plays ending in death, 128.

Before Breakfast (1916)

MAJOR PRODUCTIONS: December 1, 1916, The Playwrights' Theatre (The Provincetown Players, prod.).

PRINCIPAL CHARACTERS: Mrs. Rowland.

DRAMATIC ACTION: An aspiring poet commits suicide in response to his slovenly wife's harangue.

COMMENT: An experimental one-act in which O'Neill tried the patience of his audience to endure Mrs. Rowland's monologic diatribe against her off-stage and never seen husband. O'Neill, in his final appearance on the stage, played the part of Alfred, whose hand appears onstage at one point to accept a towel. O'Neill modeled this play after Strindberg's *The Stronger*, though not nearly to as good effect. Characterization of Mrs. Rowland as a shrew diminishes the work and puts her in line with previous female characters such as Mrs. Knapp in *Warnings* and certainly foreshadows an unseen character such as Bessie Hope in *The Iceman Cometh*. Strapping the razor, as well as gasps from the bathroom are quite effective offstage sounds. The dynamic between onstage/offstage and seen/unseen promises future expanded developments. This effort is less a play than a technical experiment and O'Neill seems to have allowed as much.

DISCUSSION: experiment with monologue, 35; early plays ending in death, 128.

Now I Ask You (1916)

MAJOR PRODUCTIONS: None.

PRINCIPAL CHARACTERS: Mrs. Ashleigh, Lucy (her daughter), Tom Drayton, Leonora Barnes, Gabriel Adams.

DRAMATIC ACTION: A mother reveals her daughter's demands for free love as an adolescent sham.

COMMENT: Fourth full-length play is a comedy, a parody of Ibsen in which the conceit of General Gabler's pistols serves as a framing device. Lucy plays part of Hedda and sports fashionable ideas of birth control and free love, and from that historical/sociological perspective the play is interesting. As a drama, it is pretty shallow. In the action, characters quote O'Neill's familiar sources such as Strindberg ("Indra's Daughter"), Nietzsche ("Big Blond Beast"), and Ibsen's *Master Builder* ("Castles in the Air") in addition to references to *Hedda Gabler*. The satire on the art/theatre world presents businessman Tom sympathetically. In that sense, the play betrays O'Neill's traditional allegiance to art and artists in the fight against bourgeois values. Here, conventional morality is upheld as an unqualified good. Still, the play doesn't take itself quite seriously and seems to provide a self-critique when one character comments upon the dialogue: "Those are strong words. I didn't think they were used any more outside of cheap melodrama."

DISCUSSION: parodic betrayal of O'Neill's artistic sensibilities, 75.

In the Zone (1917)

MAJOR PRODUCTIONS: October 31, 1917, Comedy Theater, NY (Washington Square Players, prod.); vaudeville circuit; *S.S. Glencairn* [*Bound East for Cardiff, The Moon of the Caribbees, In the Zone,* and *The Long Voyage Home* together on a single bill], 1924, Provincetown Playhouse (James Light, dir.); *S.S. Glencairn,* 1937, Lafayette Theatre (WPA Federal Theatre Project, prod.; William Challee, dir.; Canada Lee as Yank in an all–Black cast); *S.S. Glencairn,* 1948, New York City Center (New York City Theatre Company, José Ferrer, prod.); *S.S. Glencairn,* 1978, Long Wharf Theatre.

PRINCIPAL CHARACTERS: Smitty, Davis, Swanson, Scotty, Ivan, Paul, Jack, Driscoll, Cocky.

DRAMATIC ACTION: Seamen aboard an ammunition ship enter the war zone and begin to suspect that a fellow crewman is a spy.

COMMENT: Single-minded action and suspense builds to a surprising, theatrical ending. A very effective, traditional piece of writing, which earned O'Neill steady royalties for years on the vaudeville circuit. An example, according to O'Neill, of the old kind of drama in which plot drives the action. More than in any previous play, O'Neill demonstrates his technical proficiency in crafting a taut, one-act play.

DISCUSSION: an important early dramatic contribution, 128; melodramatic representation compared to *The Moon of the Caribbees,* 177–177.

Ile (1917)

MAJOR PRODUCTIONS: November 30, 1917, Playwrights' Theatre (Provincetown Players, prod.; Nina Moise, dir.).

PRINCIPAL CHARACTERS: Captain Keeney, Slocum (second mate), Mrs. Keeney.

DRAMATIC ACTION: Captain of a whaling ship must choose between turning back to protect his wife or going forward to appease his pride and to get the oil.

COMMENT: Solidly constructed melodrama in one-act in which ship's steward loads the plot, choices become very clear, and all is resolved in course of the action. Land/sea opposition made abundantly clear. Keeney's hardness and resoluteness is tragic dimension evident in later characters such as Ephraim Cabot and Lavinia Mannon. The architecture of this play allows for little tolerance: Keeney's moment of decision is followed closely by a new recognition and final reversal which makes the play highly formulaic. Emphasis upon exterior events such as the surrounding ice makes the characters victims of fate instead of combatants against it, another melodramatic aspect of the plot.

DISCUSSION: land and sea division, 105–106; early plays ending in death, 128.

The Long Voyage Home (1917)

MAJOR PRODUCTIONS: November 2, 1917, The Playwrights' Theatre (The Provincetown Players, prod.); *S.S. Glencairn* [*Bound East for Cardiff*, *The Moon of the Caribbees*, *In the Zone*, and *The Long Voyage Home* together on a single bill], 1924, Provincetown Playhouse (James Light, dir.); *S.S. Glencairn*, 1937, Lafayette Theatre (WPA Federal Theatre Project, prod.; William Challee, dir.; Canada Lee as Yank in an all–Black cast); *S.S. Glencairn*, 1948, New York City Center (New York City Theatre Company, José Ferrer, prod.); *The Long Voyage Home*, 1961, Mermaid Theatre (Torquay Company and Ruth Kramer, prod.; Paul Shyre, dir.); *S.S. Glencairn*, 1978, Long Wharf Theatre.

PRINCIPAL CHARACTERS: Mag, Olson, Driscoll, Fat Joe, Freda, Kate, Nick, Ivan, Cocky.

DRAMATIC ACTION: A sailor, on the verge of going home to his family farm, falls prey to crimpers in a low-dive London waterfront bar.

COMMENT: Straightforward narrative offers interesting psychology about Olson and the sailor's life: What keeps him at sea when he says that he wants to go home? The extent to which Olson is victimized or has willed his fate is very much in question, an ambiguity that makes this play more than it might first appear. The land/sea opposition is played out in a much more sophisticated manner than in the previous sea play. Repetition of the sailor's life as an endless circle of dives, drinks, and a return to sea is skillfully established in one act. The action shows the difficulty in breaking a familiar pattern.

DISCUSSION: an important early dramatic contribution, 128, 175.

The Moon of the Caribbees (1917)

MAJOR PRODUCTIONS: December 20, 1918, The Playwrights' Theatre (The Provincetown Players, prod.; Thomas Mitchell, dir.); *S.S. Glencairn* [*Bound East for Cardiff*, *The Moon of the Caribbees*, *In the Zone*, and *The Long Voyage Home* together on a single bill], 1924, Provincetown Playhouse (James Light, dir.); *S.S. Glencairn*, 1937, Lafayette Theatre (WPA Federal Theatre Project, prod.; William Challee, dir.; Canada Lee as Yank in an all–Black cast); *S.S. Glencairn*, 1948, New York City Center (New York City Theatre Company, José Ferrer, prod.); *S.S. Glencairn*, 1978, Long Wharf Theatre.

PRINCIPAL CHARACTERS: Yank, Driscoll, Olson, Davis, Cocky, Smitty, Paul.

DRAMATIC ACTION: A full moon watches over the *Glencairn*, at anchor off of a West Indies island.

COMMENT: The best of the *Glencairn* series, this one-act focuses on atmosphere at the expense of plot, which allows for a real sense of the sailor's life. Action contrasts isolation of one character (Smitty) with party atmosphere of the rest of the ship's crew at liberty. Characters are highly differentiated. O'Neill felt that this play illustrated the direction of the "new" drama.

DISCUSSION: poetic title/prosaic contents, 10–11; mask of bravado, 72; an important early dramatic contribution, 128; example of modern drama compared with melodrama of *In the Zone*, 175–177.

The Rope (1918)

MAJOR PRODUCTIONS: April 26, 1919, The Playwrights' Theatre (The Provincetown Players, prod.; Nina Moise, dir.); (1919) Comedy Theatre (Washington Square Players, prod.).

PRINCIPAL CHARACTERS: Abraham Bentley, Annie (his daughter), Pat Sweeney (her husband), Mary (their child), Luke Bentley (Abe's son).

DRAMATIC ACTION: Prodigal son returns home to steal his inheritance from his Old Man.

COMMENT: Conventional one-act with theatrically effective reversals and surprises reveals no new techniques. Abe, the old man, is a forerunner of Cabot and his spouting from the Bible is the most interesting aspect of the play. An undercurrent of violence runs throughout the action. With the possible exception of Bentley, none of the characters is appealing.

Beyond the Horizon (1918)

MAJOR PRODUCTIONS: February 2, 1920, Morosco Theatre (John D. Williams, prod.); 1926, Mansfield Theatre (The Actors Theatre, prod.); 1974, Princeton, NJ (McCarter Theatre Company, prod.; Michael Kahn, dir.).

PRINCIPAL CHARACTERS: Andrew Mayo, Robert Mayo, Ruth Atkins (Robert's wife), Mrs. Atkins (her mother).

DRAMATIC ACTION: Two brothers suffer the consequences of acting against their essential natures.

COMMENT: First "uptown" Broadway production of an O'Neill play led to his first Pulitzer Prize. O'Neill's best full-length work so far. O'Neill extends his story over eight years in his first play in which time really serves as the subject (novelistic experimentation). Mechanical alternation of interior and exterior scenes produced O'Neill's notion of rhythm. Consequences of a particular choice lead to a certain destiny in which all is spelled out in this early effort. There is nothing subtle about this play. Robert is another self-portrait with "a touch of the poet" about him. Andrew, the businessman, is less individuated; Ruth, the woman whom they both love, is quite similar to Maud Steele in *Bread and Butter*. *Beyond the Horizon* becomes increasingly maudlin as the action progresses and the overall poverty and despair increases. The little girl's death tries to pull at the heartstrings. There is more suffering in this play than in any other O'Neill play and it is unrelenting. There is absolutely no humor in the piece. Still, the overall sincerity is memorable. In this play, too, O'Neill displays his tragic vision most evidently. Suffering is seen as the element of mortal living that makes life worthwhile. In this novelized form, there is no real action in the play after the first scene in which Robert makes his fateful decision to marry Ruth.

DISCUSSION: self-portrait of the author, 7–8; struggles of characters mirrors playwright's struggle, 9; poetic title/prosaic contents, 10–11; love as sacrifice, 17; pipe dream or hopeless hope theme, 59; mirroring of characters 61; comparison to *The Great God Brown*, 70–71; allusions to South Sea Islands, 87; triumph through defeat at the end, 93; early plays ending in death, 128; an important early dramatic contribution, 128; shows effects of time over years, 133–134; comparison of time and the past to *Long Day's Journey Into Night*, 152; simplified version of experience, 179.

Shell Shock (1918)

MAJOR PRODUCTIONS: None.

PRINCIPAL CHARACTERS: Jack Arnold (Major of Infantry), Herbert Roylston (Lieutenant), Robert Wayne (Medical Corps).

DRAMATIC ACTION: War hero discovers the truth about his actions on the battlefield.

COMMENT: One-act that is mostly a therapy session in which a patient cures himself through talking and ties up all the loose ends within a half hour of playing time! Narrative has some suspense but no action. Recognitions and reversals in the appropriate places mark this as another conventional drama. Discussion uncovers the past in a thoroughly stagnant present.

DISCUSSION: monologue as simplified version of experience, 43–44.

The Dreamy Kid (1918)

MAJOR PRODUCTIONS: October 31, 1919, The Playwrights' Theatre (The Provincetown Players, prod.; Ida Rauh, dir.).

PRINCIPAL CHARACTERS: Mammy Saunders, "The Dreamy Kid," Irene.

DRAMATIC ACTION: A young black killer elects to stay with his dying grandmother in the face of approaching police.

COMMENT: O'Neill's first play about black experience sustains interest by developing tension between the interior space where Mammy lies, and outside the apartment where the police are gathering. Dreamy's decision to stay marks the turning point in the drama, after which he mounts a "hopeless hope" by asking his girlfriend to fetch the rest of his gang. Emphasis upon gathering forces outside enlarges the scenic space of this one-act, which ends at the precise moment in which the outside forces must come inside.

DISCUSSION: knock at the door (outside forces), 101–103, 160; early plays ending in death, 128.

Where the Cross Is Made (1918)

MAJOR PRODUCTIONS: November 22, 1918, The Playwrights' Theatre (The Provincetown Players, prod.; Ida Rauh, dir.).

PRINCIPAL CHARACTERS: Captain Bartlett, Nat Bartlett (his son), Sue Bartlett (his daughter), Doctor Higgins.

DRAMATIC ACTION: A son tries to stave off his own madness by committing his father to an asylum, but he fails to break free from the hold of his father's dream.

COMMENT: Nat gives expression to hopeless hope theme: hoping when there is no reason to hope is madness. Yet, how to live without hope? That is the question that the play poses. Bringing the ghosts onstage tests the power of theatre and illusion. As an experiment, O'Neill tried to make the audience think it was going mad by having the "green ghosts" appear onstage.

DISCUSSION: pipe dream or hopeless hope theme, 59; tensile strength of inside/outside, 103–104; early plays ending in death, 128.

The Straw (1919)

MAJOR PRODUCTIONS: November 10, 1921, Greenwich Village Theatre (George C. Tyler, prod.).

PRINCIPAL CHARACTERS: Eileen Carmody, Stephen Murray.

DRAMATIC ACTION: A writer realizes, possibly too late, that he loves the woman who inspired his best stories.

COMMENT: Action set in a sanitarium for tuberculosis patients. Writer Murray is another artist of the self-portrait variety; O'Neill clearly knew the setting from his own personal experience. The "weighing scene" in Act 2 stages simultaneous action and is one of O'Neill's best. The men line up on one side of the stage, women on the other. Suspence builds concerning the results for both Eileen and Stephen and after they're done, they have difficulty moving through the lines to meet each other. O'Neill's theme of love through sacrifice is fully evident. Once again, the self-portrait of the male writer is much more carefully drawn than the one of Eileen, who plays a victim/martyr throughout the action. One interesting development in the action is that Murray finds that he loves Eileen only after he pretends to love her, a dynamic that opens up interpretive possibilities.

DISCUSSION: self-portrait of the author, 7–8; pipe dream or hopeless hope theme, 59; mask of acting 72–73; here and there dynamic, 104; early plays ending in death, 128; an important early dramatic contribution, 128.

Chris Christophersen (1919)

MAJOR PRODUCTIONS: March 8, 1920, Atlantic City, NJ (George C. Tyler, prod.).

PRINCIPAL CHARACTERS: Chris, Anna (his daughter), Paul Andersen (Second Mate).

DRAMATIC ACTION: An old sailor tries to "swallow the anchor" in order to avoid an evil fate at sea.

COMMENT: This forerunner of *"Anna Christie"* never made it to Broadway;

it closed during an out-of-town tryout in Philadelphia. A second version became *The Old Davil* before its final incarnation. One reason for its failure is an uncharacteristic O'Neill dynamic in which the major character tries to avoid struggle and refuses to defy fate. Swallowing the anchor means shirking responsibility as Andersen, who mirrors Chris, asserts in the middle of the play. O'Neill develops this idea in his anti-tragedy, *The Iceman Cometh*, in which Hickey urges all the bums at Hope's to, in effect, "swallow the anchor." The passivity of Chris in this play turns the focus away from him and onto a more dynamic Anna, a woman of action.

DISCUSSION: theme for a novel, 28; disdain for actors, 31; romance for the past (clipper ships), 106; swallow the anchor theme related to *The Iceman Cometh*, 116–117; earlier version of *"Anna Christie"* 116; fails as Hickey's project fails, 119.

Gold (1920)

MAJOR PRODUCTIONS: June 1, 1921, Frazee Theatre (John D. Williams, prod.).

PRINCIPAL CHARACTERS: Captain Bartlett, Silas Horne, Ben Cates, Jimmy Kanaka, Mrs. Bartlett, Sue Bartlett, Danny Drew, Nat Bartlett, Dr. Berry.

DRAMATIC ACTION: Pipe dreams sustain Captain Bartlett, but knowledge brings him the peace of death.

COMMENT: This full-length play is an expanded version of *Where the Cross Is Made*. The earlier one-act is essentially the fourth act of the later effort. Neither one is a good play. In contest between knowledge and belief, belief proves stronger. In this play, too, pipe dreams are portrayed as a kind of madness. Madness, however, sustains life. O'Neill's concern with the power of illusion promotes the theatre as a powerful medium.

DISCUSSION: pipe dream or hopeless hope theme, 59–60; early plays ending in death, 128.

"Anna Christie" (1920)

MAJOR PRODUCTIONS: November 2, 1921, Vanderbilt Theatre (Arthur Hopkins, prod.; Robert Edmond Jones, settings); 1977, Imperial Theatre (José Quintero, dir.; with John Lithgow and Liv Ullmann; 1993, Roundabout Theatre (David Leveaux, dir.; with Liam Neeson as Mat Burke and Natasha Richardson as Anna).

PRINCIPAL CHARACTERS: Anna Christie, Mat Burke, Chris Christopherson, Martha Owens.

DRAMATIC ACTION: A prostitute finds love at sea and vows to marry despite portents of a not-so-happy future.

COMMENT: In O'Neill's second Pulitzer Prize winner, the so-called "happy ending" spoiled the play for him. Still, that ending contributes to the fact that the play is still frequently revived today and rates among O'Neill's most often produced dramas. Anna is O'Neill's first truly interesting female character insofar as she moves from stereotypical prostitute to individuated character. The fact that her transformation is not altogether complete adds to her interest. In *Chris Christophersen*, Anna was a school teacher from Leeds, England. The change to a prostitute from Minnesota makes her past seem much more believable as Chris' abandoned daughter. Romance between Anna and Burke dominates the action once Burke is literally dredged from the sea. His presence completely washes Old Chris to the background of the play. Theme of "swallowing the anchor" vanishes entirely. Opportunities for simultaneous action present themselves in the triangle of major characters. For example, the final image of the play has Burke and Anna together, pledging their love, while Chris, on another part of the stage, looks over the fog and gives voice to his hesitation about the future.

DISCUSSION: refused to include in collected works, 6–7; failed ending, 19; collusion of showing and telling, 43–44; land and sea opposition, 104; later version of *Chris Christophersen*, 116; problem of the "happy ending," 126–127; problem of ending solved in late plays, 135; comparison to ending of *Long Day's Journey Into Night*, 143–144; fog in, 168.

The Emperor Jones (1920)

MAJOR PRODUCTIONS: Nov. 1, 1920, The Playwrights' Theatre (The Provincetown Players, prod.; with Charles Gilpin); December 27, Selwyn Theatre; January 21, Princess Theatre; 1997, The Performing Garage (The Wooster Group, prod.; Elizabeth LeCompte, dir.; with Kate Valk and Willem Dafoe).

PRINCIPAL CHARACTERS: Brutus Jones, Smithers

DRAMATIC ACTION: A tyrannical despot tries to escape a West Indies island before his angry and rebellious subjects kill him.

COMMENT: O'Neill's first attempt to incorporate expressionistic techniques, which include nightmare flashbacks of the past, beating tom-toms that replicate a heartbeat, and action set in parts of a dark forest. Jones' progression through the forest and the gradual stripping away of his clothes alludes possibly to Jung's concept of the collective unconscious, especially as Jones sees scenes from his past in reverse order: as a Pullman porter; on a chain gang; at the slave market; on a slave ship; in Africa. Despite the narrative drive of the play, Jones actually moves in a circle and ends up where he started, a convenient pattern for staging purposes. Pronounced use of monologue in the play allows for simultaneous action with Jones on one part of the stage, separated from pantomimic action on another part of the stage. The beating tom-toms proved to be a particularly effective and innovative use of sound. Jig Cook built a plaster dome cyclorama for the original production which helped give the small theatre an illusion of tremendous space. *The Emperor Jones* is the first play to feature a major role for a black actor on the American stage. Paul Robeson took over the part from Charles Gilpin.

DISCUSSION: clothing as mask, 17; radical staging ideas, 28; approved of the acting, 30–31; dramatic function of monologues, 43; monologue as alienation, 44–47; unmasking through removal of clothes, 76; important "middle period" play, 98; deaths in "middle period" plays, 128.

Diff'rent (1920)

MAJOR PRODUCTIONS: December 27, 1920, The Playwrights' Theatre (The Provincetown Players, prod.); 1938, Maxine Elliott Theatre (WPA New York State Federal Theatre Project, prod.; Charles Hopkins, dir.; Ben Edwards, des.; Feder, lighting); 1961, Mermaid Theatre (Torquay Company and Ruth Kramer, prod.; Paul Shyre, dir.).

PRINCIPAL CHARACTERS: Emma Crosby, Caleb Williams, Benny Rogers.

DRAMATIC ACTION: A young, idealistic woman refuses to marry her fiancé because of a lone indiscretion, but over time she, too, falls victim to a lapse of judgment.

COMMENT: Another novelistic play in the sense that action covers 30 years, a space elided in the gap between the first act and second. Real interest of the piece lies in the space not represented in the drama: the gradual disintegration of Emma's character and Caleb's persistence to marry her. Caleb's annual return to ask for Emma's hand reflects the "hopeless hope" of the action. Allusions to the South Sea islands reflect O'Neill's studied oppositions between land/sea and Puritanism/freedom. From a contemporary standpoint, the sexual politics in the play are fascinating, if unenlightened. The premise of Caleb's defense of his own actions is that native women from the islands don't count as women because they're black and heathens. That opinion is not just the opinion of one character but represents the entire New England whaling community. The play is more interesting as a cultural/historical document and as it relates to other O'Neill plays than as an independent drama.

DISCUSSION: justification for inclusion, 22; references to masks in stage directions, 63; allusions to South Sea Islands, 87, 107–108; reference to South Sea Islands compared to *Mourning Becomes Electra*, 108; deaths in "middle period" plays, 128; shows effects of time over years, 133, 134.

The First Man (1921)

MAJOR PRODUCTIONS: March 4, 1922, The Neighborhood Playhouse (Augustin Duncan, prod. and dir.).

PRINCIPAL CHARACTERS: Curtis Jayson, Martha Jayson, Richard Bigelow, John Jayson, Mrs. Davidson.

DRAMATIC ACTION: An anthropologist must reconcile himself to the fact that his wife needs an independent existence.

COMMENT: The offstage labor cries that result in Martha's death haunt the entire third act of the play. Very dramatic theatrically, if not grotesque. A domestic play set in small town Connecticut, this play never escapes the Jayson household. A novel drama in the sense that the real action is the relationship between Jayson and his wife, but the drama is not ever able to portray that sufficiently. Instead, a melodrama takes over in which Jayson's extended family speculates that Curt is not the father of Martha's baby, a suspicion Jayson never harbors. O'Neill seems to take pleasure in satirizing the small town business class as he did earlier in *Bread and Butter*. Martha is a potentially interesting character until her desire for a baby completely subsumes her character. It's difficult to accept the title as satire rather than conviction.

DISCUSSION: justification for exclusion, 22; generational inheritance, 131; novelized subject of time, 134–135.

The Hairy Ape (1921)

MAJOR PRODUCTIONS: March 9, 1922, The Playwrights' Theatre (The Provincetown Players, prod.; Cleon Throckmorton and Robert Edmond Jones, des.; with Louis Wolheim as Yank); 1997, Selwyn Theatre (The Wooster Group, prod.; Elizabeth LeCompte, dir.)

PRINCIPAL CHARACTERS: Yank, Mildred Douglas, Paddy, Long.

DRAMATIC ACTION: A stoker of a ship, after feeling an insult from a rich young woman, comes above board and tries to avenge his honor and find his place in the world.

COMMENT: A combination of realism and expressionism which followed the success of *The Emperor Jones*. O'Neill's last treatment of his "Yank" character, and his last sea play. Contains some of O'Neill's most theatrically effective images: blackened stokers move about like apes in a steel cage of the ship; Yank's black and white confrontation with Mildred, who travels from the deck to the bowels of the ship to see how the other half lives; Yank's recurring pose as Rodin's "The Thinker"; Yank's trip down Fifth Avenue in New York and vain attempt to get the highbrow men and women to notice him; his final trip to the zoo and meeting with the gorilla at the monkey cage, a return to the beginning. Yank's monologues represent some of O'Neill's best work with vernacular language, particularly in the early scenes in which Yank's lengthy diatribes keep pace with the mechanistic frenzy of the stokehole. Theme of "belonging" is thoroughly explored in this long one-act of alienation. Play shows O'Neill's characteristic sympathy for the underclass, but provides no answer for social change. As in *The Personal Equation*, there is no unqualified allegiance to social change. Yank discards the viewpoint of socialist Long and fights his battle against injustice alone. Such individualism puts a barrier between O'Neill and those who argue for a socialist drama for the betterment of human society.

DISCUSSION: radical staging ideas, 28; approved of the acting, 30; dramatic function of monologues, 43; monologue as alienation, 44–47; mirroring, 61; unmasking action incites and sustains action, 76–77; mask simplifies experience, 79–80; important "middle period" play, 98; Paddy's romantic tales of past, 106; visceral quality of physical scene, 106–107; deaths in "middle period" plays, 128; individuation and oneness, 167.

The Fountain (1922)

MAJOR PRODUCTIONS: December 10, 1925, The Greenwich Village Theatre (Kenneth Macgowan, Robert Edmond Jones, Eugene O'Neill, prod.; Robert Edmond Jones, des.).

PRINCIPAL CHARACTERS: Juan Ponce de Leon, Beatriz de Cordova.

DRAMATIC ACTION: Aging Juan searches for the Fountain of Youth in order to win the love of Beatriz, the daughter of a woman who once loved him passionately.

COMMENT: Time once again the subject of this play which takes place over twenty years. Theme of eternal recurrence stated baldly in "The Flower Song." O'Neill's attempt at poetical language fails miserably.

DISCUSSION: centrifugal settings, 99–100; deaths in "middle period" plays, 128; recurring struggle to survive, 132.

Welded (1923)

MAJOR PRODUCTIONS: March 17, 1924, Thirty-ninth Street Theatre (Macgowan, Jones, O'Neill, in assoc. with the Selwyns, prod.; Stark Young, dir.; Robert Edmond Jones, des.).

PRINCIPAL CHARACTERS: Eleanor Owen, Michael Cape, John Darnton.

DRAMATIC ACTION: Husband and wife seek an ideal marriage.

COMMENT: O'Neill's pun on "Wedded" to get "Welded" is not very successful. Playwright and actress suffocate each other with their love in their apartment. The formulaic patterning of the drama (two acts, two scenes in each, duologues in each, mirroring of one scene to another) adds to the monotony of the piece. Play marks first use of thought aside technique that O'Neill develops fully in *Strange Interlude*. Battle of sexes, imitative of Strindberg, has none of the piquancy of later O'Neill. In some ways, it is a parody of O'Neill and, in that way, offers an approach to the work that might prove fruitful in performance.

DISCUSSION: auras of egoism, 27; first use of thought aside, 27; metatheatrical interpretation, 27–28; radical staging ideas, 28; references to masks in stage directions, 63–64; comparison of masking to *Mourning Becomes Electra*, 76; theme of servitude compared to *A Moon for the Misbegotten* 90; comparison of Eleanor's mask to Tyrone's in *A Moon for the Misbegotten* 81; knock at the door (outside forces), 101–102.

All God's Chillun Got Wings (1923)

MAJOR PRODUCTIONS: May 15, 1924, The Provincetown Playhouse (Macgowan, Jones, and O'Neill, prod.; James Light, dir.; Cleon Throckmorton, des.; with Paul Robeson and Mary Blair); 1975, Circle in the Square Theatre (Circle in the Square, prod.; George C. Scott, dir.; with Robert Christian and Trish Van Devere).

PRINCIPAL CHARACTERS: Jim Harris, Ella Downey, Hattie Harris.

DRAMATIC ACTION: A black man marries a white woman and they battle to sustain their relationship.

COMMENT: O'Neill's last "race" play faced censorship obstacles. Civic authorities deemed the play unsuitable for children to perform in and therefore the director, James Light, read the first scene in the play. Oppositions of black and white used expressionistically to great effect in the wedding scene in which one half of the stage is lined with black guests, and the other half is lined with whites. O'Neill dictated that the walls of Jim and Ella's apartment should close in around them. Also, the Congo mask is used to chilling effect in the play. Action of the play covers over sixteen years. Race, itself, poses as a kind of mask in this play. Play is not so much about race as it is about opposites, and alternating rhythms of attraction and repulsion that stem from that relationship. Race, black and white, is a visual reminder of those opposite sensibilities. *All God's Chillun Got Wings* is O'Neill's most interesting marriage play to date, much more satisfying than *Diff'rent*, *The First Man*, or *Welded*. Ella's mental instability mars the theme which O'Neill would develop more fully in his mature plays, notably *Long Day's Journey Into Night*.

DISCUSSION: autobiographical reading, 7; radical staging ideas, 28; use of masks, 66–67; recurring struggle to survive, 132; shows effects of time over years, 133.

Desire Under the Elms (1924)

MAJOR PRODUCTIONS: November 11, 1924, The Greenwich Village Theatre (Macgowan, Jones, and O'Neill, prod.; Robert Edmond Jones, des.); 1952, ANTA Playhouse (American National Theatre and Academy, prod.; Harold Clurman, dir.; Mordecai Gorelik, set; Ben Edwards, costumes, with Karl Malden as Ephraim Cabot); 1963 (Circle in the Square, prod.; José Quintero, dir.; David Hays, des., with Rip Torn, George C. Scott, and Colleen Dewhurst); 1984 (The Roundabout Theatre, prod.; Terry Shreiber, dir).

PRINCIPAL CHARACTERS: Eben Cabot, Ephraim Cabot, Abbie Putnam, Simeon Cabot, Peter Cabot.

DRAMATIC ACTION: Three characters vie for possession of a family farm, but only one survives the struggle.

COMMENT: O'Neill's best play to date and the closest approximation to a kind of Greek tragedy. Written in a thick New England dialect that is hard to accept at times. Brilliant design which featured a house onstage with removable walls that exposed interior parts of the house. Possibility remained for simultaneous staging in two different interior areas, as well as interplay between interior and exterior scenes. Balanced principal roles make it difficult to determine whose play it is. Ephraim Cabot emerges as the most interesting character by the end of the play, if not the most tragic. He is, after all, the only character who survives and who endures. The young lovers are believable. Their scenes together are among the most passionate in all of drama. The play is very interesting from the standpoint that it never fully resolves the oppositions that it establishes between soft/hard, youth/age. Final image of the "purty farm" successfully achieves note of irony. In a play that constantly repeats the word "purty," eyesight, or lack of eyesight, determines the action.

DISCUSSION: autobiographical reading, 7; poetic title/prosaic contents, 11; radical staging ideas, 28; approved of the acting, 30; description of elms, 32–33; important "middle period" play, 98; comparison with *Dynamo*, 98; deaths in "middle period" plays, 128; generational inheritance, 131; inability to see creates tension, 169; commingling of melodramatic and tragic elements, 180–189; compares presence of "something" to *Mourning Becomes Electra*, 190–191; comparison of Cabot to Lavinia, 195.

Marco Millions (1924)

MAJOR PRODUCTIONS: January 9, 1928, The Guild Theatre (Theatre Guild, prod.; Rouben Mamoulian, dir.; Lee Simonson, des.); 1964, (Repertory Theatre of Lincoln Center at Washington Square, prod.; José Quintero, dir.; David Hays, scenery and lighting, with Hal Holbrook, Zohra Lampert, and David Wayne).

PRINCIPAL CHARACTERS: Marco Polo, Donata, Kublai, Kukachin.

DRAMATIC ACTION: Marco Polo's zeal for business in the Far East kills a young princess with coldness.

COMMENT: Babbitt in the Renaissance, an interesting play in light of economic developments later in the decade. Elaborate spectacle in a kind of pageant form satirizes the American businessman and the hollowness of American values compared to the spiritual truths and knowledge in the Far East. Still, this play never extends beyond stereotypes. Action plays out over twenty-three years but Marco's character never changes. Only once does he almost proclaim his love for Kukachin, but a nearby accountant quickly changes the subject back to profits. Depiction of Marco as contented, bourgeois, businessman reflects an antitheatrical prejudice borne out in the epilogue, in which Marco Polo applauds his own performance before leaving the theatre in a limousine. West/East opposition is always straightforward and never nuanced which further simplifies a reading of the play.

DISCUSSION: radical staging ideas, 28–29; theatre as metaphor, 60; centrifugal settings, 99–100; deaths in "middle period" plays, 128.

The Great God Brown (1925)

MAJOR PRODUCTIONS: January 23, 1926, The Greenwich Village Theatre (Macgowan, Jones, and O'Neill, prod.; Robert Edmond Jones, dir.); 1959, Coronet Theatre (Phoenix Theatre, prod.; Stuart Vaughan, dir.; with Fritz Weaver); 1972, Lyceum Theatre (New Phoenix Repertory Company, prod.; Harold Prince, dir.; Boris Aronson, set, costumes and masks; Carolyn Parker, Tharon Musser, lighting).

PRINCIPAL CHARACTERS: William A. Brown, Dion Anthony, Margaret, Cybel.

DRAMATIC ACTION: William Brown, architect, steals the identity of his rival, Dion Anthony, but dies from the weight of the artistic mask.

COMMENT: Confusing use of masks did not take away from the success of the original production (283 performances). Despite lack of clarity, familiar O'Neill concerns surface in the play: condemnation of bourgeois values (the Brown family); sympathetic, if stereotypical, portrait of earth mother/prostitute (Cybel); romantic view of the tortured artist (Dion); split characters who mirror each other (Brown, Dion). Margaret, Dion's and later Brown's wife, is not individuated. Brown, as a major character, is as colorless as his name. Dion, the artist, is by far the most interesting character in the play and has a couple of excellent speeches that poignantly express his essential alienation. Split between Brown and Dion suggests the fragmentation of the individual but the action doesn't fully explore that theme.

DISCUSSION: apotheosis of mask technique, 16–17, 67–71; radical staging ideas, 28; mirroring of characters 61; comparison to *Lazarus Laughed*, 71; epic theme compared to later domestic ones, 74; "broken" image compared to *A Moon for the Misbegotten*, 92; deaths in "middle period" plays, 128; seasonal recurrence, 130; simplified version of experience, 179.

Lazarus Laughed (1926)

MAJOR PRODUCTIONS: April 29, 1928, Pasadena Community Playhouse (Pasadena Community Players, prod.; Gilmor Brown, dir.).

PRINCIPAL CHARACTERS: Lazarus, Miriam, Caligula, Tiberius Caesar, Pompeia.

DRAMATIC ACTION: Lazarus returns from the dead to teach humankind to laugh in the face of death.

COMMENT: O'Neill's most elaborate use of masks and most spectacular drama "for an imaginative theatre" has never been produced professionally. Among a huge cast of 159 players and 420 roles, Lazarus is the only unmasked character. The most Nietzschean of all O'Neill's drama, there is little substance to the play beyond the often repeated mantra that "Death is dead. There is only laughter!" Despite the conscious visual spectacle in the play, there is very little visually striking imagery in the text. Repetition, unlike O'Neill's better plays, seems more for its own sake here, rather than an integrated and essential element.

DISCUSSION: rationale for exclusion, 22; radical staging ideas, 28; theatre as metaphor, 60–61; masks, 71; epic theme compared to later domestic ones, 74; centrifugal settings, 98, 101; deaths in "middle period" plays, 128; repetition and eternal recurrence, 130.

Strange Interlude (1927)

MAJOR PRODUCTIONS: January 30, 1928, John Golden Theatre (Theatre Guild, prod.; Philip Moeller, dir.; Jo Mielziner, des.; with Lynn Fontanne);

1963, Hudson Theatre (Actors Studio, Inc., prod.; José Quintero, dir.; David Hays, scenery and lighting; with William Prince, Franchot Tone, Geraldine Page, Ben Gazzara, Pat Hingle, Richard Thomas, Jane Fonda); 1985, Nederlander Theatre (Keith Hack, dir.; with Glenda Jackson, Tom Aldredge, Edward Petherbridge, Brian Cox, James Hazeldine).

PRINCIPAL CHARACTERS: Charles Marsden, Professor Leeds, Nina Leeds, Sam Evans, Edmund Darrell, Gordon, Madeline Arnold.

DRAMATIC ACTION: Nina Leeds, in search of happiness, passes beyond the heat of desire into the twilight of cool evening.

COMMENT: Incredibly, this was O'Neill's most financially successful play, both with audiences in the theatre (426 performances) and with a reading public. Curtain time was 5:00 P.M. and the nine act show did not end, including a dinner break, until 11:00. Play most famous for use of thought asides, a technique to allow characters to speak their innermost thoughts directly to the audience. Novelized action takes place over twenty-five years, beginning in aftermath of World War I. Only O'Neill play to project into the future, the action ends in the 1940s. Each act is episodic and focuses on Nina's pursuit of happiness through a series of men. Play reads as a melodrama and has not borne up particularly well over the years. The "deep" thoughts of the characters which receive full expression in the play appear thoroughly conventional and tame today. Likewise, the plot itself does not carry the taint of scandal that thrilled earlier audiences. There is little action. The play is best regarded as a social/ historical phenomenon. Playing up the comic elements in the play is one solution for a contemporary producer. The action within the play takes itself very seriously, an attitude which lends itself to parody and laughter.

DISCUSSION: only play to project into future, 5; attempt to add "depth," 7; autobiographical reading, 8; poetic title/prosaic contents, 11; thought asides, 16, 27–28, 39–42; novelistic aspects, 36–42; success among reading public, 41; revivals, 41; epic theme compared to later domestic ones, 74; simultaneous staging in boat race scene, 98; generational inheritance, 131; recurring struggle to survive, 132; shows effects of time over years, 133; staging aging, 138; tremendous length of play, 139–141; comparison of time and the past to *Long Day's Journey Into Night*, 152; individuation and oneness, 167; failed pursuit of the ideal (Gordon), 179.

Dynamo (1928)

MAJOR PRODUCTIONS: February 11, 1929, Martin Beck Theatre (Theatre Guild, prod.; Philip Moeller, dir.; Lee Simonson, des.).

PRINCIPAL CHARACTERS: Reuben Light, Reverend Light, Mrs. Light, Ramsay Fife, May Fife, Ada Fife.

DRAMATIC ACTION: Reuben Light prays to new god Electricity in atonement for his sins of the flesh.

COMMENT: Originally, O'Neill proposed this play as the first of a trilogy which he never completed. *Days Without End* is the only other vestige of the original plan. This was one of the few productions that O'Neill did not over-see in rehearsal (he was living in France at the time). The sound of the dynamo was the most interesting aspect of O'Neill's conception. In other respects, the literalness of the stage picture interfered with the imagery of the action. The dynamo onstage was not accepted as a female god. Presence of two skeletal houses on stage created the possibility for simultaneous action. Yet another play in which significant time passes between acts. Sexuality is very interesting in the play. Reuben transfers his guilt and love for his own mother to his next door neighbor, Mrs. Fife, who embodies the same earth mother qualities as Cybel in *The Great God Brown*. Reuben's sexual relationship with her daughter, Ada, stirs his guilt and ends with murder. The dynamo itself is a substitute for a mother figure. Reuben's self-immolation at the end can be viewed in sexual terms as his desire to go back to the mother. All of this is difficult to take in this very unsuccessful play.

DISCUSSION: justification for inclusion, 22; radical staging ideas, 28; use of monologue, 35; failure of author against director, 42; mirroring of charac-ters 61; epic theme compared to later domestic ones, 74; Simonson's skeletal design, 98; deaths in "middle period" plays, 128.

Mourning Becomes Electra (1931)

MAJOR PRODUCTIONS: October 26, 1931, Guild Theatre (Theatre Guild, prod.; Philip Moeller, dir.; Robert Edmond Jones, des.; with Alla Nazimova and Alice Brady); 1971, Stratford, CT (American Shakespeare Festival The-atre, prod.; Michael Kahn, dir.; with Sada Thompson and Jane Alexander); 1972, Joseph E. Levine Theatre (Circle in the Square, prod.; Theodore Mann, dir.; with Colleen Dewhurst and Pamela Payton-Wright); 1997, Lansburgh The-ater, Washington, D.C. (The Shakespeare Theatre, prod.; Michael Kahn, dir.; Ming Cho Lee, set; Jane Greenwood, costumes; with Kelly McGillis as Lavinia).

PRINCIPAL CHARACTERS: Ezra Mannon, Christine Mannon, Lavinia Mannon, Orin Mannon, Adam Brant, Peter Niles, Seth Beckwith.

DRAMATIC ACTION: First a mother, then her daughter, tries to escape the death-in-life fate of the Mannons.

COMMENT: O'Neill abandons tricks for the stage such as thought asides and masks in order to produce his modern version of Greek tragedy set in the aftermath of the American Civil War. This generational saga revolves around a nuclear family with Oedipal and Electra complexes. As the action unfolds, the children become more like their parents. The dynamic between the inside and outside, a rhythmic experiment begun with *Beyond the Horizon* is perfected in this play as an issue between public and private space. Watching becomes the subject of the play and the audience is fully implicated in that project. Sex-uality and depravity are again featured subjects. Lavinia emerges as the most interesting female character in all of O'Neill's plays to date. In terms of char-acter development, she is very similar to Ephraim Cabot in *Desire Under the*

Elms. Novelized action in previous plays is shown in full melodramatic glory here (two suicides, two murders). Final image of Lavinia's self-interment is one of O'Neill's very best scenic images.

DISCUSSION: poetic title/prosaic contents, 11; as melodrama (Benchley), 20; modeled on Greek tragedy, 20; commingling of melodrama and tragedy 21; struggle to find appropriate language, 42; mirroring, 61; mirroring of characters 61; literary use of masks, 64–65; similarity to *The Great God Brown,* 68; comparison to *Lazarus Laughed,* 71; unmasking revelations, 76; comparison of unmasking action to *The Hairy Ape,* 76; mask simplifies experience, 79–80; allusions to South Sea Islands, 87, 107, 108–109; reference to South Sea Islands compared to *Diff'rent,* 108; deaths in "middle period" plays, 128; generational inheritance, 132; "ceaseless struggle" in, 136–137; staging time through generations, 138; tremendous length of play, 139–141; individuation and oneness, 167; inability to see creates tension, 169; commingling of melodramatic and tragic elements, 180, 189–196; comparison of Lavinia to Cabot, 189–195.

Ah, Wilderness! (1933)

MAJOR PRODUCTIONS: October 2, 1933, Guild Theatre (Theatre Guild, prod.; Philip Moeller, dir.; Robert Edmond Jones, des.; with George M. Cohan); 1941, Guild Theatre (Theatre Guild, prod.; Eva Le Gallienne, dir.; with Harry Carey); 1975, Circle in the Square Theatre (Circle in the Square, prod.; Arvin Brown, dir.); 1988, Neil Simon Theatre (Arvin Brown, dir.; Michael Yeargan, des.; with George Hearn and Kyra Sedgwick); 1998, Vivian Beaumont Theatre (Lincoln Center, prod.; Daniel Sullivan, dir.; with Craig T. Nelson, Debra Monk, Sam Trammell).

PRINCIPAL CHARACTERS: Nat Miller, Essie Miller, Arthur Miller, Richard Miller, Sid, Lily, Muriel McComber.

DRAMATIC ACTION: A young man rebels against the bourgeois values of his small town and proclaims burning love to his equally innocent girlfriend.

COMMENT: An anomaly in O'Neill's work, this marks his only mature comedy, a genuinely warm family play with enough disturbing elements to ward away sentimentality. Makes an excellent contrast with *Long Day's Journey Into Night.* Significantly, it is the only play in which family members gather for a meal around a table. Begins O'Neill's look back into the past. Action for the play is set on July 4th, 1906. Much smaller scope in this play, despite its rather long four act structure, signals a return to domestic themes that marked early works. Whereas O'Neill's first works are highly melodramatic, later efforts, beginning with this play, enjoy a more open structure and the characters are more fully developed and nuanced as well. While Richard Miller is the protagonist of the play, there are many excellent roles: his parents, particularly, but also the parental foils, Sid and Lily. There are no heroes or villains in the play; every character is sympathetic. O'Neill's familiar theme of youth vs. age is seen from the perspective of both youth and maturity. The theme of the play, its warm humor, an ensemble cast which places no undue burden upon any one actor, make it frequently produced by student and amateur groups. While it is more accessible for those reasons, it remains a delicate play and one that can be easily ruined by excessive sentimentality. An exploration of the dark side of the play makes it all the more rewarding to behold. The action critiques the very values that it seems to celebrate and that conflict makes for rewarding drama.

DISCUSSION: autobiographical reading, 8; part of contemporary repertory, 13; comic mask, 74–76; mirror side of *Long Day's Journey Into Night*, 74; as example of realism, 94–96; seasonal recurrence, 130–131; use of dinner table compared to *Long Day's Journey Into Night*, 153.

Days Without End (1933)

MAJOR PRODUCTIONS: January 8, 1934, Henry Miller Theatre (Theatre Guild, prod.; Philip Moeller, dir.; Lee Simonson, des.)

PRINCIPAL CHARACTERS: John, Loving, Elsa, Father Baird.

DRAMATIC ACTION: John Loving, unable to integrate two sides of his personality, threatens to destroy his marriage for fear of losing his wife.

COMMENT: O'Neill's worst failure since *Dynamo*, this play originally followed the same quest for a new religion after the death of the old God. O'Neill struggled to find an ending for his play, just as novelist John Loving struggles to end his book. O'Neill's solution fails miserably: John Loving vanquishing his alter ego at the foot of the cross produced a highly melodramatic ending. The problem of the ending is one that O'Neill eventually solved in his best plays in a format that provided closure yet simultaneously seemed to suggest ongoing life processes and endurance. Entire play can be read as a quest to find an appropriate ending, and in that respect, this play is quite interesting. The fact that the ending seems so contrived and false in the play further points the direction in which O'Neill's final and best works would go.

DISCUSSION: employed masks for last time, 17; justification for inclusion, 22; melodramatic ending, 44; novelistic detachment, 47–48; mirroring of characters 61; masks and dualism, 71; struggle to finish the play, 74; epic theme compared to later domestic ones, 74; theme of servitude compared to *A Moon for the Misbegotten* 90; 12 year gap before next O'Neill play on Broadway, 112; no death scenes in "final period" plays, 128–129.

A Touch of the Poet (1939)

MAJOR PRODUCTIONS: March 29, 1957, Dramatiska Teatern, Stockholm, Sweden; October 2, 1958, Helen Hayes Theatre (Harold Clurman, dir.; Ben Edwards, des.; with Kim Stanley, Helen Hayes, and Eric Portman); 1967, ANTA Playhouse (Jack Sydow, dir.; with Denholm Elliott); 1977, Helen Hayes Theatre (José Quintero, dir.; Ben Edwards, set; Jane Greenwood, cos.; with Jason Robards, Geraldine Fitzgerald, Kathryn Walker, and Milo O'Shea).

PRINCIPAL CHARACTERS: Cornelius Melody, Nora Melody, Sara Melody, Jamie Cregan, Deborah Harford, Nicholas Gadsby.

DRAMATIC ACTION: A poor New England tavern owner clings to the image of himself as a Byronic hero.

COMMENT: First O'Neill play to use only a single setting; offstage areas play key roles in the action of the play: the adjoining bar; the upstairs bedroom; the barn where the mare stays; the Harford estate a few miles away. Only completed play of the entire elaborate cycle of plays, tales of "possessors, self-dispossessed." Unmasking action never fully resolves and creates emotional impact. The mechanical and obvious structure of the play leads to a surprising conclusion and is a good example of O'Neill's dramatic method of super-imposing a simple structure over what turns out to be an unanswerable question, one that both the characters within the play and the audience witnessing the event must ponder at the end.

DISCUSSION: poetic title/prosaic contents, 11; posthumous production, 13; clothing as mask, 17; formulaic plot, 21; unproduced during O'Neill's lifetime, 31; Aristotelian plot, 49; failure of novelistic impulse, 49–50; pipe dream or hopeless hope theme, 59; mirrors, 61; pride as mask, 64; unmasking action, 77–80; first full-length play to have only one setting, 94; spatial design (onstage/offstage), 102–103; offstage space governs action, 109–110; offstage gunshot parodies melodramatic ending, 129; generational inheritance, 131; adheres to unities of time, place and action, 135; "ceaseless struggle" in, 136–138; individuation and oneness, 167; heavy drinking as "fog," 168–169; transcendence of melodrama, 178–180.

More Stately Mansions (1939)

MAJOR PRODUCTIONS: September 11, 1962, Dramatiska Teatern, Stockholm, Sweden; October 31, 1967, Broadhurst Theatre (José Quintero, dir.; Ben Edwards, set; Jane Greenwood, cos.; with Colleen Dewhurst, Arthur Hill, Ingrid Bergman).

PRINCIPAL CHARACTERS: Sara Harford, Simon Harford, Deborah Harford.

DRAMATIC ACTION: A young man fights to preserve his soul against his competing desire for material gains and conquests.

COMMENT: An extremely long draft of an unfinished play that O'Neill obviously intended to destroy along with his other incompleted work. Nevertheless, this play, more than *A Touch of the Poet*, reveals the pattern of the cycle plays and articulates the overall theme of *A Tale of Possessors, Self-dispossessed*. Shifting alliances between Simon and his wife and his mother are plodding, yet revelatory for the dynamic in all of O'Neill's best plays. Simon's dualism is mirrored in Sara. The two women characters are actually more interesting than Simon as they portray the split between mother/wife (lover) and actually exchange roles at various times. Integration of all aspects of personality and individuality continues to dominate as a concern, although the problem is worked out in a very formulaic fashion, an advance upon *Days Without End*, but far short of treatments of the same issues in the last plays. The design of the play remains obvious, which, in fact, is what makes the play worthy of study insofar as it reveals patterns more skillfully woven into the fabric of the final plays.

DISCUSSION: survives in draft form, 6; poetic title/prosaic contents, 11; a "lost" play, 22; dramatic function of monologues, 39; time as subject, 49; dividedness and multiplicity, 79; significance of doors, 102; marriage of Sara Melody and Harford as subject, 109; generational inheritance, 131; sprawling drama, 135; tremendous length of play, 139–141.

The Iceman Cometh (1940)

MAJOR PRODUCTIONS: October 9, 1946, Martin Beck Theatre (Theatre Guild, prod.; Eddie Dowling, dir.; Robert Edmond Jones, des.); 1956 (Circle in the Square, prod.; José Quintero, dir.; David Hays, scenery and lighting; with Jason Robards, Jr.); 1973 (Circle in the Square, prod.; Theodore Mann, dir.; with James Earl Jones); 1985, Lunt-Fontanne Theatre (José Quintero, dir.; Ben Edwards, scenery; Jane Greenwood, costumes; with Jason Robards, Donald Moffat, Bernard Hughes); 1990, Goodman Theatre, Chicago (Robert Falls, dir.; with Brian Dennehy and Jerome Kilty); 1999, Brooks Atkinson Theatre (Howard Davies, dir.; with Kevin Spacey).

PRINCIPAL CHARACTERS: Harry Hope, Larry Slade, Theodore Hickman, Don Parritt, James Cameron (Jimmy Tomorrow).

DRAMATIC ACTION: A hardware salesman visits Harry Hope's bar for his annual drunk, but this time he soberly urges the bums to give up their pipe dreams.

COMMENT: O'Neill's largest ensemble cast in one of his longest plays, set entirely within the confines of Harry Hope's saloon. One of O'Neill's most musical plays in terms of a dominant theme (role of pipe dreams) repeated with variations over four acts and played out among major and minor characters. Another retrospective play set in 1912, filled with humor in the first half which transforms into chilling action. While Hickey is the protagonist and driving force in the play, Larry Slade is the moral center of the play, and a target not only for Hickey's pitch, but Don Parritt's plea as well. The rest of the bums at Harry's fill out a rich chorus. This play is notable for its lack of women, the only three female characters are "tarts" who play secondary characters. Meanwhile three female characters who play pivotal roles in the drama do not actually appear in the action. Ending of the play resolves the action, but also questions everything that has come before. As a play that has been compared to Gorky's *The Lower Depths*, *The Iceman Cometh* exists as a paradigmatic realist text, but its action seems to refute the very tenets of realism and tragedy. The play, in the voice of Hickey, attacks O'Neill's own basis for tragedy, the need for the pipe dream, which had been established in all of O'Neill's earlier plays.

DISCUSSION: written during respite from cycle plays, 6; poetic title/prosaic contents, 11; posthumous production (1956), 12–13; tension between inside

& outside, 18; repetition, 19; formulaic plot, 21; disdain for actors, 31; dramatic function of monologues, 43; pipe dream or hopeless hope theme, 59; mirroring of characters 61; mask of pretense, 73; unmasking action, 73–74; booze has no kick (comparison to *A Moon for the Misbegotten*) 86; realistic interior set in saloon, 94; sources for settings, 94; realism as tautology, 95; critique of O'Neill's spatial dualism, 112–125; no death scenes with exception of Parritt, 129; adheres to unities of time, place and action, 135; "ceaseless struggle" in, 136–138; staging past through pipe dreams, 138; tremendous length of play, 139–141; individuation and oneness, 167; heavy drinking as "fog," 168–169; transcendence of melodrama, 178–180; Hickey's melodramatic revelation of hidden motive compared to Lavinia's final confession, 196.

Long Day's Journey Into Night (1941)

MAJOR PRODUCTIONS: February 10, 1956, Dramatiska Teatern, Stockholm, Sweden; November 7, 1956, Helen Hayes Theatre (José Quintero, dir.; David Hays, set; Tharon Musser, lighting; Motley, costumes; with Fredric March, Florence Eldridge, Jason Robards, Jr., Bradford Dillman, Katherine Ross); 1971, Promenade Theatre (Arvin Brown, dir.; with Robert Ryan, Geraldine Fitzgerald, James Naughton, Stacy Keach); 1976, Brooklyn Academy of Music (Jason Robards, dir.; with Jason Robards, Zoe Caldwell, Kevin Conway, Michael Moriarty, Lindsay Crouse); 1986, Broadhurst Theatre (Jonathan Miller, dir.; with Jack Lemmon, Bethel Leslie, Kevin Spacey, and Peter Gallagher); 1988, Neil Simon Theatre (José Quintero, dir.; with Jason Robards, Colleen Dewhurst, Campbell Scott, Jamey Sheridan).

PRINCIPAL CHARACTERS: James Tyrone, Mary Tyrone, James Tyrone, Jr., Edmund Tyrone, Cathleen.

DRAMATIC ACTION: Mary Tyrone's relapse into drug addiction plunges her family into despair and a desperate search to explain what happened and what went wrong and who's to blame.

COMMENT: Aristotelian action takes place in one day as each act centers around mealtime and moves inexorably from morning light to late at night. All the action takes place within one interior, the summer home of the Tyrones, which makes Mary the center of the play both as the traditional homemaker and as the character most alienated in the action. Mary is the only one of the Tyrones who never leaves the house. In fact, when the action begins, she has only recently returned "home" from treatment at a sanitarium. Similar to "pipe dreams" in *The Iceman Cometh*, "home" is repeated and reformulated many times throughout the action of the play. The play asks, what is a "home"? The action plays out in a series of dialogues between father/son, mother/son, mother/father, son/son and throws that question very much in doubt. Unverified accounts of past deeds make it very difficult to determine who is to blame for things that have befallen the family. The length of the play is essential to show the play from a variety of perspectives in order to gain sympathy for every character and to see how they are all caught in familial relationships of love and hate from which they cannot escape. The length of the play is necessary in order to see the action from multiple points of view, so that any one account of what happened must be interpreted in terms of who says what to whom and under what circumstances. Almost inexplicably, events in the past become more cloudy as they are brought forward for discussion.

DISCUSSION: written during respite from cycle plays, 6; illusion of definitive, autobiographical work, 7–10; struggles of characters mirror playwright's struggle, 9; poetic title/prosaic contents, 11; stammering as poetry, 11; posthumous production (1956), 13, 31; retrospective action, 19, 141–163; justification of references, 22; description of bookcases, 33–34; failure of novelistic impulse, 50; pipe dream or hopeless hope theme, 59; mirroring of characters 61; mirror side of *Ah, Wilderness!*, 74; realistic interior and only one setting, 94; source for setting is Monte Cristo Cottage, 94; contrast between interior and exterior scene, 97; here and there paradigm, 104–105; spare room and unseen upstairs as outside forces, 110–111; desire to transcend materiality, 111–112; comparison of Edmund's Act 4 speech to Larry Slade's about men's greedy hopes and fears, 115–116; Edmund's lack of theatricality compared to Slade's, 119–120; right kind of pity, 124–125; adheres to unities of time, place and action, 135; tremendous length of play, 139–141; fog in, 168; heavy drinking as "fog," 168–169; transcendence of melodrama, 178–180; autobiographical nature compared to *Desire Under the Elms*, 180.

Hughie (1942)

MAJOR PRODUCTIONS: 1958, Dramatiska Teatern, Stockholm, Sweden; 1964, Royale Theatre (José Quintero, dir.; David Hays, scenery and lighting; with Jason Robards); 1975, John Golden Theatre (Martin Fried, dir., with Ben Gazzara); 1996, Circle in the Square (Circle in the Square, prod.; Al Pacino, dir.; with Al Pacino).

PRINCIPAL CHARACTERS: Erie Smith, Night Clerk.

DRAMATIC ACTION: A down-at-his-heels two-bit gambler tries to start a conversation with the new night clerk and restore his old confidence.

COMMENT: Only one of the planned *By Way of Obit* series that O'Neill completed, this one-act is one of his most thoroughly modern, existential plays of hope and loneliness. A minimal play in every respect: minimal set, minimal cast, minimal length, minimal dialogue. Action contains some of O'Neill's best language, a musical mastery of vernacular and slang from the 1920s just before the onset of the Depression. Colorful language masks desperation of scene and dramatic situation which adds tension to the experience of the play. Thought asides are not included in spoken text, but stage directions include them as a kind of actor's subtext for the Night Clerk. Absence of dialogue in the play underscores the desire for human contact in the play. Modern feel to this play gives it a Beckettian flavor. Return to one-act form, after such long plays as *The Iceman Cometh* and *Long Day's Journey Into Night*, represents a break in style.

DISCUSSION: part of contemporary repertory, 13; novel drama 16; example of unmasking, 22; unproduced during O'Neill's lifetime, 31; failure of novel drama celebrates theatre, 51–58; mirroring, 61; realistic play with only one set, 94; unseen (offstage) perimeter spaces, 103; no death scenes in "final period" plays, 129; transcendence of melodrama, 179.

A Moon for the Misbegotten (1943)

MAJOR PRODUCTIONS: February 20, 1947, Hartman Theatre, Columbus, Ohio (Theatre Guild, prod.; Arthur Shields, dir.; Robert Edmond Jones, des.; with Mary Welch and James Dunn); 1957, Bijou Theatre (Carmen Capalbo, dir.; with Wendy Hiller, Cyril Cusack, and Franchot Tone); 1973, Morosco Theatre (José Quintero, dir.; Ben Edwards, scenery and lighting; Jane Green-wood, costumes; with Colleen Dewhurst, Jason Robards, and Ed Flanders); 1984, Cort Theatre (David Leveaux, dir.; with Kate Nelligan, Jerome Kilty, and Ian Bannen).

PRINCIPAL CHARACTERS: Josie Hogan, Phil Hogan, James Tyrone, Jr.

DRAMATIC ACTION: A dying alcoholic confesses his sins to his chaste lover.

COMMENT: A kind of sequel to *Long Day's Journey Into Night*, this play focuses on a sympathetic treatment of the elder Tyrone son. While he functions as the protagonist and the play is "his story," Josie Hogan emerges as the most interesting character in the play, and O'Neill's most nuanced, if not sometimes grotesque, portrayal of a woman. An overt melodramatic plot keeps the action going, but this play is really a character study in which all masking peels away to reveal human vulnerability. The actual resolution is not as easy as the action implies, though, and questions remain about identity and individuality at the end of the play. The action seems to travel from pretense to reality, but the nature of that reality continues to shift through the surprising and painful conclusion. This play was not received well when it first opened, nor on its subsequent revival. Critics considered it a small play in comparison to *Iceman* and *Long Day's Journey*. The 1973 production with Quintero directing Robards and Dewhurst restored opinion of this play as one of O'Neill's best. More than any other O'Neill play, a single production changed the critical estimation of a work. This is fitting since *A Moon for the Misbegotten* is about, as much as anything else, acting, and the action plays out as an elaborate play-within-a-play.

DISCUSSION: poetic title/prosaic contents, 11; posthumous production, 13; metaphorical mask, 16–17; formulaic plot, 21; example of unmasking, 22; unproduced in New York during O'Neill's lifetime, 31; description of Josie Hogan, 34–35; collision of novelistic and dramatic, 50–51; unmasking action, 80–92; action set exclusively on Hogan farm, 94; Tyrone's anger against mother similar to Don Parritt's in *Iceman*, 123–124; no death scenes in "final period" plays, 129; adheres to unities of time, place and action, 135; evoking past through alcohol, 138; heavy drinking as "fog," 168–169; transcendence of melodrama, 178–180.

Notes

Introduction: The Director's Perspective

1. The quotation marks surrounding the title signify that Anna Christie is only the nickname of Anna Christopherson. In the first act, Anna says that she called herself by that shorter name in Minnesota (where she worked as a prostitute). It is the only reference to Anna Christie in the entire play. O'Neill paid careful attention to his titles; the quotation marks emphasize important themes of identity, redemption, and fate.

2. The volume of plays, selected by O'Neill with an introduction by Joseph Wood Krutch, is titled *Nine Plays* (New York: Horace Liveright, 1932). The contents include *The Emperor Jones, The Hairy Ape, All God's Chillun Got Wings, Desire Under the Elms, Marco Millions, The Great God Brown, Lazarus Laughed, Strange Interlude*, and *Mourning Becomes Electra*. This volume is still in print today (New York: Modern Library, 1993).

3. According to Doris Alexander, O'Neill woke up with a dream of a dead baby on New Year's morning, 1924. See her analysis of *Desire Under the Elms* in *O'Neill's Creative Struggle: The Decisive Decade 1924–1933* (University Park, PA: Pennsylvania State University Press, 1992) 23–39.

4. Originally published in the *Boston Evening Postscript*, Oct. 31, 1925; rpt. Isaac Goldberg, *The Theatre of George Jean Nathan* (New York: Simon and Schuster, 1926); rpt. Cargill 102.

5. See Eugene O'Neill, *The Unfinished Plays: Notes for "The Visit of Malatesta," "The Last Conquest," "Blind Alley Guy,"* Ed. Virginia Floyd (New York: Continuum–Frederick Ungar, 1988).

6. For O'Neill as a failed poet, see John Henry Raleigh, *The Plays of Eugene O'Neill*, 209. See also Mary McCarthy, "Dry Ice," *Partisan Review* 13 (Nov.-Dec. 1946) 577–579; rpt. Raleigh, *Twentieth Century Interpretations of "The Iceman Cometh"* (Englewood Cliffs, NJ: Prentice-Hall, 1968).

7. Originally published in *The Nation*, March 3, 1956; rpt. Harold Clurman, *Lies Like Truth* (New York: Macmillan, 1958).

8. In *Eugene O'Neill and the American Critic* (2nd ed.; New York: Archon, 1973), Jordan Y. Miller records the following production record (75–78): *The Iceman Cometh* opened on May 8, 1956, at Circle in the Square in Greenwich Village and played 565 performances; *Long Day's Journey Into Night* opened on November 7 at the Helen Hayes Theatre and ran 390 performances; Carmen Capalbo independently staged *A Moon for the Misbegotten* at the Bijou Theatre on May 2, 1957, in a short run that lasted 68 performances; *A Touch of the Poet* opened October 2, 1958, also at the Helen Hayes Theatre, and played 284 performances.

9. Henry Alford's amusing satire replaces O'Neill's dialogue with his famous stage directions. Here's a taste: "He begins to laugh, softly at first — a laugh so full of a complete acceptance of life, a profound assertion of joy in living, so devoid of all self-consciousness or fear, that it is like a great bird song triumphant in depths of sky, proud and powerful, infectious with love, casting on the listener an enthralling spell."

10. See Eugene O'Neill, "Memoranda on Masks," *The American Spectator* 1 (Nov. 1932): 3; "Second Thoughts" (Dec. 1932): 2; "A Dramatist's Notebook" (Jan. 1933): 2; rpt. Cargill 116–122; rpt. Eugene O'Neill, *The Unknown O'Neill*, ed. Travis Bogard (New Haven: Yale University Press, 1988) 404–411.

11. O'Neill would have won the Nobel in 1935, but for the lukewarm response of Hallström, president of the Nobel Committee. As a result, no award was given that year. While he praised O'Neill for his "original conception of tragedy" in making the 1936 presentation, Hallström had this to say in the previous year: "[O'Neill] is unquestionably a remarkable dramatist in his impulsive power, but he quickly exhausts his audience's interest by his obsessions, by his complicated plots, and by his technical tricks, which rarely come off. He has great gaps in his general culture and an almost total lack of taste, which does not make him particularly well known in his own country" (*Nobel Prize Library* 195).

12. *Lost Plays of Eugene O'Neill* (New York: New Fathoms Press, 1950), an unauthorized edition of early plays "found" with an expired copyright in the Library of Congress, included *Abortion, The Movie Man, The Sniper, Servitude*, and *A Wife for a Life*. The volume *Ten "Lost" Plays* by Eugene O'Neill (New York: Random House, 1964) is a posthumous collection of early works, lost only in the sense that the plays embarrassed the author and he refused to publish them. Mrs. O'Neill allowed them to be "found" after his death. The volume includes nine one-acts (*Thirst, The Web, Warnings, Fog, Recklessness, Abortion, The Movie Man, The Sniper, A Wife for a Life*) and one full-length play (*Servitude*). O'Neill did publish a limited edition (1,000 copies) of the first five of these plays as a young man, at the expense of his father, under the title *Thirst and Other Plays* (Boston: Gorham Press, 1914). This volume did not sell well and O'Neill chose never to publish them again.

Chapter 1: Writing a Novel Drama

1. Ronald Wainscott notes in *Staging O'Neill: The Experimental Years, 1920–1934* (New Haven: Yale, 1988), 131, that the first edition of *Welded* did not include stage directions for followspots as "auras of egoism." Nor did the first production make use of such lighting effects. O'Neill added this written direction in editions subsequent to the production.

2. See SL 97–118.

3. See Bogard, *Contour in Time* 183 and Doris Alexander, *O'Neill's Creative Struggle* 189. Other marriage plays written during this same period include *Diff'rent* (1920), *The First Man* (1921), and *All God's Chillun Got Wings* (1923).

4. The phrase, "antitheatrical prejudice," borrows from Jonas Barish's excellent book of that same name. See *The Antitheatrical Prejudice* (Berkeley: University of California, 1981). On O'Neill, Barish mentions him in the introductory pages of his chapter called "Jonson and the Loathèd Stage": "Eugene O'Neill, for example, registered repeated dismay at what he scathingly called the "show-shop" of the theater, recording his sense of betrayal at what actors, including the most gifted and dedicated actors, made of the characters he had forged in the silence of his imagination" (133).

5. O'Neill later learned, according to Travis Bogard's notes (CP1 1101), that the proper spelling of the surname is "Christopherson," and he made the change when he wrote *"Anna Christie."*

6. See "On the Tragedies of Shakespeare considered with reference to their fitness for stage representation" in Charles and Mary Lamb, *Works*, ed. E. V. Lucas, 5 vols. (New York, 1903) 1: 99.

7. Originally published in an interview in the *New York Herald Tribune* March 16, 1924.

8. *The Emperor Jones* is generally acknowledged as the first American play to feature a black actor in a leading role. O'Neill ultimately replaced Gilpin with Paul Robeson. Gilpin never played another major role in New York and died a few years later on his farm in New Jersey at the age of fifty-one.

9. O'Neill made these comments in an article for the playbill for *The Spook Sonata*, which opened as the first production by Experimental Theatre, Inc., January 3, 1924.

10. To Macgowan, O'Neill writes in 1926: "Has it ever been produced as I wrote it? Never! (I'm leaving acting out of this dope, as a necessary uncertainty.) There have never been the elm trees of my play, characters almost, and my acts were chopped up into four distinct scenes through lack of time to get the changes perfected in black-outs, the flow of life from room to room of the house, the house as character, the acts as smooth developing wholes have never existed" (SL 213).

11. CP3 724. "The Moor, I know his trumpet." This early quote from *Othello* is significant because James will later relate the high point of his theatrical career as playing Othello and Iago in repertory with Edwin Booth. There is a further parallel in the relationship of James/Mary and Othello/Desdemona.

12. CP3 759. "God is dead: of His pity for man hath God died" (Part II, chapter 3). Jamie sneers at Edmund's reading of Nietzsche out of jealousy, while the elder Tyrone equates Edmund's reading such philosophy with Jamie's Broadway loafing and scolds them both for flouting the Catholic Church.

13. CP3 825. From *Poems and Ballads*. Jamie, not Edmund, quotes from Swinburne, a detail that ties the two brothers together. Despite Jamie's jealousy of his younger brother, it is clear that they share similar tastes and this quotation verifies that Jamie introduced Edmund to literature. To paraphrase an earlier dialogue: Jamie is Edmund's Frankenstein.

14. I am spurred on with this idea by a paper presented by Thierry Dubost, "Portrait of a Beauty," O'Neill Panel, American Literature Association Convention, Renaissance Harborplace Hotel, Baltimore, May 28, 1999. He, too, sees the stated contradictions in Josie's description as a warning to the director/reader: "If, following your own conception of beauty, you were tempted to define Josie Hogan as a mannish person, you are wrong. She may not be Miss America, but possesses a womanly beauty of her own."

15. See Edna Kenton, "The Provincetown Players and The Playwrights' Theatre 1915–1922," ed. Travis Bogard and Jackson Bryer, *The Eugene O'Neill Review* 21, nos. 1 & 2 (Spring & Fall 1997) 47–48. Also, see Bogard quoting Kenton in *Contour in Time*, 78–79.

16. In the 1985 revival at The Nederlander Theatre, Edward Petherbridge as Marsden received glowing notices as a driving force behind the successful production. See "Marsden Revisited," interview by Yvonne Shafer with Edward Petherbridge, 26 May 1998, Brooklyn Academy of Music, *The Eugene O'Neill Review* 21, nos. 1 & 2 (Spring & Fall 1997) 163–171.

17. Jamie, horribly drunk, returned with his mother's body on a train to New York on the night of *The Hairy Ape*'s opening performance. O'Neill, as usual, didn't go to the play, but he didn't meet the train either. Later, when his brother lay blind and dying painfully from alcoholism in a sanitarium bed, O'Neill refused to visit him.

Chapter 2: Masks and Mirrors

1. Wainscott 110. Masks were not O'Neill's idea, but costumer Blanche Hays', for the Fifth Avenue chorus in scene 5 (117). Wainscott emphasizes the collaborative nature of this successful and influential production: "The work of director, designers, and actors melded most perfectly here [scene 5] in capturing an unforgettable style which was not only emblematic but also established a stylistic staging model for American expressionism of the 1920s" (118).

2. See Wainscott 147–156. The mayor prevented children from acting in the first scene of the play, ostensibly because they were "too young"; consequently, director James Light read the scene to the audience. Most of the critical commentary focused on the racial issue.

3. The number of masks reached 300 for the initial production in Pasadena (Wainscott 221).

4. See Miller 363–364. The first production of this play was staged on April 9, 1928, by the Pasadena Community Playhouse in California, directed by Gilmor Brown. Fordham University produced the play in 1948, but both play and production received poor reviews in the New York premiere.

5. See O'Neill's letter of 1926 to Kenneth Macgowan explaining the novelty of the play (SL 204). One of the biggest obstacles in staging the play was that O'Neill could think of no actor who could play the title role (SL 207). In a letter to Benjamin De Casseres, O'Neill suggested the Russian actor Chaliapin for the role, but he didn't speak English (SL 246). In a letter to critic Barrett Clark in 1930, he thought Paul Robeson would be a good Lazarus, though he thought his race might be disconcerting (SL 365). In a letter to Lawrence Langner in 1943, O'Neill puts forward the unlikely candidacy of Spencer Tracy for the part (SL 548).

6. In a letter to Eugene O'Neill, Jr., dated November 11, 1932, O'Neill tells his son that he wrote the first draft of *Ah, Wilderness!* in one month.

7. This interview in 1948, the second in a three part series in *The New Yorker*, was the last one ever granted by O'Neill.

8. See Thomas F. Van Laan, "Singing in the Wilderness: The Dark Vision of O'Neill's Only Mature Comedy," in Bloom 99–108 for analysis of the unresolved social ills depicted in the play.

Chapter 3: Beyond the Proscenium

1. Jimmy-the-Priest's, also the scene of Act 1 in *"Anna Christie,"* was a dive on the Lower East side on Fulton Street. The Golden Swan, a.k.a. The Hell Hole, was on the corner of 6th Avenue and 4th Street in Greenwich Village. The Garden Hotel, on the N. E. corner of 27th St. and Madison Ave., was located across the street from the original Madison Square Garden. O'Neill frequented all these establishments between 1910 and 1920.

2. See www.eugeneoneill.org/mcc.htm for visitor information. The Eugene O'Neill Theater Center owns and operates the site and claims: "Visitors from around the world see the living room furnished according to O'Neill's vivid description in *Long Day's Journey Into Night* as well as O'Neill's seaman's bag and desk."

3. Mielziner was a very young designer whose famous style, "selective realism," had not yet developed. In addition, *Strange Interlude's* multiple settings (6) and nine acts created technical problems for scene changing. Wainscott notes that Act 8, the yacht scene, was the only one erected independently and thus presented visual relief from the other rectangular, box settings (237).

4. Adding to the recipe of failure for *Dynamo* was the fact that O'Neill did

not personally oversee rehearsal, an anomaly for him. He was living in France and traveling with Carlotta at the time while waiting for his divorce from Agnes Boulton to become official.

5. See Edna Kenton, "The Provincetown Players and The Playwrights' Theater 1915–1922," ed. Travis Bogard and Jackson R. Bryer, *The Eugene O'Neill Review* 21 Nos. 1 & 2 (Spring/Fall, 1997) 88–89. Kenton quotes O'Neill: "I want to see whether it's possible to make an audience go mad too. Perhaps the first rows will snicker—perhaps they won't. We'll see" (89). Apparently they did, not surprisingly, since the first rows were only four feet from the stage.

6. Kenton's remarks that the three ghosts were composed of fish net and seaweed, augmented with orange, green and purple paint, produces a theatrical image worthy of the Count of Monte Cristo emerging from the briny sea to proclaim: "The world is mine!"

7. Clipper ships recalled O'Neill's past and his love of sailing. Travis Bogard records in *Contour in Time* (388) that O'Neill ordered models of ships built when he was writing *The Calms of Capricorn*, one of the unfinished cycle plays, and that these models were mounted on the walls of his study at Tao House.

8. Sexual and racial politics might astonish the modern reader. Caleb argues, for example, that the native woman with whom he had relations was a heathen and therefore barely human. Indeed, the New England community regards the practice of men having sexual relations with such women as nothing more than male weakness. Emma's decision not to marry Caleb, then, defies the standards of her society.

9. Michael Kahn's production of *Mourning Becomes Electra* at the Shakespeare Theatre in Washington, D.C., in 1997 made sexual revulsion palpable in the morning after scene in which Christine rose from Mannon's bed in the early morning hours and washed herself at a basin. This gesture, not in the stage directions, added tremendously to an understanding of a woman's life in the Mannon household.

10. See, for example, Anthony S. Abbott, *The Vital Lie: Reality and Illusion in Modern Drama* (Tuscaloosa: University of Alabama Press, 1989).

11. See Cyrus Day, "The Iceman and the Bridegroom: Some Observations on the Death of O'Neill's Salesman," *Modern Drama* 1 (May 1958) 3–9; also Joseph Wood Krutch, "Drama," *Nation* 163 (26 Oct.) 481–482.

12. In Matthew 5:6: "And at midnight there was a cry made, 'Behold, the bridegroom cometh; go ye out to meet him." The joke alluded to in the play is one associated with Hickey, one he always tells, about the iceman cheating with another man's wife. The set-up for the joke spots the return of a man from work who calls upstairs to his wife: Has the iceman come yet? She replies: "No, but he's breathing hard."

Chapter 4: Plays Without End

1. In his letter to Nathan, O'Neill wrote: "The happy ending is merely the comma at the end of a gaudy introductory clause, with the body of the sentence still unwritten" (SL 148). O'Neill considered calling the play *Comma* at one time.

2. See Virginia Floyd, *Eugene O'Neill at Work* 228–229; also see Stephen A. Black, "O'Neill's Dramatic Process" *American Literature* 59 (March 1987): 58–70.

3. See SL 554 for O'Neill's argument that Barrett Clark's analysis of deaths in the plays is skewed because the early works are included. In O'Neill's letter to R. W. Cottingham in 1944, he says of his friend (Clark): "To make a good case, he includes the earliest, most immature stuff, attempts at plays written when I was still trying to become a playwright. That these would-be plays were ever published is my misfortune. But published or not, anyone can see they are merely preliminary amateurish-melodramatic junk and should no more be considered as adult works than diapers should be rated as trousers."

4. The two contemporary writers who are most often compared to O'Neill are August Wilson, who is writing his own elaborate cycle plays of African-Americans in the 20th century, and Tony Kushner, whose *Angels in America*, in two parts, approached the epic size of *Mourning Becomes Electra*.

5. For example, *Wit*, the 1999 Pulitzer Prize winning play by Margaret Edson, enjoyed great success at the Union Square Theatre with a running time of 90 minutes.

6. See Michael Manheim, "The Transcendence of Melodrama in *Long Day's Journey Into Night*," *Perspectives on O'Neill*, ed. Shyamal Bagchee (University of Victoria, B.C., Canada: English Literary Studies, 1988) 33–42, for his excellent analysis of melodramatic elements in the play.

7. Judith Barlow makes a convincing argument in *Final Acts: The Creation of Three Late O'Neill Plays* (Athens: University of Georgia Press, 1985) that Mary has not taken drugs prior to Act 1. In her analysis, the suspicions of the family and endless watching of her cause her to relapse after her first appearance on stage: "By keeping her drug-free during the first act, O'Neill can show that there is a basis for her complaints: we actually see the men scrutinizing and doubting an as yet innocent Mary" (79).

8. In this most autobiographical play, one conspicuous fact of O'Neill's life is not mentioned in Edmund's background. While his suicide attempt is recorded, as well as his life of dissipation in Buenos Aires, there is no reference to a failed marriage and an unwanted child.

9. This same story is reconfigured in *A Moon for the Misbegotten*, in which Hogan is the tenant farmer who battles with T. Stedman Harder.

Chapter 5: Tragic Vision

1. Although rumors fanned by George Jean Nathan had O'Neill expelled for throwing a beer bottle through then university president Woodrow Wilson's window, the Gelbs set the record straight by noting that O'Neill was not asked to return for his second year because of "poor scholastic study." He did not take any of his final exams (116–117).

2. See Albert E. Kalson and Lisa M. Schwerdt, "Eternal Recurrence and the Shaping of O'Neill's Dramatic Structures," *Comparative Drama* 24 (Summer 1990) 133–150 in which they note the cyclical form in O'Neill's drama and cite the influence of Strindberg, in addition to Nietzsche.

3. Thierry Dubost records overt use of fog in *Bound East for Cardiff*, *Fog*, *The Long Voyage Home*, *"Anna Christie," The Hairy Ape, Mourning Becomes Electra*, and *Long Day's Journey Into Night* (199).

4. René Charles Guilbert de Pixérécourt (1773–1844), author of 120 works, is the acknowledged "father of melodrama." The rise of the genre in Post-Revolution France is directly connected to the fall of the aristocracy and a new political intent to legislate morality and, above all, to make that morality visible.

5. See Michael Manheim, "O'Neill's Transcendence of Melodrama in *A Touch of the Poet* and *A Moon for the Misbegotten*," *Critical Approaches to O'Neill*, ed. John H. Stroupe (New York: AMS Press, 1988) 147–159; "The Transcendence of Melodrama in *Long Day's Journey Into Night*," *Perspectives on O'Neill: New Essays*, ed. Shyamal Bagchee (University of Victoria, B.C., Canada: English Literary Studies, 1988) 33–42; "The Transcendence of Melodrama in O'Neill's *The Iceman Cometh*," *Critical Essays on Eugene O'Neill*, ed. James J. Martine (Boston: G. K. Hall & Co., 1984) 145–157.

6. See Stephen A. Black, "'Celebrant of Loss': Eugene O'Neill 1888–1953" *The Cambridge Companion to O'Neill*, ed. Michael Manheim (New York: Cambridge University Press, 1998) 4–17. See also Doris Alexander, *Eugene O'Neill's Creative Struggle: The Decisive Decade, 1924–1933* (University Park: Pennsylvania State University Press, 1992).

Conclusion: Resonant Emotion

1. See Richard Gilman, *The Making of Modern Drama* (1972; New York: Plenum–Da Capo Press, Inc., 1987) vii.

2. See letter to George Jean Nathan about "science and materialism" (SL 311).

Works Cited

Alexander, Doris. *Eugene O'Neill's Creative Struggle: The Decisive Decade, 1924–1933*. University Park: Pennsylvania State University Press, 1992.

Alford, Henry. "Unspoken O'Neill." *New Yorker*. 30 Oct. 1998: 68.

Atkinson, Brooks. "Ennobeling O'Neill." *New York Times*. 22 Nov. 1936, sec. 11: 1.

Barish, Jonas. *The Antitheatrical Prejudice*. 1981. Berkeley: University of California Press, 1985.

Barlow, Judith E. *Final Acts: The Creation of Three Late O'Neill Plays*. Athens: University of Georgia Press, 1985.

Barnes, Clive. "Positively Misty Over 'Christie'." Review. *New York Post*. 15 Jan. 1993: 26.

Barthes, Roland. "The Reality Effect." *French Literary Theory Today: A Reader*. Ed. Tzvetan Todorov. Trans. R. Carter. Cambridge: Cambridge University Press, 1982.

Basso, Hamilton. "Profiles: The Tragic Sense—II." *New Yorker*. 6 Mar. 1948: 34–49.

Benchley, Robert. "Top." *New Yorker*. 7 Nov. 1931: 28; rpt. *The Passionate Playgoer*. Ed. George Oppenheimer (New York: Viking Press, 1958). 581.

Bentley, Eric. *The Life of the Drama*. 1964. New York: Atheneum, 1970.

_____. "Trying to Like O'Neill." Raleigh. *Twentieth Century Interpretations* 37–49.

Berlin, Normand. "O'Neill the Novelist." *Modern Drama* 34 (1991): 49–58.

_____. *O'Neill's Shakespeare*. Ann Arbor: University of Michigan Press, 1993.

Black, Stephen A. "O'Neill's Dramatic Process." *American Literature* 59 (1987): 58–70.

_____. "Tragic Anagnorisis in *The Iceman Cometh*." *Perspectives on O'Neill*. Ed. Shyamal Bagchee. University of Victoria: English Literary Studies, 1988. 17–31.

Bogard, Travis. *Contour in Time: The Plays of Eugene O'Neill*. Rev. ed. New York: Oxford University Press, 1988.

Brooks, Peter. *The Melodramatic Imagination.* New Haven: Yale University Press, 1976.

Brustein, Robert. *The Theatre of Revolt: An Approach to the Modern Drama.* 1964. Chicago: Ivan R. Dee, 1991.

Cargill, Oscar, N. Bryllion Fagin, William J. Fisher, ed. *O'Neill and His Plays: Four Decades of Criticism.* New York: New York University Press, 1961.

Carpenter, Frederic I. *Eugene O'Neill.* Rev. ed. Boston: Twayne, 1979.

Chabrowe, Leonard. *Ritual and Pathos—The Theater of O'Neill.* Lewisburg: Bucknell University Press, 1976.

Chothia, Jean. *Forging a Language: A Study of the Plays of Eugene O'Neill.* New York: Cambridge University Press, 1979.

Clurman, Harold. "Long Day's Journey Into Night." Review. Cargill 214–216.

Daly, Augustin. *Under the Gaslight.* Gerould 135–182.

Day, Cyrus. "The Iceman and the Bridegroom: Some Observations on the Death of O'Neill's Salesman." Raleigh, *Twentieth Century Interpretations* 79–86.

Downer, Alan S. "Eugene O'Neill as Poet of the Theatre." Cargill 468–471.

Dubost, Thierry. *Struggle, Defeat or Rebirth: Eugene O'Neill's Vision of Humanity.* Jefferson, NC: McFarland, 1997.

Editorial. *New York Times* 14 Nov. 1936: A18.

Egri, Péter. *The Birth of American Tragedy.* Budapest: Tankönyvkiadó, 1988.

Eisen, Kurt. *The Inner Strength of Opposites: O'Neill's Novelistic Drama and the Melodramatic Imagination.* Athens: University of Georgia Press, 1994.

Engel, Edwin A. *The Haunted Heroes of Eugene O'Neill.* Cambridge, MA: Harvard University Press, 1953.

Estrin, Mark W., ed. *Conversations with Eugene O'Neill.* Jackson: University Press of Mississippi, 1990.

Eugene O'Neill: A Glory of Ghosts. By Paul Shyre. Dir. Perry Miller Adato. Prod. Perry Miller Adato and Megan Callaway. Perf. Colleen Dewhurst and Jason Robards. *American Masters.* PBS. WNET, New York. 1985.

"Eugene O'Neill Wins Nobel Prize." *New York Times.* 13 Nov. 1936: 1+.

Fechter, Charles. *The Count of Monte Cristo. Best Plays of the Early American Theatre: From the Beginning to 1916.* Ed. John Gassner. New York: Crown, 1967.

Fergusson, Francis. "Melodramatist." Cargill 271–282.

Fleche, Anne. *Mimetic Disillusion: Eugene O'Neill, Tennessee Williams, and U.S. Dramatic Realism.* Tuscaloosa: University of Alabama Press, 1997.

Floyd, Virginia. *O'Neill at Work: Newly Released Ideas for Plays.* New York: Frederick Ungar, 1981.

_____. *The Plays of Eugene O'Neill: A New Assessment.* New York: Frederick Ungar, 1985.

Frye, Northrop. *Anatomy of Criticism: Four Essays.* 1957. Princeton: Princeton University Press, 1973.

Gassner, John. "The Nature of O'Neill's Achievement: A Summary and Appraisal." Gassner 165–171.

_____. *O'Neill: A Collection of Critical Essays*. Ed. John Gassner. Englewood Cliffs, NJ: Prentice-Hall, 1964.

Gelb, Arthur, and Barbara Gelb. *O'Neill*. 1962. New York: Harper & Row, 1973.

Gerould, Daniel C., ed. *American Melodrama*. New York: Performing Arts Journal Publications, 1983.

Glaspell, Susan. *The Road to the Temple*. London: Ernest Benn Limited, 1926.

Goethe, Johann Wolfgang Von. "Epic and Dramatic Poetry." In *European Theories of the Drama*. Ed. Barrett H. Clark. Rev. ed. 1918. New York: Crown, 1969.

Habermas, Jürgen. *The Philosophical Discourse of Modernity*. Trans. Frederick G. Lawrence. Cambridge, MA: MIT Press, 1993.

Hallström, Per. "Nobel Prize Presentation." *Eugene O'Neill's Critics: Voices from Abroad*. Ed. Horst Frenz and Susan Tuck. Carbondale: Southern Illinois University Press, 1984. 63.

Heilman, Robert Bechtold. *The Iceman, the Arsonist and the Troubled Agent: Tragedy and Melodrama on the Modern Stage*. Seattle: University of Washington Press, 1973.

_____. *Tragedy and Melodrama: Versions of Experience*. Seattle: University of Washington Press, 1968.

Hinden, Michael. *Long Day's Journey Into Night: Native Eloquence*. Boston: G. K. Hall & Co.–Twayne, 1990.

Hoffman, Gerhard. "Eugene O'Neill: America's Nietzschean Playwright." *Nietzsche in American Literature and Thought*. Ed. Manfred Pütz. Columbia, SC: Camden House, 1995.

Ibsen, Henrik. *The Complete Major Prose Plays*. Trans. Rolf Fjelde. 1965. New York: Penguin-Plume, 1978.

Jiji, Vera. "Reviewers' Responses to the Early Plays of Eugene O'Neill: A Study in Influence." *Theatre Survey* 29 (1988): 69–86.

Kalson, Albert E., and Lisa M. Schwerdt. "Eternal Recurrence and the Shaping of O'Neill's Dramatic Structures." *Comparative Drama* 24 (1990): 133–150.

Langner, Lawrence. *The Magic Curtain*. New York: E.P. Dutton–Story Press, 1951.

Lukács, Georg. *The Historical Novel*. Trans. Hannah and Stanley Mitchell. Boston: Beacon Press, 1963; Lincoln: University of Nebraska Press, 1983.

Manheim, Michael. *Eugene O'Neill's New Language of Kinship*. Syracuse, NY: Syracuse University Press, 1982.

_____. "O'Neill's Transcendence of Melodrama in *A Touch of the Poet* and *A Moon for the Misbegotten*." *Critical Approaches to O'Neill*. Ed. John H. Stroupe. New York: AMS Press, 1988. 147–159.

_____. "The Stature of *Long Day's Journey Into Night*." *The Cambridge Companion to Eugene O'Neill*. Ed. Michael Manheim. New York: Cambridge University Press, 1998. 206–216.

_____. "The Transcendence of Melodrama in *Long Day's Journey Into Night*." *Perspectives on O'Neill: New Essays*. Ed. Shyamal Bagchee. University of Victoria, B.C., Canada: English Literary Studies, 1988. 33–42.

_____. "The Transcendence of Melodrama in O'Neill's *The Iceman Cometh.*" *Critical Essays on Eugene O'Neill.* Ed. James J. Martine. Boston: G. K. Hall, 1984. 145–157.

McCarthy, Mary. "Eugene O'Neill—Dry Ice." Raleigh, *Twentieth Century Interpretations* 50–53.

Miller, Jordan Y. *Eugene O'Neill and the American Critic.* 2nd ed. Hamden, CT: Archon Books, 1973.

Moeller, Philip. "Silences Out Loud." *New York Times.* 26 February 1928, sec. 8: 4.

Mullett, Mary B. "The Extraordinary Story of Eugene O'Neill." Estrin 26–37.

Murphy, Brenda. *American Realism and American Drama, 1880–1940.* New York: Cambridge University Press, 1987.

Nietzsche, Friedrich. *The Birth of Tragedy* and *The Case of Wagner.* Trans. Walter Kaufmann. New York: Vintage–Random House, 1967.

_____. *On the Genealogy of Morals* and *Ecce Homo.* Ed. and trans. Walter Kaufmann. 1967. New York: Vintage–Random House, 1989.

_____. *The Portable Nietzsche.* Ed. and trans. Walter Kaufmann. 1954. New York: Viking-Penguin, 1982.

"Nobel Prize Is Won By Eugene O'Neill." *New York Times.* 13 Nov. 1936, late ed.: A2+.

Nobel Prize Library: Faulkner, O'Neill, Steinbeck. New York: Helvetica, 1971.

O'Neill, Eugene. *Complete Plays.* Ed. Travis Bogard. 3 vols. New York: The Library of America, 1988.

_____. "Damn the Optimists." Cargill 104–106.

_____. "Memoranda on Masks." Cargill 116–122.

_____. "O'Neill Talks About His Plays." Cargill 110–112.

_____. "Playwright and Critic: A Letter to George Jean Nathan." Cargill 101–103.

_____. *Selected Letters of Eugene O'Neill.* Ed. Travis Bogard and Jackson R. Bryer. New Haven: Yale University Press, 1988.

_____. *The Unfinished Plays: Notes for "The Visit of Malatesta," "The Last Conquest," "Blind Alley Guy."* Ed. Virginia Floyd. New York: Continuum–Frederick Ungar, 1988.

_____. "What the Theatre Means to Me." Interview with Oliver Sayler. Cargill 107–108.

Pfister, Joel. *Staging Depth: Eugene O'Neill and the Politics of Psychological Discourse.* Chapel Hill: University of North Carolina Press, 1995.

Postlewait, Thomas. "From Melodrama to Realism: The Suspect History of American Drama." *Melodrama: The Cultural Emergence of a Genre.* Eds. Michael Hays and Anastasia Nikolopolou. New York: St. Martin's Press, 1996. 39–60.

Quintero, José. Playwrights Theater Forum. Provincetown Playhouse, New York. August 9–27, 1998.

Raleigh, John Henry. "Eugene O'Neill and the Escape from the Château d'If." Gassner 7–22.

_____. *The Plays of Eugene O'Neill*. 1965. Carbondale: Southern Illinois University Press; London: Feffer and Simons, 1967.

_____, ed. *Twentieth Century Interpretations of The Iceman Cometh*. Englewood Cliffs, NJ: Prentice-Hall, 1968.

Remshardt, Ralf Erik. "Masks and Permutations: The Construction of Character in O'Neill's Earlier Plays." *Essays in Theatre* 8 (1990): 127–136.

Rich, Frank. "Theater: A Fresh Look for O'Neill's 'Interlude'." Review. *New York Times*. 22 Feb. 1985: C3.

Robinson, James A. *Eugene O'Neill and Oriental Thought: A Divided Vision*. Carbondale: Southern Illinois UP, 1982.

Scholes, Robert, and Robert Kellogg. *The Nature of Narrative*. New York: Oxford University Press, 1966.

Shakespeare, William. *As You Like It*. Ed. Agnes Latham. The Arden Shakespeare. 1975. New York: Methuen, 1986.

Shapiro, Gary. "In the Shadows of Philosophy: Nietzsche and the Question of Vision." *Modernity and the Hegemony of Vision*. Ed. David Michael Levin. Berkeley: University of California Press, 1993.

Sheaffer, Louis. *O'Neill: Son and Artist*. Boston: Little, Brown, 1973.

_____. *O'Neill: Son and Playwright*. Boston: Little, Brown, 1968.

Simonson, Lee. *The Stage Is Set*. 1932. New York: Theatre Arts Books, 1970.

Szondi, Peter. *Theory of the Modern Drama*. Ed. and trans. Michael Hays. Minneapolis: University of Minnesota Press, 1987.

Tiusanen, Timo. *O'Neill's Scenic Images*. Princeton, NJ: Princeton University Press, 1968.

Van Laan, Thomas F. "Singing in the Wilderness: The Dark Vision of O'Neill's Only Mature Comedy." *Modern Critical Views: Eugene O'Neill*. Ed. Harold Bloom. New York: Chelsea House, 1987. 99–108.

Wainscott, Ronald Harold. *Staging O'Neill: The Experimental Years, 1920–1934*. New Haven: Yale University Press, 1988.

Waith, Eugene M. "Eugene O'Neill: An Exercise in Unmasking." Gassner 29–41.

Wikander, Matthew H. "Eugene O'Neill and the Cult of Sincerity." Manheim, *The Cambridge Companion to Eugene O'Neill* 217–235.

Williams, Raymond. *Drama from Ibsen to Brecht*. Rev. ed. New York: Oxford University Press, 1969.

Woollcott, Alexander. "*Anna Christie*." Review. *New York Times*. 13 Nov. 1921, sec. 6: 1.

Index

Entries below in boldface refer to the Play Abstracts in Appendix II. Concluding those abstracts are "DISCUSSION" sections, giving references to more specific and detailed analyses of the plays in the main text of this book. Page numbers in italics indicate photographs.

251